BREAD UPON
THE WATERS

BREAD UPON THE WATERS

the developing law of the sea

Charles Fincham
and
William van Rensburg

TURTLEDOVE PUBLISHING

JERUSALEM   LONDON   MONTREAL
FOREST GROVE, OREGON
1980

First published: January 1980

ISBN 965-20-0009-4

TURTLEDOVE PUBLISHING
P.O.B. 18086, Jerusalem; P.O.B. 8044, Ramat Gan, Israel.
3 Henrietta Street, London WC2E 8LU.
2182 St. Catherine Street West, Montreal, Que. H3H 1M7.
2130 Pacific Avenue, Forest Grove, Oregon 97116.

Printed in Israel by Kal, Tel Aviv.
Bound by Lipschitz, Tel Aviv.

0 9 8 7 6 5 4 3 2 1

Cast thy bread upon the waters,
for thou shalt find it after many days
Ecclesiastes 11:1

Contents

Foreword

The Third United Nations Conference on the Law of the Sea, UNCLOS III as it is commonly known, now in its seventh session, is certainly one of the most complex instances of international negotiation of modern times, if not of all time. The Conference commenced at the end of 1973, on the basis of incomplete preparatory work which started as far back as 1967. What is more, the fact that four of its six sessions to date have been "off the record" and closed to the press and public, with results appearing in relatively obscure U.N. working papers of limited circulation, has kept much of the work that has been done from the eyes of the general public. Even persons generally well informed on current international affairs are frequently at a loss to describe with any degree of accuracy what is at stake, what are the objectives, what has been achieved and what the general picture will be of the restructured law of the sea that will emerge from this gargantuan and unique conference. It is, regrettably, only tragedies like the *Torrey Canyon* disaster some eleven years ago, or the *Amoco Cadiz* catastrophe off the coast of Brittany, that thrust into prominence some major aspects—here the protection of the marine environment, the social and economic interests dependent upon it and the freedom of international maritime communications—of the agreed international regulations of the sea and its multifarious and often conflicting uses, which is what this Conference is really about.

My official position makes it necessary for me to make the traditional disclaimer, that my words of introduction and commendation here do not mean that I necessarily identify myself with the theses and doctrines advanced.

It is the merit of the authors of this important book, Dr Charles Fincham and Dr William van Rensburg—both of them have in the past represented their country in different international meetings devoted to problems of the sea—that they have succeeded in compressing within its few pages and in an intelligible form enormous quantities of highly skilled learning and international experience, and not merely

diplomatic experience, in dealing with the sea and related matters —
political, administrative, military, economical, recreational, ecological,
scientific and what you will.

They have avoided technicalities and abstractions and have thus
managed to present important facts and arguments in an eminently
readable way. They have done that in a form which should commend
itself to the inquisitive layman, especially the politician, the diplomat
and government official, the journalist, and the informed proverbial
man-in-the-street. The lawyer and student of the law too, whether or
not he is an international lawyer, will draw much benefit from this
work which, I may venture to add, has every chance of becoming for
this complicated topic of the Law of the Sea an introduction of classical
standing.

Shabtai Rosenne
Jerusalem 1978

Introduction

The Palais des Nations in Geneva has corridors which are paved with granite and marble from all over the world. There are conference rooms panelled in richly grained hardwoods, tapestries and ceramics, paintings and furnishings contributed by member States of the old League of Nations—a testament of faith in the proposition that man's affairs can be resolved by reason under the law.

From the restaurant terrace, delegates to numberless conferences have gazed across the still waters of Lac Leman to the mountains beyond, receding rank upon rank into the haze, and dominated on a clear day by the pure snowcapped profile of Mont Blanc.

It is a setting in which initiatives which might otherwise have seemed Utopian acquire a measure of credibility. In a country where order, reason and a pervading awareness of natural beauty are so much a part of daily life, it is easy to believe that these qualities must come to govern man's affairs in a global context.

And indeed these old headquarters of the League of Nations which now house the European Office of the United Nations and provide its main international meeting place outside New York, have seen the first stirrings of ideas which have since become part of our history. Many a compromise has been born in these corridors—outside the inhibiting influence of the conference halls with their official records and procedures. Most of them have been stillborn, but some have progressed from the private meeting of minds to the discussion of proposals in debate and finally to the stage of adoption by the international community.

But for every initiative which has been successfully launched, a far greater number of ideas which might have enriched the quality of man's life and eliminated at least some of the deadly conflicts by which he is diminished, have languished.

No doubt national rivalries and conflicts of interest have played their part; but too often the blame must be laid upon the inertia of governments and their unwillingness (or inability) to face the real issues in an international line-up, especially if the issues are complex and interrelated, involving a number of disciplines and disparate, sometimes conflicting, national groups.

The idea of this book was born in Geneva in the Spring of 1971, at a session of the Sea-Beds Committee, officially and more ponderously known as the "Enlarged United Nations Committee on the Peaceful Uses of the Sea-Bed and Ocean Floor Beyond the Limits of National Jurisdiction." This became a preparatory commission, meeting twice a year for six or seven weeks at a time over a four year period, for the Third Law of the Sea Conference.

Convinced that the issues were of great importance to our country, as indeed they were to the world at large, we had persuaded our Government to let us attend the conference as observers.

As such we were not involved in the protracted negotiations which had to be concluded before the conference proper could begin — bargaining sessions behind closed doors on such issues as which country should provide the chairman of this committee or sub-committee, and how the other spoils of office should be divided among the States participating.

Day followed day and week followed week and our participation in the conference by which we had set such store was confined to marching up and down the corridors which by this time had become synonymous in our minds with the graveyard of so many of man's hopes.

As the conference progressed and debates on the substance began to supplant the long procedural hassle, we went through the evolution which most delegates to international conferences undergo. We started to make contacts. In the course of informal meetings in the coffee-shop of the delegates' lounge, and at interminable beer-drinking sessions on the square in the Old Town, friendships were sealed which might have surprised the governments which had sent their representatives to Geneva. It was during one of these extracurricular night sessions in the Old Square that we made what to us was a momentous discovery — we found that we were not alone in searching for a rationale for the conference!

As an international lawyer and as a mineral economist, we had some background on the legal issues involved and some insight into the economic potential of the sea-beds and the scope and complexity of the task of exploiting them. We realised however that this was only a part of the picture. What we had seen stirring in Geneva was the first ground-swell of a tidal wave of history. Mankind was beginning to address himself, as yet uncertainly, to the question of what to do with the vast resources lying beneath the seas and oceans which cover four-fifths of our planet and which for the first time were being brought within reach of his exploitation.

In the broadest sense, what seemed to be emerging was a conflict in a new dimension. On the one side stood the seafaring nations, with their entrenched interest in the freedom of navigation; and on the other, the rest of the international community including the Third World, with their interest in the bread-and-butter questions of what sources of wealth might be locked up in the seabeds and in the waters lying above them.

More specifically, the issues were more than politico-legal. They related also to geology and economics and the technology of exploiting the mineral and energy riches of the oceans. Scientific research, pollution, marine ecology, espionage, naval and strategic issues, the control of vital fishing resources and technical problems of deep-sea mining were involved.

Seldom has man been confronted with a task of such complexity and seldom have so many distinct but interrelated disciplines been brought under the umbrella of a single conference.

From the point of view of many delegates, the problem resolved itself into two phases; first, to try to understand the problems and their ramifications and second, to reduce the issues to understandable form, so that governments could decide on them. If the synthesis is difficult to achieve on an international level, it is no easier in the national context.

It is easy enough for a delegation to convince a government minister that he should endorse a particular line in regard to issues falling within his purview. A minister responsible for trade and shipping policy could readily be persuaded that freedom of navigation must be treated as the highest priority; a minister of defence would tend to think that strategic issues had overriding importance; and a minister of mines might well look with excitement and some alarm at the prospect of minerals, key metals and sources of energy being recovered from the sea-beds. The nub of the problem was not how to promote the interests of a single department, but how to convince governments as a whole that resolution of the issues would demand a package deal in which one Department might lose and another gain, in the national interest or in the interest of all mankind.

In some countries, the difficulty in framing a national policy was compounded by the fact that special interest groups applied pressure on their governments to follow policies which were mutually exclusive, even in relation to a single issue. Countries with extensive fishing resources off their own coasts would be disposed to favour exclusive fishing rights in a wide belt—but the very same countries could have fishing fleets operating off foreign shores, whose owners would not unnaturally favour narrow limits to the jurisdiction of coastal States.

One senior United Nations official remarked that the documentation of the Sea-Beds Committee is more than a man can physically lift, let alone digest. Outside the conference, much was being written in many languages. There was no lack of learned expositions, reflecting a high degree of competence and expertise, but each written within a particular discipline. Nowhere could we find a comprehensive book to which the layman—and this without disrespect includes cabinet ministers and others in the decision-making levels of government— could turn for a synoptic presentation of the main issues. Ministers are busy people working under internal and external pressures. If an issue is not clear-cut, they avoid committing themselves.

These were the considerations which moved us to set down our thoughts on one of the most important and least understood issues of our time.

Whatever the outcome of the Third United Nations Conference on the Law of the Sea, it is most important that informed public opinion should take a close look, before it is too late, at the world of waters which surrounds us. Must the oceans become the battleground of warring national claims—their gloriously rich and complex life decimated, their pure waters defiled and polluted? Or will governments be able to rise to the challenge of working out a regime in which all can share in the benefits and bear their part of the responsibility for preserving this, our greatest heritage? The authors believe that such a regime is possible, but only if we, nations and individuals, have the courage to heed the biblical injunction to cast our bread upon the waters.

Charles Fincham   William van Rensburg

BREAD UPON
THE WATERS

Chapter One
How It All Began

Every so often, as the process of history unfolds, it happens that a person of vision puts his finger on the nub of what is happening, summing up in a few words what has gone before and what is to follow. When this occurs, the pieces fall into place and arrange themselves into a pattern which, while no less complex, becomes more susceptible of study because the parameters are known.

It would be hard to imagine a less auspicious setting for a history-making statement of this nature than the United Nations General Assembly session of the year 1967, or a less exciting occasion than the speech of the Delegate of Malta, Ambassador Arvid Pardo, who is known more for his insight and eloquence than for the brevity of his interventions.

But one sentence in the draft resolution he was presenting electrified the Assembly and the world; and if it is too early to say that it changed the course of history, it can certainly be said that it put the cat among the pigeons and ensured that man's attitude towards the 60% of the earth's surface which is covered by water would be subjected to a scrutiny by the organs of the international community which can have few parallels.

The idea which Ambassador Pardo dropped into the pond of a somnolent Assembly, creating ripples which have been bouncing back and forth ever since, was that the resources of the seas and oceans, beyond the limits of national jurisdiction, should be regarded as the "common heritage of mankind," to be exploited cooperatively for the benefit of all, with special reference to the needs of the developing countries. The phrase itself was not a new one; it had indeed been used

1

by Prince Wan in his speech accepting the presidency of the First Law of the Sea Conference in 1958—but in the new context it had a new, and dramatic, impact.

The draft resolution introduced by Dr. Pardo set in motion a long chain of events, the ramifications of which have not yet become clear. The immediate effect was the setting up of an *ad hoc* Committee of 35 members, which in 1968 became a Standing Committee rejoicing in the somewhat ponderous title of the "Committee on the Peaceful Uses of the Seabed and Ocean Floor beyond the Limits of National Jurisdiction." For the sake of brevity, the Committee, which was expanded in 1970 to 36 member States and again in 1971 to 91 members, will be referred to henceforth by the name in most common use by the delegates — the "Seabeds Committee." The five conferences of the enlarged Seabeds Committee (starting with the Spring session in 1971), which became in effect a preparatory commission for the Third Law of the Sea Conference, were followed by eight sessions of the Plenipotentiary conference. More is to follow, since agreement is not yet in sight.

Seldom has the international community devoted so much time and energy to a single task. Ambassador Pardo's statement could not have set in motion such a series of events if it had not given expression to currents which were already gathering force under the surface. It is these currents which provide the key to an understanding of the complex of issues now being examined by the Conference, and outside the Conference by the chanceries of the member States. At this stage, the issues are only partly of a legal nature—the community of States is deeply divided on a range of interconnected questions which relate as much to politics and economics, strategy and the balance of power, navigation, mining, technology, scientific research, marine biology and the integrity of the marine environment as they do to the Law of Nations.

From the point of view of the jurist, the question which at once arises is why the Pandora's box should have been opened in the first place. The International Law of the Sea was adequately codified in the 1958 Geneva Conference—the First Law of the Sea Conference— in the form of four international conventions. These Conventions impose, as it were, a uniform code of behaviour governing man's use of the seas and oceans. Their provisions lay down a regime for the Territorial Sea and Contiguous Zone; for the High Seas; for the Continental Shelf; and for Fisheries and the Conservation of the Living Resources of the Sea.

Together, the four Geneva Conventions on the Law of the Sea, to which there will be occasion to return later in this book, represent what many regard as the greatest achievement of the international community in its efforts to codify the rules of international law.

This assessment holds despite the fact that the 1958 conference, which is very clear on the rights and duties of States in the Territorial Sea, failed to reach agreement on what the breadth of the territorial belt should be—a failure which gave rise two years later to the Second Conference on the Law of the Sea which, since it did not solve the issue, must be written off as abortive.

Our hypothetical jurist, puzzled at the fact that the 1958 Conventions, despite their evident success, were considered only ten years later to be inadequate, might well start looking round for a scapegoat. One such excuse was that the 1958 Conventions performed rather badly in practice, in that they were ratified by a limited number of States. (At the time of writing the Territorial Sea Convention had attracted only 42 ratifications, the Continental Shelf Convention 50, the High Seas Convention 50, and the Fisheries Convention 32).

It is doubtful if anyone who had worked on the day-to-day application of international law in a foreign ministry would be impressed by such an argument. It is well known that States tend to drag their feet about ratifying international conventions and treaties which they have signed, and in the preparation of which they have played a part. This does not mean that a convention, even if it remains unratified by the country concerned, can simply be ignored. The 1958 Conventions, under international conventional law, are binding only on those States which have signed and ratified them; but this is not the whole story. They have a residual importance deriving from the fact that they represent the "greatest measure of agreement which could be attained among States" (a phrase beloved by the International Law Commission) and would therefore add up to persuasive if not to conclusive evidence of customary international law on the subjects with which they deal. And in the last resort, as every foreign ministry official knows, customary international law is one of the things that any kind of tribunal for the settlement of disputes, from an *ad hoc* conciliation commission all the way up to the International Court of Justice itself, must take into account.

As with other multilateral treaties codifying law and practice in the international community, the 1958 Conventions on The Law of the Sea were much more successful, and much more widely observed, than the number of ratifications would suggest. The reason for their early obsolescence, when it seemed that they were all set to govern man's activities in, under and over the seas and oceans of the world for many years, and perhaps generations to come, must be sought elsewhere.

Clearly some new elements in the international balance of powers, interests, needs and capabilities must have intruded themselves to have upset a code which represented the culmination of centuries of practice and many years of study, analysis, compromise and negotiation, and which so admirably suited the needs and interests of the signatory States. But the very strength of the Geneva Conventions — the fact that they were tailor-made for and by the States participating in the 1958 Conference — proved to be their undoing. The community of States was undergoing a profound change in which the newly independent and developing countries — loosely referred to as the Third World — were becoming a majority in the United Nations.

The Third World, by and large, wanted no truck with the Geneva Conventions, in the framing of which they had had no part and which were associated in their minds with colonialism. No doubt there were features of the regime established in Geneva which added fuel to the fire of their discontent. The presence of foreign fishing fleets operating just outside their territorial belts was no doubt a provocation. In some cases, the suspicion that they might be losing out economically may have been reinforced by the desire to "get even" with their erstwhile exploiters, and to assert their new found strength. Whatever the reasons, it became clear very early in the deliberations of the Seabeds Committee that the Third World wanted not so much to revise and update the 1958 Conventions as to examine anew the whole field of inter-State relations affecting the Sea.

Most of the developed countries — a group which included those which had played a part in framing the 1958 Conventions — would have preferred a simple review Conference. They argued, not without some cogency, that the 1958 Conventions were a solid point of departure and that insofar as they fell short of meeting present day realities they could be amended, the lacunae filled in and the faults corrected, without discarding everything which had been so laboriously built up over the years. A phrase heard often during the first meetings of the Seabeds Committee, was that great care must be taken lest the baby be thrown out with the bathwater.

In his last speech to the nation from his exile in Switzerland, after the defeat of his people in the Anglo-Boer War, President Kruger of the

Transvaal adjured his countrymen to "Take what is best out of your past, and build upon it for the future." This was clearly not the temper of the majority in the United Nations with regard to the Law of the Sea. The emphasis was on a new approach.

Apart from the psychological factor, other pressures were building up against the old or "classical" regime established by the Geneva Conventions of 1958—a regime of narrow territorial seas, and of maximum freedom on the high seas, which favoured the maritime powers and those with the financial and technical ability to exploit, close to the shores of other States (including some developing countries), the wealth of fish in the waters. It also put them in a position to provide, by agreement of course with the coastal States, the technology and finance to exploit the latter's oil and mineral resources below the waters.

Populations were growing, especially in developing countries, more rapidly than the food supply. Foreign fleets operating from distant home bases, and equipped with technical aids of hitherto unheard of sophistication, were catching and processing the living resources of the sea at a rate which could only lead to the extinction of some species and the serious depletion of others. And the fruits of their labour were going mostly to the developed countries, the flag-states of the fishing fleets, and not to the poorer coastal countries which lacked the financial and technical capacity to take their share. To cap it all, countries with an advanced marine technology were poised for what may well prove to be amongst the most exciting developments of our own generation; no less than the exploitation of the vast and hitherto untapped resources which lie on and under the deep sea-beds, far beyond the reach of man's technology as it existed when the Geneva Conventions were signed in 1958.

Clearly the framework of needs and capabilities, of the aspirations of people around the world, had been knocked out of kilter and the 1958 Conventions would no longer serve.

It should be stressed at this stage that, when it comes to establishing a code of behaviour for those who go down to the sea in ships, an international convention is not the only way, the sine qua non without which anarchy must reign in the seas and oceans of the world. The Law of the Sea—which means neither more nor less than the rules of the game in the maritime sphere—has evolved over centuries of strife, trial-and-error, conciliation and compromise. A body of law and practice existed before the Geneva Conventions of 1958, and it will exist even if the current efforts to agree on a new regime, and to embody it in an international Convention, should fail. If that should happen, the Conventions of 1958 would remain in force, modified and supplemented by an accretion of new law.

This is not to suggest that the current efforts to arrive at a comprehensive new code of law are misplaced. It remains true that a new Convention—if mankind can achieve one—would compress into a few years a process of evolution which might otherwise have taken a much longer time. This is so because in the international sphere there is no organ which fulfils the role that a sovereign and a legislative assembly or parliament perform in a national context. Once the legislative authority in a given country has passed a law, it has the backing of the whole machinery of the State; it is enforced by the police, and interpreted and refined as needed by the courts of the land, and there is no escaping it. International law, having neither legislature nor simple straightforward machinery for enforcement, must needs grow more slowly. In the international sphere the nearest approach to legislation as we know it in our own countries is the complex process by which sovereign States, of their own free will and in the exercise of their sovereignty, agree to bind themselves in an international convention or treaty. Once they have done so, the practice followed by the decision-making organs of States, and the law which is applied by national courts and, on the international level, by courts of arbitration, conciliation and judicial process, tend to fall into line. Soon a formidable body of law and practice is built up. The 1969 Vienna Convention on the Law of Treaties, another outstanding achievement of the treaty-making process, was 20 years in the framing; surely but "an evening past" in the time-scale of international law, considering that it placed the seal on hundreds of years of chequered evolution, focussing in a single code the experience of centuries and providing a sound and carefully constructed base for future adaptations.

There can be no doubt of the superiority of the treaty-making process, as compared with all other means by which international law is advanced. Certainly this applies to the whole complex of legal and related issues considered under the heading of the Law of the Sea. The law will exist and even advance without a new Convention, but a Convention would be infinitely better.

It is therefore of some importance to try to assess where man stands in relation to the current effort to rewrite the Law of the Sea in a new convention conforming more closely with the emerging pattern of inter-

State relationships. This will require the balancing of conflicting claims and needs: on the one hand, the creation of an acceptable machinery and frame of reference to give meaning to Dr. Pardo's vision of the resources of the deep sea-beds as the "common heritage of mankind"; on the other, a recognition of the claim of coastal States to a greater share in the living and non-living resources off their shores; finally, a better and more responsible use by mankind of resources which are of crucial importance in these times of impending famine, but which are threatened by pollution, over-fishing and other forms of abuse. In the process, a wide variety of States' interests will have to be accomodated—including the interests of landlocked States and States which have been placed at a disadvantage in other respects through the accidents of geography.

It is a formidable task. Formidable because of the intrinsic difficulty of the subject-matter, because of the deep division of interest between States and groups of States, and because a whole new jurisprudence will have to be built up before shape and legal consistency can be given to principles and norms which differ, at times crucially, from those which informed the classical Law of the Sea, as laid down in the four Geneva Conventions.

But as if the task were not already difficult enough, history and circumstances have imposed on the Third Law of the Sea Conference a *modus operandi* and rules of procedure which make the resolution of differences, even on small matters of detail, peculiarly time-consuming and difficult.

It has been said that the achievement of the Hague Conference of 1958 and of the International Law Commission, in giving birth to the four Geneva Conventions on the Law of the Sea, was unparalleled in the history of international code-making. So much so that it set the pattern for all subsequent codifications of international law, such as the Vienna Conventions on Consular (1963) and Diplomatic (1961) Relations, and the Vienna Convention on the Law of Treaties of 1969.

We could do worse than take a look at the way in which the four Geneva conventions of 1958 came into being, since their history provides some illuminating contrasts with that of the new convention which is striving to be born.

The International Law Commission, an independent body of jurists elected by the United Nations on the grounds of their individual competence in international law, decided as far back as 1949 to give priority to one of the tasks assigned to it by the General Assembly—the codification of the body of law governing the High Seas and the Territorial Sea.

The fact that they did so suggests that some more or less urgent problems were beginning to appear, which were straining the fabric of international sea law as States understood it. These problems sprang from unilateral claims being made by coastal States to the resources of their continental shelves; and from the fact that the growing threat to the marine ecology, though it had not yet assumed crisis proportions, was already causing concern.

The International Law Commission spent a great deal of time drafting and re-drafting the articles of a proposed Code or Codes; after eight years, during which time States had an opportunity to comment and the Commission to react to their comments, it was in a position to lay on the table 73 draft articles for consideration by the Plenipotentiary Conference. After such long and thorough preparation in which Governments were also involved it is not perhaps surprising that the 73 draft articles already embodied a substantial measure of agreement between States.

This, then, brings us to the first element in the "classical" procedure for codification of international law: the Conference starts off with a draft prepared by a body like the International Law Commission, which has already brought to bear upon it a fund of experience and of legal and technical expertise which it would be hard to equal.

The first stage of the Plenipotentiary Conference is usually devoted to a clause-by-clause examination of the draft in a main Committee, or Committee of the Whole, in which all delegations are represented. After every delegation wishing to do so has spoken on the article, the Chairman may call upon a person with particular expertise in the field—the Special Rapporteur of the International Law Commission— who may explain to delegates what the Commission had in mind in framing the draft article as it did, and may comment upon some of the arguments raised by delegates during the debates. After having heard the Special Rapporteur, the Conference may decide (at this stage, by a simple majority vote) to retain the draft article in the form in which the Commission presented it, to delete the article, or to send it to the drafting Committee for such amendments as would reflect most accurately some new trend revealed in the debate.

Once the Committee of the Whole has voted on every article, including those re-submitted (perhaps more than once) by the Drafting

Committee, the text goes to the Plenary where each and every article must be adopted by a majority of two-thirds of the representatives present and voting. To the articles which emerge from the Committee of the Whole, are added such amendments as delegates may wish to propose. Sometimes a single article attracts a whole string of amendments which, following accepted rules of procedure, are then voted on one by one, in a sequence (established by the Chairman and seldom challenged) based on the principle that the amendment furthest removed in substance from the basic text, should be voted upon first.

All this is possible, however, because at each successive stage there is a single text which the Conference can add to, take away from, amend or otherwise modify, acting all the time under rules of procedure which are clear, consistent and well understood by delegates.

This does not mean that decisions at codification conferences following the "classical" procedure were easily arrived at; it means rather that under the stimulus of need, a procedure was evolved by which the international community could reach agreement in a reasonable time, the intellectual efforts of the delegates being devoted to the solution of questions of substance rather than being dissipated in procedural wrangles.

If the international community managed to forge such an effective instrument for the codification of areas of international law as important and as complex as the Law of the Sea (as it was understood in 1958) and the Law of Treaties, why could the same instrument not be used in the new and adventurous task of updating the Law of the Sea in the seventies?

The reasons are not at once apparent; but without knowing what caused the international community to be landed with the present *modus operandi*, it is not possible to understand the magnitude of the task faced by the Third UN Conference on the Law of the Sea, or the snail's pace of progress which the present rules impose upon it.

In framing the earlier codes, the task of the International Law Commission and of the Plenipotentiary Conferences which were to follow, was to identify and formulate rules and principles of international law which were already established in the practice of States; where the practice conflicted, to try and reconcile them by negotiation and compromise; and where no established practice could be found, to endeavour by provisions *de lege ferenda* to bridge the gap in such a way as not to vitiate accepted rules of law but rather to make them workable.

This tried and tested procedure was denied to the Conference mainly because of the political reasons to which reference has been made — the States of the Third World wanted to re-examine not only the existing Law of the Sea but the very postulates on which it was based.

The dilemma is summed up in a lucid article by the then Legal Counsel of the United Nations, C. A. Stavropoulos, in an issue of the *UNITAR News* which appeared before the opening of the Caracas session in 1974, in the following words:

> When there is an effort to change existing rules of law, particularly rules of the greatest importance, it is obviously indispensable to have the widest measure of agreement among States. If any significant part of the world community were to operate under old rules of law while the other parts followed a new rule, the conflicts would be manifold and, in a vital area like the Law of the Sea, might even endanger world peace and security. Two separate systems of law on the subject might well amount in practice to no law at all. Anarchy would prevail and it would be left to each State to assert and enforce its claim by the means available to it...149 States have been invited to the (Caracas) Conference. The two-thirds majority voting rule followed in plenary by almost every previous UN Conference, including all the codification conferences, would obviously not be satisfactory if an alternative were to be available, since to adopt a rule over the opposition of as many as 50 States might be only a dangerous mockery.[1]

With these considerations in mind the General Assembly produced what became known as the "Gentlemen's Agreement" which provides in effect that since the problems of ocean space are clearly interrelated and must be considered as a whole, and since it is important that a Convention on the Law of the Sea should have the widest possible acceptance, "the Conference should make every effort to reach agreement on substantive matters by way of consensus; there should be no voting on such matters until all efforts at consensus have been exhausted."[2]

Following the guideline laid down by the General Assembly, the Seabeds Committee and the Conference have followed the consensus procedure, with one or two exceptions, throughout their deliberations over the last eight years. It is a rather curious development of the democratic process.

It is easier to say what a consensus is not than to define it, although there is some United Nations practice to go by. To say that a consensus has been reached does not mean that States are unanimous on the point at issue. Stavropoulos has described it, rather tentatively, as meaning that "a minority of delegations that do not fully support a text are willing to state their reservations for the record, rather than insisting on voting against.... It is, essentially, a way of proceeding without formal objection."[3]

There are some intriguing analogies with the process by which, in a one-party State, all shades of opinion are expressed, and hotly contested, at meetings which take place at all levels from the village pump upwards—but the decision which finally emerges is unanimous or (a better word) uncontested. This does not mean that there has been no disagreement, but only that issue has been joined, and conflicts resolved, at levels below that of the confrontation between parties.

There are both advantages and disadvantages in the consensus procedure. A point in its favour is that it avoids the confrontation implied in a head-count. This is useful in the earlier stages of a conference when it is important that States should not foreclose their options by taking up too rigid a stance. In a long series of conferences such as the present one, delegations put their case not once but several times over, depending on their degree of involvement and other factors. Their point of view may shift, sometimes slowly and by subtle gradations, from one conference to the next in the light of what happened at the previous conference and of how delegates and the Governments to which they report assess the international community's mood and their chances of balancing the various pressures upon them so as to advance their own interests as far as possible. It is no use adhering to one's initial view if in the meantime it has become clear that the tide has set against it and that there is no chance of changing other delegates' minds.

The hoary old quip about the delegate who implored other delegates not to confuse him with facts, as his mind was already made up, is not without a grain of truth. If there is to be a change in a State's policy on issues related to the Law of the Sea, it is seldom effected in the course of debate. It is more likely to take place at the national level, in the period between conferences. A delegate may have little room for maneuvre during the session. If his views carry enough weight back home, he may have played a part in the decision-making bodies in which his Government's policy was hammered out, so that the brief to which he speaks may be at least partly of his own creation. But a brief is a brief, and it must be adhered to until the whole process can be repeated and revised instructions issued.

This may help to explain why so many visitors to the United Nations come away from listening to their first debate with a feeling of unreality and disillusionment. Too often, it seems, a speaker will say what he had planned to say despite the fact that the preceding speaker has already cut the ground from under his feet. The observer is left with the disquieting impression that very little that anyone says has any influence on anyone else. The impression is misleading — it would be nearer the mark to say that there is a delayed reaction. The point is that according to the consensus procedure a delegate's statement does not bind him, or his delegation, or his Government to the same extent as would have been the case had the vote been recorded.

The consensus procedure has in fact enabled States to shift their positions, through the years of debate on the regime of the seas and oceans, almost from one pole to the other. There are no votes on earlier positions to be explained away, since no votes are taken.

Anyone who has followed the Seabeds Committee debates since Spring 1971 will know that some States (including some of the most important maritime powers) have changed their stand on certain key issues such as the 200-mile economic zone to the extent that their attitude today is hardly recognisable compared with their stand in 1971. Some of the most doughty protagonists of the three-mile limit to territorial waters and of the maximum possible area of High Seas have seen the writing on the wall and come round to espousing the 200-mile zone instead. It is doubtful whether this evolution from the traditional Law of the Sea to acceptance, with however loud a protest, of its opposite would have been possible without the consensus procedure.

There is another major advantage to the consensus procedure. A State which accepts a decision arrived at by a consensus in which it has had ample opportunity to take part is more likely to feel bound by it than would have been the case had the conference been bulldozed into a decision by the vote of a technical majority (i.e., a numerical majority of States which may not represent anything very substantial in terms of power, influence, wealth or responsibility). And the essence of a Treaty which is made to last is that the parties intend to honour the arrangement, which must have been arrived at freely.

There is no need to be pessimistic about the outcome of the Third Law of the Sea Conference. But to expect speedy results in the codification of such complex rules, many of which have still to be agreed and formulated, is to misunderstand the magnitude of the task as well as the time-table which the consensus procedure imposes upon the law-making process.

The task of following the long and often involved deliberations of UNCLOS III—the Third United Nations Conference on the Law of the Sea—is not made easier by the fact that part of the Second Session, and the whole of the Third, Fourth, Fifth and Sixth Sessions, were held "off the record" without the meetings of the main Committees being fully documented. Much of the work was done in informal negotiating groups, with few or no records being kept of the proceedings.

The first substantive session, held in Caracas in 1974, was on record and some of the reports—not least the Main Trends Working Paper of the Second (Legal) Committee—have provided a useful basis for further discussion.

In the absence of an agreed text for UNCLOS III, the Conference produced, in 1975, an "Informal" Single Negotiating Text (ICNT) which formed the basic document of the session (the first part of the Seventh Session), held in Geneva, from 28 March to 19 May 1978.[4]

Lest there be any misunderstanding, these texts are merely a device to focus the attention of delegates on the issues. Although they are drawn up in the form of draft articles for a new and comprehensive convention on the Law of the Sea, they do not purport to reflect a consensus. At best they are a statement of the views of chairmen of the main committees as to what might, or might not, be trends emerging from the debates, as they perceive them.

Notes

1. *Stavropoulos, Constantin A*. Procedural Problems of the Third Conference on the Law of the Sea. Article in *UNITAR NEWS* Vol 6 No. 1 1974.
2. *"Gentlemen's Agreement"*—The understanding is embodied in United Nations Document A/9278, para 16.
3. *Stavropoulos, Constantin A*. Op cit.
4. United Nations Press Release Sea/785 19 May 1978

Chapter Two
The International Community And The Lawmaking Process

In any attempt to assess the "state of play" in regard to the manner and direction in which the Law of the Sea is moving, reference will have to be made to some of the institutions by which the Law of Nations is advanced and modified.

It has been pointed out in the first chapter that this is not a legal treatise; but even when trends are described in general terms, questions may arise in some readers' minds about the alchemy which transforms ideas and tendencies into hard-nosed legal rules which are firmly entrenched in the practice of States and enforceable by a hierarchy of courts, whether municipal or international, and by arbitral tribunals set up either by the international community, or on an *ad hoc* basis by the States parties to a treaty to ensure the settlement of such disputes as may arise under its provisions.

There are no doubt some readers whose interest lies in the broader issues embraced by the Law of the Sea, and who have had no occasion to consider how the rules of international law are conceived and formulated, and how and through what instrumentalities they are applied. It is precisely for such readers that this chapter has been written.

The sources of law which the International Court of Justice is enjoined to take into account in reaching its decisions are summarised in Article 38 of its Statute in the following words:

> The Court . . . .shall apply
> (a) International Conventions, whether general or particular, establishing rules expressly recognised by the contesting States.

15

(b) International custom, as evidence of a general practice which
is accepted as law

(c) The general principles of law recognised by civilised nations

(d) Subject to Article 59 (providing that a decision of the Court
has no binding force except between the parties and in respect of
that particular case), judicial decisions and the teachings of the
most highly qualified publicists of the various nations, as sub-
sidiary means for the determination of rules of law

This provision shall not prejudice the power of the Court to
decide a case *ex-aequo et bono*, if the parties agree thereto.[1]

The Court's statute is part of the United Nations Charter, and
one could do worse than take this re-statement of the sources of
international law as a starting-point·for a thumbnail sketch of how the
Law of Nations is developed and applied by and to the world
community.

It is an axiom that since international law concerns the relations
between sovereign States, the rules which govern their intercourse
must be based, in the first place, on consent. Consent is clearly the
basis of conventional or treaty law, by which States agree to bind
themselves in a solemn undertaking, which must be ratified by
whatever process their constitutions prescribe. Less obviously but no
less compellingly, it is the basis of customary international law; for if
States have allowed a certain custom to develop in their relations one
with another, it must be assumed that they consented to practices
which they followed and helped to establish.

In the course of their relations and inter-relations over a long
period of history, States came to observe certain rules of conduct which
eventually hardened into custom. The growth of such rules of customary
international law was however, of necessity a slow and uncertain one.
Since States are sovereign, each in its own right, there is no overall
authority, such as the legislature which exists in a single State, to
impose rules of conduct upon them.

During the Middle Ages, writers including the Dutch jurist Grotius,
who is often dubbed "the father of international law" because of
the influence which his teachings came to wield, began to supplement
the growth of customary international law, and to lay the foundations
for its future development, by drawing upon moral, religious and
philosophical models and the lessons of history. The system of
jurisprudence, or philosophy of law, which Grotius and his followers

built up, was known as the Law of Nature — *ius naturale* — and although it has been largely supplanted by later developments in jurisprudence, there can be little doubt about the importance of the role which his philosophy played in promoting the idea (in theory if not always in practice) that States should be governed by the Law of Nations in their dealings with one another. Without going into the controversy between the Natural Law and the Positive Law schools of jurisprudence, a controversy about which many volumes have been written — it is perhaps enough for our purpose to point out that the Natural Law doctrine filled what would otherwise have been a lacuna in the development of legal thought. By postulating certain eternal and immutable values which must underlie all civilised legal systems and, *a fortiori*, the Law of Nations, it provided a focal point around which legal systems could grow and by reference to which they could be tested.

It is therefore not surprising that the most celebrated text in the Law of Nations, and its first systematic compilation, should be found in Grotius' treatise on the laws of war and of peace — "De Jure Belli ac Pacis" — which was published in 1625. The absence of anything like an international legislature gave added weight to the writings of scholars and publicists, who could devote their time to the study of the rules of international conduct, elucidating them by reference to present need and the fund of past experience, and thus providing a rationale on which decision-makers in government could base themselves, and by reference to which they could justify their actions in the complicated and sometimes dangerous field of interstate relations.

A development of capital importance occurred in the 19th century, when the family of nations, instead of being content to allow customary international law to develop at its own slow pace, made deliberate attempts to expand it by way of treaties which they would draw up after sometimes lengthy periods of study, negotiation and compromise. In this way a body of "conventional" international law was built up, in which new rules, or newly systematised ones, were laid down. The distinction is not without importance. Codifications of international law normally contain two elements — those provisions which express and define rules already widely accepted, the *lex lata*, and provisions *de lege ferenda* — rules agreed upon by the States parties to the Convention not because they express accepted law, but because they are necessary to give cohesion and consistency to the law. Such provisions are in effect new law, which States by their free choice and in the exercise of their sovereignty have agreed to make binding on themselves.

There are certain conventions which are so important, and so widely accepted, that their influence reaches beyond the perhaps limited circle of the original parties. Treaties are binding in a strictly formal sense only on States which have signed and ratified them; but it is unthinkable that a State accused of genocide, slave-trading or piracy, would rely on the defence that it was not a party to the treaties outlawing these crimes against humanity. This is only another way of saying that the original treaties formed the basis of universally respected rules (again, in principle if not always in practice) which thus passed into the body of customary international law. This process may be illustrated by the judgment of the International Court in the North Sea Continental Shelf case (Chapter 6). Conventional and customary international law exist side by side, and they react upon each other.

There is another route by which rules of international law, once accepted either in treaties or as customary law by a limited number of States, may earn a wider recognition. When the community of States admits a new member (and the majority of members of the United Nations today fall into this category), it does so on the basis that the newcomer will accept the body of international law binding on the community. Indeed, ability and willingness to do so are among the main criteria which a State must fulfil before being admitted to the "club."

In the international context, the Courts play a key role in applying and elucidating the rules. This is true not only of the international courts and arbitral tribunals, but also of municipal courts, i.e., courts within individual States. The relationship that exists between municipal law and international law has given rise to a great deal of controversy, the background to which is clearly set forth in the famous Oppenheim/Lauterpacht treatise, which has been the standard work for generations of students of the Law of Nations, and in the voluminous literature which he cites.[2]

Leaving aside the theoretical basis for the relationship, including the well-documented argument between the dualist and monist schools of thought, one is left with the fact that a large number of States, including the USA, Great Britain and France, recognise customary and conventional international law as part of the law of the land. It follows that cases decided by municipal courts, in so far as questions of international law are involved, are not without their influence upon the development of the Law of Nations. The International Court itself may consider them under Article 38 of its Statute—quoted above—either as revealing principles of law recognised by civilised nations (para c.), or as the kind of judicial decisions envisaged under paragraph (d). The sheer volume of cases involving points of international law decided by municipal courts around the world is far in excess of the volume of cases dealt with by international courts and tribunals of one kind or another. The reader may be referred to the table of municipal cases given by D. P. O'Connell in what is widely held to be the leading modern textbook on international law, listing about two thousand cases decided in the municipal courts of no less than 70 countries—a formidable body of jurisprudence.[3]

International Tribunals for
the Arbitration of Disputes

It is perhaps not surprising that the variety of tribunals set up under international agreements should be limited only by the needs of the agreement concerned, and by the imagination of the jurists and diplomats negotiating the treaty.

Machinery for the settlement of disputes arising out of a specific treaty is normally provided for in the treaty itself; and since the treaty is purely a matter for agreement between the two or more States concerned, it follows that they can agree to settle such differences as may arise, by whatever means seem fit.

Arbitration has played a distinguished—if not always well-publicised—role in the settlement of disputes, with the period immediately preceding World War I being one of the most productive. After the Treaty of Versailles of 1919, the community of States had other options which supplemented the method of arbitration, without however replacing it. The literature on the subject is voluminous, and a bibliography can be found in any standard textbook on the Law of Nations. A selected few of the leading authorities are listed in the notes.

One of the earlier, and doubtless most important, arbitrations took place between Great Britain and the United States under the Jay Treaty of 1784, in which Commissions were set up to arbitrate such disputes as might arise on boundary questions, breaches of neutrality and the exercise of belligerent rights.[4] A Commission, under Article VII, was to consist of two arbitrators chosen by each of the litigants and a fifth who would be chosen by lot. Both in Europe and on the American Continent this model was widely but by no means slavishly followed—at the other end of the scale one could still find an atypical treaty like that of 1879 between France and Nicaragua, providing that disputes should be submitted to the Cour de Cassation in France.[5]

It was perhaps to be expected that techniques of arbitration as developed under arbitration clauses in bilateral and multilateral treaties should in due course be generalised and applied to a wider class of disputes. On a bilateral basis, this could be done by two States concluding a treaty of friendship in which they agreed to submit certain general classes of disputes, with no connection whatsoever to specific treaties, to arbitration; and on the multilateral plane it could be done by a group of States, or the Community of States as a whole, agreeing to submit to arbitration disputes that might arise between them about the interpretation of a general lawmaking convention.

By the turn of the century the value of arbitration as a means of settling disputes had been well established. A landmark was the Disarmament Conference which met in the The Hague in 1899 at the instance of Czar Nicholas of Russia. There emerged from this Conference a most important instrument—namely the "Convention for the Pacific Settlement of International Disputes" signed by 27 Powers—a respectable enough number in those times when the international commmunity was so much smaller.

The convention provided for the creation of a panel of qualified persons, not more than four of whom could be the nominees of any one State. From this panel, the litigants could by mutual agreement select a board. If unable to agree, each of the litigants could appoint two arbitrators and the four so chosen could by unanimous vote appoint a fifth as umpire. The terms of reference of the Court so assembled were laid down in a document known as the "compromis," signed by the parties involved, before the arbitration began.

The success of the Court—which still exists as the Permanent Court of Arbitration—is attested by the fact that when the next Hague Conference met in 1907, the number of adherents had increased from the original 27 States to 46. Over a score of cases have been settled by the Permanent Court of Arbitration, which has thus made a solid contribution to the body of jurisprudence and illuminated some of the darker areas in the Law of Nations.

It is significant that there are very few cases on record of a State failing to honour an arbitral award—and equally significant that what failures have occurred seem to follow from a breakdown in the consent which lies at the base of all treaty-making. Where the arbitrators exceed their competence as laid down in the compromise, or where some other serious irregularity such as bribery of one of the arbitrators occurs, a litigant State may be justified in claiming that its consent to be bound by the award has been vitiated. Saving these rare exceptions, the "stickability" of arbitral awards is no doubt due in large measure to the fact that a State would be hard put to it to repudiate a decision arrived at by a Court to whose composition and terms of reference it had agreed in advance. The rule laid down in Article 37 of the Hague Convention of 1907 is indeed a healthy one—"international arbitration has for its object the settlement of disputes between States by judges of their own choice and on the basis of respect for law."

Pre-war treaties for the peaceful settlement of disputes addressed themselves mostly to specific classes of disputes. After the First World War, an advance was made in that these systems were based more and more on the assumption that *all* international disputes should be subjected to some kind of settlement procedure. It is no accident that many pre-war treaties provided for the arbitration of "differences which may arise of a legal nature or relating to the interpretation of treaties" (the wording is from the Anglo-French Arbitration Treaty of 1903, but similar formulae appear in a large number of treaties concluded during this period); whereas in post-war treaties this qualification did tend to give way to provisions allowing the Tribunal, where no clear rules of law were applicable, to decide "ex aequo et bono," or on grounds of common sense and equity. This was a clear advance on the old type of arbitration treaty, and it prepared the way for the next phase, which one could describe as the modern approach to the settlement of international disputes.

The League of Nations and the United Nations

The two most important treaties in history are undoubtedly the Covenant of the League and the Charter of the United Nations. Each of these instruments arose, like the Phoenix of legend, from the ashes of a world-wide conflagration. Each was designed, first and foremost, to ensure that such a cataclysm would not again overtake the world; and to this end each sought to strengthen the forces making for peaceful co-operation between nations and peoples, and to create a machinery and lay down procedures by which States could settle their differences peacefully and with respect for Law. The provisions in the Covenant and the Charter for the peaceful settlement of disputes, the practices of the League and of the United Nations which grew up around them, and the judicial decisions and learned studies by which both the treaty provisions and the subsequent practices were interpreted, are a study in themselves.

For our purposes, what is important is that the community of States, in these two treaties, agreed to follow certain procedures and to exhaust a very comprehensive set of remedies, before resorting to force. Voluntarily, in the exercise of their sovereignty, they agreed to limit their own freedom of action in certain spheres. It could indeed be said that as a sovereign act they agreed to place a limit on their own sovereignty. Since this touches on the most jealously guarded attributes of statehood, they did not do so lightly; and the "thin red line" dividing issues which fall within the purview of the organised international community from those essentially domestic in character were, and are, and perhaps always will be a sensitive issue. At what point does a question cease to be only a statistic and become a matter of legitimate concern to the international community?

Some of the most difficult issues of international law are centred around this distinction.[6]

The Charter of the United Nations provides in Article 2, paragraph 7 that:

> Nothing contained in the present Charter shall authorise the United Nations to intervene in matters which essentially are within the domestic jurisdiction of any State or shall require the Members to submit such matters to settlement under the present Charter; but this principle shall not prejudice the application of enforcement measures under Chapter VII.

From the outset this provision, like the similar provision in Article 15, paragraph 8 of the Covenant of the League, gave rise to difficulties.

The paragraph prohibits intervention by the world body in certain classes of disputes. But what is meant by "intervention"? In the literature of international law, the word has a very precise meaning. It covers dictatorial or forceful interference on the physical plane; it most emphatically does *not* cover a resolution or recommendation by the United Nations or one of its organs. Must it be accepted that the delegations which took part in the framing of the Charter, and which included some of the leading jurists of the day, were using a word with a precise legal connotation in an imprecise manner, and in effect saying something which they did not mean to say? In such cases it is legitimate, according to the rules for the interpretation of treaties, to look at the records of the preparatory work and of the debates, in order to establish what the framers of the treaty had in mind. Unfortunately this test too, is inconclusive; the records show that different delegations expressed different views, and most of them expressed no view at all.

And what is meant by the term *essentially* within the domestic jurisdiction of States? There are a few issues which would be generally recognised as being of domestic concern, at least *prima facie*. Immigration policy is such an issue, it being widely conceded that every State may decide for itself whom it will admit to the rights and duties of its citizenship, and under what conditions. There could be a point however, at which even an "essentially" domestic matter might spill over into the sphere where it becomes a matter of concern to the international community. In an extreme case it is at least arguable that a State could apply an immigration policy which was a gross violation of human rights, and which conflicted with its international treaty obligations in a manner which removed the issue from the purely domestic sphere and involved the Community of Nations. It is logical that questions of fundamental human rights, and matters involving a State's treaty obligations, should be regarded as being of international rather than purely domestic concern. But what is important here is that we are dealing not with absolutes, but a shifting frontier, as exemplified by the authoritative opinion given in 1923 by the International Court of Justice in the case of the Nationality Decrees in Tunis and Morocco:

> The question whether a certain matter is or is not solely within the domestic jurisdiction of a State is an essentially relative question; it depends on the development of international relations.[7]

Be that as it may, and for better or for worse, the practice of the League and the United Nations shows that the interpretation of this key provision devolves not upon the State relying upon it, but on the organ of the international community seized of the question. The practice of the two world bodies, and the interpretations given by the Court, tend to give a restrictive meaning to the clause and thus, indirectly, to expand the sphere of competence of the United Nations at the expense of the domain reserved by individual States to themselves under the Charter.

As one of the authors of this study wrote in 1948, when the practice of the United Nations had not yet settled down:

> For a variety of reasons, including the loose and ambiguous wording of the text, its inherent conflict with the spirit of the Charter, and the rules of voting according to which it must be upheld or rejected by the organ seized of the dispute, the domestic jurisdiction clause is tending to become a dead letter.[8]

This early assessment has been amply confirmed by subsequent experience.

An international body like the United Nations is created by the agreement of States expressed in a Treaty. As such, it is the creature and servant of its sponsors. In terms of positive law, it can have no powers other than those which States have conferred upon it. Nevertheless, by a combination of subtle processes, the world body tends, over a period of time, to assume powers which go beyond what its founders had envisaged.

From the point of view of the development of international law, and the peaceful ordering of the affairs of man, this process of "creeping jurisdiction" is not without its advantages; the dichotomy between world order and the absolute sovereignty of States must be resolved progressively in favour of the former.

But the process is not without dangers which are particularly germane to the organisation which must eventually be set up to regulate man's activities in and under the sea. The issue of where the writ of the Seabeds Authority will run, where its authority will cease and that of States and consortia will begin, is indeed one of the central issues which may decide the fate of present-day efforts to reach an international accord on the Law of the Sea.

The International Law Commission[9]

It may be said that the practice of States, acting either individually or through the organs of the International Community, are the raw material from which international law is built. The International Court is the highest judicial tribunal of the Community and interprets and consolidates the law which emerges. Between the two, completing the circle, is the International Law Commission which fulfils the vitally important role of the "think tank" of the world community, doing the ground work and preparing the drafts for the treaties by which States codify the areas of law on which they are able to agree, and laying the foundations for futher agreements.

The Charter requires that the General Assembly "initiate studies and make recommendations for the purpose of...encouraging the progressive development of international law and its codification." It was with this task in mind that the Assembly in 1947 established the International Law Commission. It held its first sessions in 1949, and has since prepared studies and draft articles on over a score of topics of international law. Drafts prepared by the Commission have formed the basis of a number of codification treaties which have passed into the main body of international law. Apart from the four Geneva Conventions of 1958 on the Law of the Sea which are of direct relevance to the present study, these include the Convention on the Reduction of Statelessness (1961), the Vienna Convention on Diplomatic Relations (1961) and on Consular Relations (1963), and the Vienna Convention of 1969 on the Law of Treaties which must be counted amongst its greatest achievements.

The Commission is undoubtedly one of the most successful bodies ever to be set up under the aegis of the United Nations. It is submitted that its success is due in no small measure to certain features in its make-up and its manner of operating which single it out from the general run of United Nations bodies.

The Commission's statute lays down simple and clear rules for the election of its 25 members. They are to be chosen by the General Assembly (not, like the judges of the International Court, by the Assembly and Security Council jointly) on the basis of their individual competence in the field, and with due regard to the principle that the membership of the Commission as a whole should be representative of the main forms of civilization and the principal legal systems of the world. Candidates are nominated by States, but once elected they serve in their individual capacities, as jurists. They serve for five years, on a part-time basis (normally one ten-week session per annum).

A further provision, which turned out to be of cardinal importance, was that casual vacancies occurring between sessions of the General Assembly, when the elections take place, may be filled by the Commission itself. This means, in effect, that if the Commission is seized of a difficult topic, and a vacancy occurs, it can co-opt into its ranks whichever expert it thinks most likely to be able to contribute to the task in hand. In this respect it is uniquely fortunate among UN bodies.

Elections in the General Assembly are hampered by the practice of horse-trading, under which State X may promise its support of a candidate put up by State Y, in return for the latter's support for its candidate for some other office. The result is not always a happy one — a candidate belonging to a State which is unpopular in the Assembly may stand no chance of being elected even if on merit he is the obvious choice. Elections to the International Law Commission are not exempt from this practice, although less vulnerable to it than elections to more "politically charged" bodies.

It is a basic principle of treaty law, applying to multilateral "Law-making" treaties as much as to bilateral agreements, that they must be entered into voluntarily by States in the exercise of their sovereignty. A Convention which is steamrollered through by a majority of States against the will of an important minority has little chance of passing into the body of international law. There is nothing to compel the dissidents to fall in with the majority. One of the strengths of the Commission came from the fact that it decided early in its existence to give full effect to the principle that a Convention must enjoy as wide support as possible, and not merely the support of a "technical majority" of two-thirds of the Members, which need not necessarily include the most important States. In preparing its draft articles for consideration by a plenipotentiary conference, it made a practice of consulting Member States — of going back, as it were, to the constituency — and of giving effect whenever possible to their views and comments. In this manner it ensured that by the time its draft articles were submitted to the Conference, they would already reflect the greatest measure of agreement which could be achieved among States at that stage in the development of international relations — to use one of the favourite phrases of the Commission itself. In addition to written comments received from member States on its drafts and revisions of drafts, the Commission benefitted from the debates in the Sixth (Legal) Committee of the Assembly, when its annual report came up for review.

Finally, the Commission as it became more experienced moved gradually away from the practice of voting on each article in a draft (a practice which was still followed in preparing the draft articles for the 1958 Law of the Sea Conference, some aver to the detriment of the Conventions which eventually emerged), and came more and more to follow the more laborious but more certain consensus procedure. The pros and cons of the consensus procedure are discussed elsewhere. At this stage it is perhaps enough to point to the psychological effect on States of a formulation reached by common consent, rather than in a mechanical fashion by a prescribed majority of votes.

The International Court of Justice[10]

There are no great differences between the International Court of Justice, whose Statute is annexed to and incorporated by reference in the United Nations Charter, and the old Permanent Court which was the highest judicial authority before the Second World War, in the time of the League of Nations. This is no mere accident; it was the intention of the framers of the Charter that the new Court should function in the tradition of its distinguished predecessor, building on the foundation of jurisprudence which had been developed in the years between the wars.

The Charter provides that all members of the United Nations are *ipso facto* parties to the Court's Statute, and that non-members may be admitted. Members—by the mere fact of becoming parties to the Charter of the United Nations—undertake to comply with decisions of the Court in any cases to which they are a party, failing which Security Council action may be taken.

The role of arbitral and other tribunals created or to be created by agreement between the Members is safeguarded in Article 95: the intention clearly is that the Court should supplement and not supplant existing machinery for the settlement of disputes.

Only States may be parties to disputes brought before the Court, but Article 96 of the Charter contains a provision which is of some importance: it provides that the Assembly and the Security Council may request the Court to give an advisory opinion on any legal question, and that other UN organs and the Specialised Agencies, if duly authorised, may request an advisory opinion on legal questions within the scope of their activities.

The Court's Statute provides in Article 36 that States which are parties to it "may at any time declare that they recognise as compulsory, *ipso facto* and without special agreement, in relation to any other State accepting the same obligation, the jurisdiction of the Court in all disputes concerning:

(a) the interpretation of a treaty;
(b) any question of international law;

(c) the existence of any fact which, if established, would constitute a
      breach of an international obligation;
(d) the nature and extent of the reparation to be made for the breach of
      an international obligation."

As of 1974, 57 States had deposited declarations accepting the
compulsory jurisdiction of the Court (or of the old Permanent Court).

As might have been expected, given the sensitivity of States to
anything which looked like signing away their options, a number of
these declarations are hedged by the reservation that their consent to
the compulsory jurisdiction of the Court does not extend to matters
falling essentially within their domestic jurisdiction. It is significant
that even within these parameters there are degrees of caution in the
wording of the reservation. Eighteen States concede the paramountcy
of law by referring to disputes which *by international law* are essentially
within their domestic jurisdiction; while six make the reservation as
comprehensive as possible by referring to disputes which *in their own
opinion* are essentially domestic. This is known as keeping all options
open!

It will be seen that consent to the Court's jurisdiction is not
universal or automatic—a fact which must inevitably resrict the
number of cases decided by it, and thus its role in the consolidation
and elucidation of international law.

The General Assembly has indeed expressed its desire that full use
should be made of the Court's services, exhorting organs of the UN and
the Specialised Agencies, to review legal problems arising from their
activities and consider whether they could not be referred to the Court
for an advisory opinion; pointing out the virtue of States' accepting the
compulsory jurisdiction of the Court with as few reservations as
possible; and encouraging States, when concluding conventions or
treaties having clauses for the settlement of disputes, to provide for
such disputes to be submitted to the Court (Resolution 171 (II) of 14
November 1947). A similar theme occurs in later Assembly resolutions.

Although the Court would, without doubt, be a far more effective
instrument had it more cases to decide, it has nevertheless built up an
important body of jurisprudence since the First World War.

According to Rosenne, 66 new cases were filed with the Permanent
Court in the period between the wars; 12 were discontinued, and the
Court gave 27 advisory opinions, 32 judgments and 137 orders. The
present Court, in the period 1946 to 1973, had 60 new cases filed with

it; gave 15 advisory opinions, 34 judgments and 186 orders; seven cases were discontinued, and eight removed from the list by the Court.[11]

Among the most important cases from the point of view of the Law of the Sea are the Corfu Channel case of 1949, which has a bearing on passage through straits, the 1951 Anglo-Norwegian Fisheries case, which established that States with an indented coastline may measure their territorial sea from straight base-lines joining headlands; and the North Sea Continental Shelf Cases of 1969 to which reference is made in the next Chapter. Such is the authority and prestige of the Court that its decisions in these cases have already found their way into various drafts of the new Code.

A Note on Codification

The point of departure at the beginning of this Chapter was the variety of different sources of international law, all of which have something to contribute: the practice of States, accepted over a period of time; the decisions of a whole hierarchy of international tribunals, permanent or *ad hoc*, including not only arbitral tribunals but also courts for the judicial settlement of international disputes; the decisions of municipal courts around the world; the writings of scholars and publicists; the United Nations and the family of its organs and specialised agencies, as unifying factors in State practice.

The crowning achievement in this process is the codification of whole areas of international law, in the form of international conventions to which all or a large number of States are parties.

It would be hard to find a better example of the codification process at work than the Vienna Conference of 1969 on the Law of Treaties. In the stages leading to the final Convention, all the processes outlined above can be seen at work. The practice of States in treaty-making, over the centuries, was the raw material; the decisions of courts and arbitral tribunals over a long period were concerned to a large extent with the interpretation of treaty provisions and the settlement of disputes arising from treaties; on the municipal level, treaties to which the State is a party must in most civilised countries be taken into account by municipal courts. Scholars have devoted much attention to treaty problems over the years; the International Law Commission, whose members include some distinguished scholars, worked for 20 years on the draft, referring it back repeatedly to Governments where treaty and legal divisions in foreign ministries around the world studied the successive drafts and commented upon them clause by clause. At the same time, scholars in universities and learned institutions contributed their views and international law journals and other publications aired their opinions. Finally, delegates representing over 100 countries (the list reads like an international Who's Who of legal scholarship) met in Vienna to debate the International Law Commission draft, in two long sessions in the summer of 1968 and 1969. The Vienna Convention on the Law of Treaties which emerged from these sessions is indeed a monumental achievement.[13] It will be studied in the foreign ministries of the world, and will undoubtedly set the pattern for many years to come—not only for those States which have ratified it, but for the "lesser breeds without the Law" which may hesitate to formalise their adherence to the Convention but will follow it more or less faithfully, if not because they are bound by its provisions in any literal sense, then because it represents the most thoroughgoing statement of customary international law on the subject to be found to-day.

The Convention on the Law of the Sea, if and when it comes, will draw on the same sources; like a river, it will fuse and unite in itself many streams and trickles.

Will it come, in the fullness of time, to express such a formidable consensus that no respectable State would wish to be seen to go against it?

Notes

1.   The Statute of the International Court appears in Annexure 1, as part of the Charter of the United Nations.

2.   Oppenheim, L. *International Law.* Edited by H. Lauterpacht. Vol 1, Ch. IV.

3.   O'Connell, D.P. *International Law.* 2nd. ed. Stevens and Sons, London, 1970.

4.   De Lapradelle, A., and Politis, N. *Receuil des Arbitrages Internationaux.* Paris, 1905. (Background to the Jay Treaty).

5.   La Fontaine, H. *Pasicrisie Internationale, 1794-1900 (Histoire Documentaire des Arbitrages Internationaux)* Berne, 1902.

6.   Trindade, A.A. Can4cado. "The Domestic Jurisdiction of States in the Practice of the United Nations and the Regional Organizations." *International and Comparative Law Quarterly*, London, 1976.

7.   Permanent Court of International Justice. *Advisory Opinion in the Case of the Nationality Decrees in Tunis and Morocco.* PCIJ Series B, no. 4. (7 February 1923.)

8.   Fincham, C.B.H., *Domestic Jurisdiction.* A.W. Sijthoff, Leiden, 1948. (Reviewed in the British Yearbook of International Law, 1948.)

9.   International Law Commission. United Nations Publication 67. V. 4. Office of Public Information.

10.   Lalive, J.-F. "La Jurisprudence de la Cour Internationale de Justice." *Annuaire Suisse de Droit International* Vol VI, 1949. Zurich, 1950. (See also n. 12.)

11.   Rosenne, Shabtai. *Documents on the International Court of Justice.* Sijthoff—Oceana, Leiden and New York, 1974.

12.   Hambro, Edward. *The Case Law of the International Court.* A.W. Sijthoff, Leiden, 1966.

13.   Rosenne, Shabtai. *A Guide to the Legislative History of the Vienna Convention.* Sijthoff-Oceana, Leiden and New York, 1970.

Chapter Three
Where Land Meets Sea

Internal Waters, The Territorial Sea and the Contiguous Zone

In broad terms, it may be said that the internal waters of a State are part of its territory, over which it exercises jurisdiction as complete and unfettered as the sovereignty which it enjoys in respect of the land; the territorial sea is a zone which may be regarded as the seaward extension of its territory, over which it exercises a sovereignty which is qualified only by the "right of innocent passage"—the right which foreign vessels enjoy to navigate on the surface under certain conditions; and the contiguous zone is the seaward extension of the territorial sea, in which the coastal State may exercise only such rights as are accorded to it by international law, for certain limited purposes.

It follows that a ship leaving harbour would normally pass through three distinct zones on its way to the high seas, each zone having its own distinct status under the Law of the Sea.

Internal waters include those harbours, bays and inlets the openings of which are of a certain breadth, and bear a certain relationship to the area enclosed; the so-called "historical bays" which, although not conforming to these standards, have long been recognised as belonging to the coastal State whose jurisdiction over them has never been effectively challenged, and all areas of sea to the landward side of a line which the law allows the coastal State to draw as the baseline from which it is entitled to measure its territorial belt.

More obviously, internal waters include waters which are fully enclosed in the land territory, including waters which lie within the territory of the coastal State and have only a narrow channel to the open sea, which channel falls within its territorial waters.

For the purposes of this study, the regime of internal waters may be left aside; it has more to do with the internal jurisdiction of States

33

than with the Law of the Sea. There will be occasion to return to it, however, in connection with the consensus which is emerging in regard to the status of the waters of archipelagos, which are the subject of another chapter.

The concept of the territorial sea goes back a long way, although it is only in the last few centuries that it has acquired anything like the present form and content. The Israeli jurist Shabtai Rosenne has found in the Talmud what must surely be the earliest recorded reference to a zone of State sovereignty extending into the sea:

> What is deemed to be the land of Israel, and what is deemed foreign parts? Whatever slopes down from the mountains of Ammanus inwards is the land of Israel, and outwards is foreign parts . . .we imagine a line drawn from the mountains of Ammanus to the Brook of Egypt [the Wadi-el-Arish? the Nile delta?]. All within that line is considered to be the Land of Israel . . .[1]

Apart from this rather isolated case, there is little sign that the jurists of antiquity had given thought to the matter. Even the Roman Law, whose writ ran over most of Europe, the Middle East and North Africa, and which may be regarded as one of the most durable legal systems in history the effects of which are still felt to-day, has little to say on the subject.

This is perhaps not surprising. Until comparatively recent times, the sea was regarded as a hostile element peopled by legendary monsters, subject to storms and fickle winds and calms, and incapable of being subjected to man's will in the way that the land could be tamed by the sword, the plough and the controlled use of fire.

Besides, the hegemony of Rome—the classical example of a legal regime based on conquest and the exercise of power—left little room for argument as to which countries' ships could operate in which waters, and under what rules. The use of the sea was free to all, provided only that it did not conflict with the one overriding regime. Whatever served the Pax Romana was legitimate, and what did not must be suppressed—a rule-of-thumb which had the merit at least of simplicity. It was only centuries later, in the context of competing nationalities and spheres of interest, that it became important to sort out the ground rules and draw the boundaries of States' control of the seas and oceans.

The notion of the territorial sea and the concomitant right of "innocent passage" was established in the nineteenth century. Its birth was not without incident and some travail, but the law and practice of States has crystalised over the years until the outlines are today fairly clear.

How do we come to the idea of a territorial sea in the first place? When the onion-skins of argument and theory are peeled off, we are left with a simple pragmatic answer. A coastal State has interests in a belt of sea or ocean off its coasts, however broad or narrow it may be. It has ports which must be defended against seaborne invaders, against pestilence, against outsiders engaged in traffic in harmful drugs, or bringing arms which may threaten its security. It has fisheries, the peaceful use of which requires that its fishermen should not suffer interference in its coastal waters; it has the right to defend itself, which means it should be able to deploy its naval and military forces around its shores and to carry out maneuvres even if its waters have to be temporarily closed to foreign vessels; it has fiscal and health regulations to enforce, and an interest in preventing the pollution of its beaches, its fisheries and its shore installations.

In short, the sovereignty of a coastal State over its land territory would be weakened, perhaps fatally, if it did not exercise a similar authority in a belt of sea immediately adjacent to its coasts.

The idea of such a belt emerged as a marriage of pragmatic need and legal theory, which is typical of the evolution of the Law of the Sea.

The nub of the problem is simply that at some point in the shifting and trackless waters, a legal regime of State sovereignty must give way, abruptly, to its opposite—a regime of free passage on the high seas, with all that this implies. Small wonder that the dividing line between two such distinct juridical regimes—the line which coincides with the outer limit of the territorial sea— should have been the subject of so much controversy.

The question of who should control or appropriate the sea erupted in the seventeenth century. In the "battle of the books," to which reference is made in Chapter 4, it was Grotius' doctrine of the freedom of the high seas which prevailed and became one of the king-pins in the classical Law of the Sea. The argument reflected a real dichotomy. On the one hand there was the interest of coastal States in maintaining control of such part of their coastal waters as would make their control of the land mass secure and meaningful; on the other, there was the interest of all States, members of the international community, in being able to move freely in peace and in war, over and under the waters, in being able to harvest the wealth of the sea (which until recently meant its living resources) and to develop whatever mineral resources might be available.

It is the point of contact or "interface" between these two sets of interests which has hitherto defied the efforts of the international community to establish it, but which is now for the first time in sight of being fixed.

The seventeenth and eighteenth centuries were the centuries of exploration and expansion, and the maritime nations had a vested interest in keeping their options open. Most of these options were tied up with narrow jurisdictional limits; such limits suited their book, and when it came to finding a suitable philosophy as a peg on which to hang practices which they favoured, one peg was as good as another. In this way, the three-mile limit became something of a sacred cow.

Before the codification conference held in The Hague in 1930 there was already a move afoot to recognise a contiguous zone—a zone in which the coastal State could exercise certain limited and clearly defined rights, which however would fall short of the sovereign rights it had over its territorial sea. The purpose of such a zone would be essentially practical. It is difficult to exercise proper control for fiscal, immigration, sanitary and other purposes if the authority of the coastal State is abruptly terminated when the outer limit of the territorial sea is reached. To deal with infringements within the territorial sea it is sometimes necessary to intercept offenders before they enter the territorial sea or after they have left it.

The genesis of this idea—like that of other ideas relating to anything as elusive as the principles of maritime law—was somewhat confused. There was much talk of territorial rights for certain purposes only, e.g., for fiscal or sanitary control, for the protection of fish stocks or for the control of pollution. The trouble about such a fragmented approach is that it runs into difficulties of legal theory which are almost insuperable. The very idea of sovereignty for certain purposes only is a contradiction in terms, since the concept of sovereignty as it has evolved over the centuries, implies full and unfettered control by the State. It was the great French jurist, Gidel, who cleared up the muddle in a course of lectures which he gave to the Academy of International Law in The Hague in 1934. The gist of his argument, which is now generally accepted, is simply that the rights which the coastal State enjoys in the contiguous zone do not flow from its sovereignty over the land mass and the territorial sea. On the contrary, the contiguous zone is part of the high seas, which are open to all; and such limited rights as the coastal State may exercise in the zone are a derogation from the freedom of the high seas and can only be justified by international agreement, whether by way of treaties or by virtue of rules of customary international law which are widely accepted.[2]

It is this concept which takes shape in the 1958 Convention, where it is provided that:

> . . .in a zone of the High Seas contiguous to its territorial sea, the coastal State may exercise the control necessary to (a) prevent infringement of its customs, fiscal, immigration or sanitary regulations within its territory or territorial sea.

This is followed by the express provision that:

> . . .the contiguous zone may not extend beyond 12 miles from the base lines from which the breadth of the territorial sea is measured.

The 1958 Convention on the Territorial Sea and the Contiguous Zone is a truly remarkable achievement. Shabtai Rosenne describes the four Geneva Conventions on the Law of the Sea, of which this is one, as "in their way, a monument to the skill of those who initiated the United Nations codification process . . ."

For those readers upon whom the language of treaties has a soporific effect, it may be useful at this stage to highlight some of the main features—the more so as the law which is laid down in this particular Convention is unlikely to be very substantially changed in our time.

The sovereignty of a State extends to a belt adjacent to its coast, known as the territorial sea, to the airspace above it and the seabed and subsoil below; it is measured, normally, from low water mark. Where the coast is deeply indented or otherwise confused from the point of view of the map maker, the method of straight base lines (hallowed by the International Court in 1949 in the Anglo-Norwegian Fisheries Case) may be used—i.e., one may measure outwards from straight lines joining appropriate headlands or islands, provided the general conformation of the coast is followed.

Whatever falls to the landward side of such a base line comes under the regime of internal waters (through which there is no right of innocent passage). The waters of a bay the coasts of which belong to a single State may in principle be regarded as internal waters. There are articles defining when a bay is a bay (a shallow curvature of the coast does not qualify) and a reservation in favour of "historic" bays, which may not conform to the criteria laid down in the Convention but are nevertheless entitled to the status of bays because of long usage, widely accepted and acquiesced in by the community of States.

Roadsteads normally used for the loading and unloading of ships may be regarded as territorial waters, even though falling outside the limits — i.e. in the high seas adjacent to territorial waters.

There are articles defining an island (not an easy task, but a task of some importance. Islands possess a territorial sea whereas elevations which are exposed at low tide but submerged when the tide is high may or may not affect the measurements of the territorial sea depending on where they are situated. Drying rocks situated outside the territorial sea belt do not, in general, have a territorial sea of their own).

As between States whose coastlines face each other over a relatively narrow sea, amounting to less than twice the breadth of the territorial sea, the territorial sea of each extends, in principle, to the median line.

The coastal State exercises sovereignty over its territorial sea, subject to the right of other countries to move their shipping through it in conformity with the regulations of the coastal State and with rules which are fairly clearly defined in the Convention. This is known as the Right of Innocent Passage. In order for passage to qualify as innocent, there are four sets of rules which apply to four classes of vessel—all ships, merchant ships, government ships and warships. These rules are largely a matter of common sense. As the phrase suggests, passage is innocent only if it poses no threat to the coastal State's security or its fishing or other activities and does not pollute its waters. Submarines, for example must navigate on the surface and show their flag.

The Right of Innocent Passage does not include the right to fly over the territorial sea and warships may be required to leave the territorial sea if they fail to comply with the regulations of the coastal State.

It will be noted that these articles, which say a great deal about the legal regime of the territorial sea and about the points or baselines from which it should be measured, do not lay down what the breadth of the territorial sea should be. A long series of conferences, including the Codification Conference held in The Hague in 1930, the 1958 Geneva Conference which produced the convention summarised above, the

1960 Conference which was convened to settle this very point, the numerous sessions of the Seabeds Committee and, latterly, the six successsive meetings of the Third Law of the Sea Conference, have failed to come up with an agreed answer, although it seems one is now in sight.

In the absence of agreement on this rather important detail, the practice of States has varied all the way between the two extremes. At the one end of the scale, the traditionalists claimed only a territorial sea of three miles and used all their influence to discourage other States from claiming a wider belt. The three-mile limit, which was never universally accepted but which enjoyed wide observance during the period of mercantile expansion when freedom of navigation seemed the most important aim, was based on the so-called "cannon-shot" rule. The Dutch jurist van Bynkershoek, basing himself on the undoubtedly sound principle that the sovereignty of a State can extend only as far as its long arm will reach, came up in the eighteenth century with the somewhat less sound idea that the effective range of a shore based cannon was three miles. This may have been true in his time, but such a limit would have little relevance today.

At the other end of the scale, one or two of the Latin American countries staked a claim — some felt against all reason and modesty — to a territorial sea of 200 miles.

Since no agreement on the breadth of the territorial sea had been reached at the 1958 Conference (or at the 1960 Conference which was called specifically to try to overcome the deadlock) States felt free to make their own dispositions. Most of them accepted that 12 miles should be the limit, although they felt justified in putting together the combination which suited them best within that framework. A large number declared a territorial sea of six miles and a contiguous zone of six miles — adding up to the 12 miles beyond which the 1958 Convention said the contiguous zone should not extend. A proposal to adopt this "6 + 6" formula failed by only one vote to achieve the necessary two-thirds majority at the 1960 Conference. This meant that it did not come to be written into the existing Convention; but the mere fact that a majority of States favoured the "6 + 6" formula lent it respectability and encouraged other States to extend their jurisdiction in one form or the other to the 12-mile limit. Some preferred a territorial sea of three miles with a contiguous zone of nine miles, or some other combination suited to their conditions.

At the time of writing, no less than 60 States have adopted either a 12-mile limit to their territorial waters, or a combination adding up to 12 miles and embracing a belt of full sovereignty and a contiguous zone in which limited rights of surveillance will be exercised. Other States which have not yet claimed 12 miles in one form or another would be happy to go along with a universal 12-mile limit.

There can be little doubt that the Third Law of the Sea Conference will produce a consensus of States in favour of a 12-mile limit to the territorial sea, thus exorcising the ghost which has frustrated man's efforts for so many years.

If there is a grey area of uncertainty, it is in relation to the exact nature of coastal States' rights within the 12-mile zone. As we have seen, the 12-mile limit crept into the practice of States through several back doors and is in itself a somewhat mixed notion. The limited rights appertaining to the contiguous zone were part of the total area of mixed jurisdiction claimed by many States; and even these rights were but poorly defined before 1958. It is of interest to note that at the Hague codification conference in 1930, there was some controversy as to whether the need to proclaim exclusive or preferential fishing zones was sufficient justification for a State's claim to a contiguous zone. The majority at that conference were against such a notion.

In sum, the 12-mile limit to the territorial sea may well have come to stay if—and it is a large "if"—a satisfactory answer can be found to the problems which an extension of the existing limits may create in straits used for international navigation. There will be more to say on this question in the chapter which follows.

Notes

1. Rosenne, Shabtai. "The Concept of 'Territorial Sea' in the Talmud." *Israel Law Review*, vol. 10, no. 4, October,1975.

2. Gidel, Gilbert. "La Mer Territoriale et la Zone Contigué." *Receuil des Cours de L'Academie de Droit International*,1934, vol.II (No. 48): Librairie du Receuil Serey, Paris.

Bibliography

Oppenheim, L. *International Law*. ed., H. Lauterpacht. Longmans.

Bourquin, Maurice. "L'Organisation de Voies de Communication." *Receuil des Cours* (op cit), 1924, IV, (No. 5)

Fernandez, Javier Illanes. *El Derecho del Mar y sus Problemas Actuales*. Editorial Universitária de Buenos Aires, 1974.

Paolillo, Felipe H. "El Mar Teritorial y la Zona Contigua." In *Tendencias del Derecho del Mar Contemporaneo*, edited by Francisco Orrego Vicuña. Buenos Aires, 1974 (UNITAR Publication.)

Reuter, Paul. *Droit International Public. Deuxième Partie–Communications*. Presses Universitaires de France, 1976 (5th ed.)

O'Connell, D. P . *International Law*. Recent ed. Stevens & Sons, London, 1970.

O'Connell, D. P. *The Influence of Law on Sea Power*. Manchester University Press, 1975.

Blum, Yehuda. *Historic Titles in International Law*. (especially Ch. VI.) Martinus Nijhoff, The Hague, 1965.

Barrie, George N. "Historical Bays." *Comparative and International Law Journal of Southern Africa*. May, 1973.

Smetherman, Bobbie B. and Robert M. *Territorial Seas and Inter-American Relations: With Case Studies of the Peruvian and United States Fishing Industries*. Praeger Publishers, New York, 1974.

Oudenijk, J. K. *Status and Extent of Adjacent Waters–A Historical Orientation*. A. W. Sijthoff, Leiden, 1970.

Chapter Four
The Legal Status of Islands

The 1958 Convention describes an island as "a naturally formed area of land, surrounded by water, which is above water at high tide."

The Informal Composite Negotiating Text produced after the Sixth Session of the Law of the Sea Conference in July 1977 is a document of nearly 200 pages containing the draft texts (suggested by the Chairmen of the main Committees) of some 303 Articles, together with several annexes.

The draft is divided into fourteen parts, of which Part VIII consists of a single article devoted to the regime of islands. The first paragraph of this article defines an island in terms which follow, verbatim, the wording of the 1958 Convention.

To point this out is merely to emphasise that the basic concepts for determining what is or is not an island have remained pretty well unchanged. The old definition will serve, and serve admirably; all that is needed is to bring it into relation with the new concept of the 200-mile economic zone which is discussed in Chapter 9.

In the latest draft, two very important principles are enunciated in the paragraphs which follow the definition of an island.

The first dramatically affects the area of the high seas which will be left to be exploited as the Common Heritage of Mankind; it provides that islands have their own territorial sea, contiguous zone, continental shelf and—here is the rub—economic zone.

The second provides, quite simply, that "rocks which cannot sustain human habitation or economic life of their own shall have no exclusive economic zone or continental shelf" (This does not mean that they cannot be taken into account in drawing baselines round highly indented coasts, or round archipelagos).

43

The fact that even a very small island may claim an economic zone stretching for 200 miles in all directions around it, or may be sitting on top of a continental shelf which is even more extensive, could give a new look to the map of the oceans. This is graphically illustrated in Fig. 1, which shows how the Pacific Ocean (admittedly the most extensive of the oceans, and the one most richly endowed with islands and archipelagos) may look when all the islands which qualify for economic zones of 200 miles, have claimed them.

This may well be a case where, in the Biblical phrase, "the last shall be first". How many islands lie scattered over the oceans, whose inhabitants eke out a bare subsistence at present, but are the heirs to a potential fortune? Some, though by no means all of them, have oil or natural gas on their continental shelves, which they have not yet discovered or are not yet able to exploit through lack of funds or technology, although they are, in fact, entitled to so so in terms of the 1958 Convention on the Continental Shelf. Others, being merely the tips of underwater mountains rising steeply from the ocean floor, have no continental shelves but will now be able to lay claim to the resources of the deep sea-bed within a radius of 200 miles. The fact that they themselves are not able to exploit such resources need not be crucial; they can do so in co-operation with an advanced country, or with the international seabeds authority which it is hoped that the Convention will bring into being.

In terms of the ratio of land area to (potentially) valuable undersea resources, islands stand to gain most, proportionately, from the emerging regime.

Recent history has shown how a factor like the energy crisis—long predicted but largely ignored in the West—can alter the balance of economic and political power around the world. Few could have foreseen, a generation ago, that obscure desert sheikdoms whose parched and dusty sands produced barely enough to keep man and beast alive, could by today have attained to such wealth as would have made King Croesus look like a small-time operator, and such economic leverage as would cause the chanceries of the world to tremble, and to vie with one another to do obeisance at the cost of principles and traditions which had been centuries abuilding.

It is to be hoped that the world will not be treated, as the new Law of the Sea emerges, to another spectacle of surrender to expediency and the ethics of the marketplace. But if the 200-mile economic zone is to become law, and if the zones are as important as we believe them to be,

Figure 1

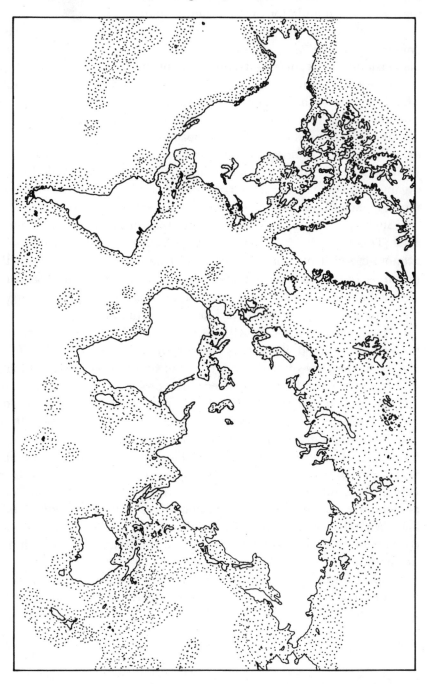

then clearly a certain shift of economic, political and strategic advantage will take place in favour of islands, perhaps out of all proportion to the size of the populations which they sustain.

An island, as defined in the article quoted earlier, must be a "naturally formed" area of land. This clearly excludes artificial or man-made islands. For centuries, islands have been constructed in relatively shallow seas by dumping quantities of rock and soil. The artificial islands so formed have been used as platforms for seabirds producing valuable guano, or to enable shafts to be sunk to mine such resources — mostly coal — as might lie below the seabed. In recent times, real-estate firms have been offering custom-made islands, to be constructed in shallow seas according to the purchaser's specifications. Who has not dreamed, at some stage, of retiring to an island, and visualised how it might look, and perhaps even longed to design it?

Such artificial islands have neither territorial sea nor contiguous zone. This being so, it is hardly to be expected that they would have economic zones of their own or would be able to lay claim to the resources of their continental shelves. The same would apply to such artificial platforms as a coastal State might construct for prospecting, as meteorological stations or for various monitoring purposes.

From the foregoing it will be seen that the regime of islands, however chequered its history may have been, is emerging fairly clearly in the Law of Nations and in the new dispensation which is shaping up. It is to be expected that problems will arise at the "interface" where it may be argued that a specific island does or does not fit the definition — but this type of problem will always be with us. A more challenging group of problems will come to the fore when the international community adopts 12 miles as the maximum limit which States may claim to their territorial sea, and when a number of islands which have hitherto lain outside the three- or six-mile zone of a neighbouring State suddenly find themselves within the new 12-mile belt. What happens to the territorial sea, the contiguous zone, the continental shelf rights and the economic zone of an island which now lies within the territorial waters of another State?

There are legal problems here which are of absorbing interest but to which justice could be done only by devoting more space to the question than is available here.

Chapter Five
Related Groups of Islands—
The Special Case of Archipelagos

Archipelagos come in different forms and sizes. Consider, at the one extreme, Greece which consists of a relatively large area of the European mainland; of the Peloponnese, which were joined to the mainland by the narrow Isthmus of Corinth until the Canal, which had been dreamed of by the Caesars and the digging of which was started abortively by Nero, was completed just before the turn of the century; and of some hundreds of islands in the Ionian Sea, the Cretan Sea, the Mirtoan Sea and the Aegean; islands varying from Crete which was large enough and fertile enough to sustain one of the great civilizations of antiquity, all the way to barren and uninhabited rocks; islands which stand alone or are clustered in groups, surrounded by relatively open areas of the sea; and islands which are so close to the shores of other countries as to impinge upon their territorial waters so that special agreements, arbitrations, or judicial decisions have been necessary to demarcate the boundaries.

Countries like Greece, which combine the features of a continental State with those of a State having important groups of islands scattered over a wide area of the seas, are in a category of their own.

Consider, at the other extreme, what may be described as the typical ocean archipelagos; groups of islands like the Galapagos, Mauritius, the Seychelles or the Fiji Islands—simple uncomplicated groups of islands standing in relative isolation, far from any mainland State.

Different considerations of law and policy apply to these two types of archipelagos. One thing they have in common, however, is that they

pose problems to the international community which cannot always be
resolved by the rules of classical international law.

There is a dichotomy between the desire of an archipelago State to
keep its scattered territory together, and the interest of the community
of States to keep the sea-lanes open. For the archipelago States tend to
sprawl over areas of water which are of vital importance to navigation.
Indeed, as a glance at Figure 2 will confirm, some of the most
important archipelagos not only lie athwart the trade routes but form
the very crossroads where such routes converge. The legal status of the
waters between the islands is therefore of direct concern to the
community as a whole. To quote McDougal and Burke:

> The possible effect of enclosing archipelagic waters as internal
> waters is dramatically illustrated by the estimate that in the case
> of Indonesia, access to an area of water 3,000 miles in length
> could be closed to foreign navigation at the discretion of local
> authorities.[1]

It is only in recent years—indeed only since the First World
War—that the international community has begun to address itself
seriously to the question of archipelagos. The problems were perhaps
less urgent, though no less complex, in the case of archipelagos
situated in relatively "crowded" areas; some of them had long since
been compelled by the pressures of history to seek accomodation with
their neighbours, whether based on conquest or on the unchallenged
exercise of sovereignty over the islands which they claimed as their
own. The problems were, in a sense, more urgent in the case of
the ocean archipelagos which, because of their isolation, had not
yet succeeded in sorting themselves out vis-à-vis the international
community, whose demands were sometimes sharply opposed to their
own interests.

It is in relation to the ocean archipelagos that the progress made
during successive sessions of the Law of the Sea Conference, and of the
Seabeds Committee which preceded it, can be most clearly discerned.
It could indeed be said that the attention given to this type of
archipelago by the Conference is somewhat out of balance compared
with the interest shown in other archipelagic problems. Perhaps a
contributing factor is that it is possible to study the underlying legal
issues with more hope of success in the case of isolated groups of
islands; once the legal principles have been hammered out, they could

be applied or adapted to the far more complex situations found in the "mixed" archipelagos. Whatever the reasons however, the Conference has not yet produced a single draft article on the "mixed" archipelagos.

Two opposing views emerged in the studies which led up to the Hague Conference of 1930 for the Codification of International Law. They continued, with minor modifications, until the present day— through the work of the International Law Commission which preceded the Geneva Conference of 1958, through the Conference itself, and through the lengthy deliberations of the Third Law of the Sea Conference and its equally lengthy build-up in the Seabeds Committee.

Essentially, the one view which was canvassed in 1930 was that the islands forming part of an ocean archipelago were sufficiently protected by existing rules in the classical Law of the Sea. Each of the islands would be entitled to a territorial sea of its own, and to its internal waters where the definition fitted (i.e., waters to the landward of such baselines as the law allowed the islands to draw for the purpose of measuring their territorial sea). Where islands were so far apart that their territorial seas did not meet or overlap, there would be an area of the high seas in which all the freedoms of navigation and overflight, which were later to be so clearly set forth in the 1958 Convention on the High Seas, would apply. Vessels passing through the territorial sea of islands forming part of an archipelago, would enjoy the right of innocent passage as they would in any other territorial sea.

In contrast to this view the archipelagic States, led by Fiji, the Phillipines, Indonesia and others, have, with increasing cogency, been putting forward the case for a special status to be given to archipelagic waters.

Their argument is that where the national territory is fragmented over a group of islands, often small individually and scattered over a wide area, the sea between is as much a part of the national territory as are the islands themselves. Some of the ocean archipelagos like Iceland are heavily dependent on fishing for their livelihood. Others, being less compact than the Icelandic Archipelago, find that control of the sea between their islands is essential for defence, for communications, for administrative control, and for the enforcement of their laws on immigration, health, fiscal, customs and pollution control matters. By the very facts of geography, the archipelago States must always stand with one foot in the water and one on land.

As early as the 1930 Codification conference at The Hague, where the "conventional" view discussed above was brought forward, the idea was mooted that archipelagic States should be entitled to establish the baselines for measuring their territorial waters by drawing straight lines joining the outermost islands and drying rocks of the archipelago. Everything falling within such closing lines should have the status of internal waters; and outward from the closing lines the territorial belt would be measured. In the areas so demarcated, the normal rules would apply; in territorial waters, vessels of all flags would enjoy the right of innocent passage, whereas their presence in and passage through internal waters would be subject to the absolute discretion of the coastal State.

This idea failed to gain the necessary support in 1930; but it has steadily gained ground until today a consensus is emerging with a few modifications. What factors could have brought about such a change? First among them is undoubtedly the shift of emphasis in recent years from the freedom of navigation which is so important to the maritime powers, to the rights of coastal States which are essentially resource-orientated.

The decision of the International Court in the 1951 Anglo-Norwegian Fisheries Case[2] helped to provide a rationale and a juridical basis. It is a short step from the Court's now well-known ruling that the baselines for measuring Norway's territorial waters could be drawn by joining the outermost islands and headlands of her coast, to the idea that the same principle could be applied to groups of islands standing alone—the ocean archipelagos.

And lastly, decisions of the international or any other community depend not only on the merits of the case, objectively considered, but also on the skill with which the case is presented.

Credit must be given to those (and not least to the attorney-general of Fiji) who have kept the special interests and problems of the archipelago States before the international community in session after session of both the Seabeds Committee and the Conference.

To say that the international community has finally come to recognise the justice of the archipelago States' claim to a special status for their waters is not to say that the issues have been thought out to their legal conclusions. The "Informal Composite Negotiating Text" which emerged from the Sixth Session of the Conference in July 1977 contains draft articles on archipelagos which few jurists could accept as being satisfactory.

Article 47 of the draft, for instance, allows archipelagic States to draw straight baselines joining the outermost islands and drying reefs,

Figure 2

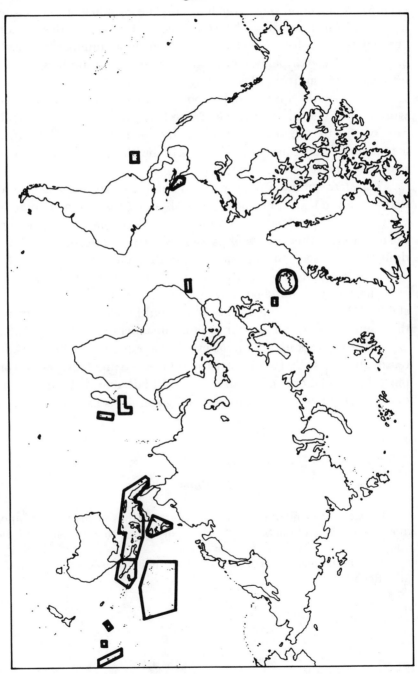

provided that such baselines enclose the main islands "and an area in which the ratio of the area of water to the area of land, including atolls, is between one to one and nine to one." The Article goes on to provide that such baselines should not be more than 100 miles in length "except that up to three per cent of the total number of baselines enclosing any archipelago may exceed that length, up to a maximum length of 125 nautical miles."

Such criteria appear to be too arbitrary, and too precise, to be worthy of universal acceptance. There is nothing sacrosanct about the ratio of nine to one, nor about the distance of 100 or 125 miles, and it is a fair guess that these provisions will be the subject of some hard bargaining before an agreed text emerges.

The status of the waters within an archipelago is not satisfactorily defined in the text. It has been clear all along that the maritime States would accept a special regime for archipelagic waters only if, and to the extent that, their rights of passage were not adversely affected. The draft Articles seek to balance the requirements of the international community against the equally real needs of the archipelagos.

The fact that no clear concept has emerged to explain the legal status of the waters in an archipelago should not cause undue concern; there will be occasion to refer to other instances of a legal norm being created *after* the community has evolved a regime to fit its needs. It is a reasonable guess that attempts to adapt the existing legal framework to meet the special case of archipelagos will fail, and that a new concept of archipelagic waters as unique— *sui generis* —is hatching.

Notes

1.   McDougal and Burke. *The Public Order of the Oceans: A Contemporary International Law of the Sea.* Yale University Press, New Haven and London, 1965.

2.   International Court of Justice. "The Anglo-Norwegian Fisheries Case." *I.C.J. Reports*, 1951.

Chapter Six
Straits

The idea that the breadth of the territorial sea should be fixed across the board at 12 miles is one of the few rules which seem at this stage to be reasonably certain of acceptance by the international community. Such a rule would merely set the seal of respectability on what has become the practice of coastal States.

But there is a caveat. Maritime powers, which have a vested interest in the freedom of navigation, have made it clear that their acceptance of a universal 12-mile limit of territorial waters is contingent upon a workable system of guarantees to secure their right of passage through straits.

Straits are the crossroads, as it were, on the way from one ocean to another, or from the open sea to the territorial waters of riparian States. Ships proceeding from the Indian Ocean into the Red Sea must be able to pass freely through the straits of Bab-el Mandeb; and those bound from the Atlantic to the Mediterranean must be assured of unimpeded passage through the Straits of Gibraltar.

Maritime powers insist that such rights of passage must not be subject to any but the absolute minimum of regulation; and that it matters not whether the vessel is a warship or a merchantman, what flag it is flying and whither it is bound. Freedom of navigation must be maintained, subject only to the physical security of the riparian State, and it must prevail over local and temporary political rivalries or states of belligerency.

There are 116 straits around the world (Fig. 1) which are generally admitted to be straits used for international navigation. The list could

57

be shrunk or expanded—but only marginally— according to how the term "international navigation" is circumscribed. Such straits occupy a position of crucial importance to the freedom of navigation, which remains the most basic of the rules of the Law of the Sea, without which the orderly regime which has evolved over the centuries would collapse.

The practice of States in regard to the right of passage through straits, and the law which protects and rationalises that practice, have evolved through centuries of war and diplomacy, arbitration and the decisions of judicial tribunals, custom and treaty-making, and today the main features can be fairly clearly discerned.

Where a strait is broader than the combined breadth of the territorial waters of the riparian States on either side of it, so that there is a zone of high seas passing through the strait, there is normally no problem; the strait is merely a continuation of the high seas which are open to all. Even in such a case there may be complications which are the exception rather than the rule; as where the zone of high seas forms an isolated pocket, as it were, surrounded on all sides by territorial waters; or where the zone which qualifies by its geographic position as "high seas" is shallow or otherwise unsuitable for navigation, so that ships are compelled to pass through the territorial belt of one or other of the riparian States. These are special cases which in the future as in the past may call for special solutions by means of treaty arrangements between the States most concerned.

Without going into details, it will be seen that the adoption of a universal limit of 12 miles to the territorial sea will eliminate the corridor of high seas passing through a number of straits which are less than 24 miles in breadth, but broader than the sum of the territorial belts on either side at present claimed by the riparian States.

By way of illustration, one could visualise a strait just 15 miles broad at its narrowest point, the shores of which belong to two countries each claiming a territorial sea of six miles. There would be a corridor of high seas, three miles broad, passing between the two territorial belts and having the status of high seas. If a universal belt of 12 miles were adopted the corridor of high seas would disappear and the strait would then become a territorial strait with a median line to demarcate where the territorial sea of the one state becomes the territorial sea of the other.

In the case of straits which are narrow enough to be encompassed by overlapping zones of territorial waters, i.e., territorial straits, the rights of passage are analogous to those which apply in any territorial sea. Ships may exercise the right of innocent passage—a right which is clearly circumscribed in the Law of Nations and which if reduced to its essentials means simply that foreign ships may pass through the territorial waters of a coastal State provided that they do so in such a way as not to threaten its security. The coastal State does however have the right to suspend temporarily the right of foreign vessels to pass through its territorial waters fronting on the open sea—as for example during naval maneuvres. Not so, however, if its territorial waters form part of a strait. Here the global imperatives of navigation take priority.

Where both shores of a narrow strait belong to a single country, the strait is part of the territorial waters of the country concerned. This is the case with both the Bosphorus and the Dardanelles, which lead from the Mediterranean and the Aegean Sea to the Black Sea, both shores of which form part of Turkish territory.

The Turkish Straits provide a particularly interesting case-study, both because of the change in their status which took place in the eighteenth century, and because of the treaty law which has grown up around their use.

So long as Turkey was in possession of all the shores of the Black Sea, it could be argued that the Straits gave access only to the internal waters of Turkey. She was therefore free, if she so chose and did not voluntarily sign away her rights in treaty arrangements, to exclude foreign vessels from the Bosphorus and the Dardanelles.

The position changed when Russia became a Black Sea power in the eighteenth century; the Black Sea ceased to be internal waters under the absolute sovereignty of Turkey. Treaties were concluded between Turkey and various foreign powers, allowing free passage to merchantmen (but not to naval vessels) through the Straits. The exclusion of foreign men-of-war was confirmed by several subsequent treaties, but was largely rescinded in 1923 by the Treaty of Lausanne which demilitarised the Straits, placing them under the supervision of an International Commission, under conditions which secured for the Black Sea States a greater measure of freedom to move their ships both to and from the Mediterranean.

The 1936 Convention of Montreux (between Turkey, France, Bulgaria, Greece, Roumania, Russia, Yugoslavia, Japan and, later, Italy) established a new regime which still applies today. It provides a model which is of lasting interest, in that it manages to achieve a workable balance between the security interests of a country in control of a strait

(Turkey), the needs and interests of neighbouring countries dependent upon the straits for access to the world's seas and oceans (the Black Sea States), and the interest of the international community in freedom of navigation.

The Treaty allows merchant ships to pass freely through the Straits in peace and in war, but allows Turkey as the riparian State to refuse transit to merchant ships of countries with which she herself is at war, and to levy certain charges and enforce sanitary measures. Warships, in time of war, may be denied transit of the Straits if Turkey is a belligerent or if she feels that her security is threatened — though in such case the League of Nations (and now, presumably, the United Nations) could decide by a two-thirds' majority to overrule that measure. Apart from this, warships of belligerents may have freedom of passage, but only if the errand upon which they are bound is in conformity with the Covenant or pursuant to a treaty of mutual assistance binding upon Turkey.

In peacetime, the access of foreign, non-Black Sea warships is rationed on a quota basis. Men-of-war of the Black Sea powers, however, may have unlimited transit through the Straits if they pass through singly, escorted by not more than two destroyers.

The regulation of transit through the Bosphorus and the Dardanelles has demanded a great deal of skill and statesmanship over the years. It has resulted in a treaty which, if it at first sight seems rather complicated, has worked remarkably well. It is not surprising, therefore, that it has been the subject of a number of studies from the diplomatic, historical and especially from the juridical angle.

By contrast, the Straits of Gibraltar, which, by their position as a potential bottleneck between the Mediterranean and the Atlantic, must be ranked among the most important straits in the world, have given rise to little controversy through the years. There is precious little in the way of treaty law and no international court cases from which the status of the waters could be deduced. In the "Entente Cordiale" of 1904 between Great Britain and France, there is a short paragraph in which both parties, in order to assure free passage through the Straits, undertake not to allow the construction of fortifications of any kind on the coast of Morocco coast, which was then under French sovereignty. That is about all.

It is of some importance that the waters of the Strait at one point are as narrow as 7½ miles. Since Spain claims a territorial sea of six miles and Morocco one of three miles, it will be clear that no ship can pass through the Straits of Gibraltar without entering the territorial waters of one of these States. The fact that ships have passed freely since ancient times, and that they continue to do so with a minimum of fuss, is as strong an argument as one could desire for the existence of a rule of customary international law assuring free passage through straits in all but the most exceptional circumstances.

Not all the 116 straits used for international navigation are subject to a regime laid down in treaties, whether between members of the international community at large or between two or more of the States most intimately affected. Many of the world's straits—both those having a corridor of the high seas passing through them and those whose waters are made up of the territorial sea of one or more countries—are regularly used by merchantmen and warships relying upon the protection afforded by customary international law.

Since the emergence, and eventual acceptance of rules of customary international law tends to be a slow process (hampered as it is by the lack of an international legislature to enact new laws) the jurist must take a hard analytical look at such leading cases as may have been decided by competent international tribunals. As far as the right of passage through straits is concerned such a case is to be found in the decision of the International Court of Justice in the Corfu Channel case. This decision is indeed a watershed, the more so as the Court rejected the arguments of both parties and proceeded to lay down principles which had until then been somewhat uncertain.

The facts of the case are simply stated. On their way through the narrow channel which divides Corfu from the Albanian mainland, two British warships were damaged by mines planted by Albania in her own territorial waters. Relying on the right of free passage, and the concomitant right to take the necessary steps to ensure it, British naval vessels thereupon carried out a minesweeping operation without permission from Albania.

Among the principles which the Court laid down were the following;

It reaffirmed the principle that foreign men-of-war must be allowed the right of transit through straits used for international navigation; that the right of innocent passage may be exercised without previous authorization by the coastal State; that the coastal State may not prohibit such passage in time of peace although it may, if the circumstances warrant it, regulate such passage by imposing reasonable conditions on the foreign vessel. Not least, the Court rejected attempts to narrow the principle down in specific cases, by holding that it was not necessary that the strait should be the only, or even the best route between two parts of the high seas; it was sufficient that it provided an alternative route and that it was in fact used for international navigation.

It was on this decision that the International Law Commission based itself in formulating what was later adopted by the Law of the Sea Conference in Geneva in 1958 as Article 16(4) of the Convention on the Territorial Sea and the Contiguous Zone. This paragraph states quite simply that "there shall be no suspension of the innocent passage of ships through straits which are used for international navigation between one part of the high seas and another part of the high seas, or the territorial sea of a foreign State."

Thus it was that the customary law principle, as laid down by the Court in the Corfu Channel case, passed into the body of conventional law, where it is binding at least on the 44 States signatories of the Convention, and has considerable persuasive force as a precedent and as evidence of a rule of customary law. Somewhere between the International Law Commission draft and the text finally adopted by the Plenipotentiary in Geneva, a word was suppressed. The draft of the Commission referred to straits *ordinarily* used for navigation. In eliminating this word, the Conference rejected what would have been a somewhat more restrictive definition than that used by the Court.

A brief look at the Single Negotiating Text issued at the May 1976 session of the Conference shows that the principles enshrined in the 1958 Convention, in customary international law and in a number of treaty arrangements, are likely to form the basis of whatever new regime emerges. Indeed, one could go further and hazard the guess that a regime ensuring freedom of passage through straits, on the basis of the established principles, will be the condition precedent, *the sine qua non*, for acceptance of any new Convention by the major seafaring and trading nations of the world. And without their support the Convention, will never come into being, or if it does, will be still-born.

The point has been made in other chapters that the Single Negotiating Texts have no status in the sense that they do not reflect a consensus among the States taking part in the Conference; as the term indicates they are a basis for negotiation and no more. Nevertheless they do reflect what in the judgement of the Chairmen of the main Committees are the main currents of thought which have manifested themselves during the years of discussion in the Plenipotentiary

Conference and in the many long sessions of the Seabeds Committee which preceded them.

The main features of the Single Negotiating Text as it applies to the straits question have been summarised in a United Nations document as follows:

In the case of straits over which sovereignty is exercised by coastal States (i.e., territorial straits) the Convention will not affect most internal waters within such straits, the status of waters beyond the territorial sea of countries bordering straits, or the regime of long-standing conventions governing passage through such straits. Nor would there be any change where a similar and equally convenient route through a given strait exists.

Where a strait links two areas of the high seas, or affords passage from the high seas to an exclusive economic zone, ships and aircraft would have freedom of passage and overflight "solely for the purpose of continuous and expeditious transit." It follows that they must proceed without unnecessary delays, and refrain from any action which might threaten the independence or sovereignty of the coastal State.

Riparian countries in control of straits would be entitled to designate sea lanes and to prescribe traffic separation schemes, once these had been adopted by the "competent international organization"; they could prescribe certain conditions relating to safety of navigation and pollution control, prohibit fishing and impose customs and sanitary regulations. States using the strait should cooperate with the controlling State in improving navigational aids and preventing pollution by ships.

The crucial provisions are that transit through straits may not be hampered or suspended and that the rules of innocent passage would apply to certain straits including those leading from the high seas or an economic zone to the territorial sea of a foreign State.

It remains to be seen whether the formula proposed in the Single Negotiating Text of 1976 can be made to satisfy both sides in the controversy.

The question of navigation through straits may seem at first sight to be a relatively simple one. It should not be beyond man's ingenuity to devise a regime for straits which would reconcile the interests of countries facing upon straits with those of countries which are dependent upon passage through straits, in peace and in war.

In practice however, the question is by no means simple, and some pundits would go so far as to say that it might prove the toughest nut of all to crack. One has only to consider the two extremes in the confrontation which is shaping up, and to realise the number and the ramifications of the positions in between. Compromise is always possible, especially when it involves some kind of arithmetical mean. But the interests involved are vital interests, touching upon issues both of national sovereignty and national security — the kind of interests on which governments cannot or dare not compromise.

At the one extreme there is the interest of the State in control of a strait used for international navigation to safeguard its own safety. Unrestricted freedom of passage for foreign ships — including warships — could in times of conflict or even in times of undeclared war, of tension and of mutual distrust, mean freedom to carry out espionage, to move weapons of mass destruction into place for an attack on the coastal State or even to move vital supplies to a country with which it is at war. Small wonder then that they should want to restrict the passage of foreign vessels to proportions which they are able to control. The right of innocent passage, and such other rights as already exist under customary or treaty law are as much as they would want to concede to vessels passing through their straits.

On the other hand, from the point of view of the maritime States, the imperatives of maximum freedom of passage are just as compelling. The United States, as a superpower with a vital interest in being able to move its fleet to where it is needed and to supply its allies in time of crisis, made its position very clear in the 1971 Conference when it proposed that the right of passage through straits used for international navigation should be the right which a State enjoys on the high seas, rather than the more limited right of innocent passage which it now exercises in the territorial waters of a coastal State. This would include the right to overfly the straits and the right of submarines to go through submerged.

The right of innocent passage as laid down in the 1958 Convention on the Territorial Sea requires that submarines must navigate on the surface and show their flag. A reasonable enough requirement from the point of view of the coastal State; but not so satisfactory from that of the naval power concerned. Submarines, which are particularly vulnerable to attack from above, rely more than anything else upon concealment. By showing themselves they would greatly facilitate the enemy's task of pinpointing their position and progress. Nuclear submarines in particular, have a virtually unlimited cruising range and can remain submerged for long periods. There is a very real strategic hazard in surfacing and enabling enemy patrols to zero in on them with all the sophisticated tracking devices at their disposal. Furthermore under the regime of innocent passage as laid down in the 1958 Convention "the coastal State may take the necessary steps in its territorial sea to prevent passage which is not innocent." This leaves it open to the coastal State to determine (within the limits of the Convention, it is true, but there is always room for a subjective element) that a particular passage is not innocent. It is at least arguable that a coastal State could prevent the passage of a nuclear powered vessel, or a ship carrying a potentially dangerous cargo, or a vessel bound for a country with which it was at war.

Finally, there is nothing in the 1958 Convention to say that the right of innocent passage includes the right to overfly the territorial waters of the strait State. This could be a serious shortcoming. As recently as the Yom Kippur war of October 1973, the United States overflew the Straits of Gibraltar (and hence, necessarily, the territorial waters of one or the other of the riparian States) when air-lifting vital supplies to Israel.

In the case of those straits which previously contained a corridor of high seas and which under the new 12-mile limits would become territorial straits the major maritime powers may be expected to insist that nothing less than the freedom of the high seas which they have hitherto enjoyed in passing through such straits will suffice. There are various ways in which this could be achieved in an international convention; the problem is not so much one of legal drafting or of constitution-making, but rather of how the main contestants can be brought to agree on the outlines of a new dispensation.

Failure to reach agreement would almost certainly mean that the mixture as before will be administered — which may be summed up as follows:

Straits less than six miles wide will continue to fall into the territorial sea of the coastal State, if the strait concerned passes through its territory; or into the territorial waters of the riparian States if two or more States are involved, the boundary between the two or more territorial belts being determined in accordance with the median-line principle, or otherwise regulated by treaty between the riparian States. Rights of passage through such straits will continue to be regulated by international convention or by customary international law: they will not automatically carry the right to overfly or to navigate below the surface.

Where a strait is more than six miles wide, i.e., more than the sum of the two territorial belts measured from either shore, the international community will insist on retaining rights of passage not less favourable than those it now enjoys, whether or not the universal 12-mile limit to the territorial sea replaces the multiplicity of regimes we have today.

It is a curious anomaly that the three-mile limit to territorial waters, which was widely observed until recently although it never attained the status of a rule of international law, is nevertheless well entrenched in its application to straits.

It has been suggested in a previous chapter that the consensus which has now emerged in favour of a universal 12-mile limit to the territorial sea may be a result of one of those false turnings which history has a way of taking. In 1971, when the Enlarged Seabeds Committee first met in Geneva it seemed that agreement on a 12-mile limit—an agreement which had eluded the First and Second Conferences on the Law of the Sea held in Geneva in 1958 and 1960—would be a good step forward.

The idea of a 200-mile zone had not yet gained respectability and its advocates were referred to in some quarters—off the record of course—as the "lunatic fringe." As new ideas and new positions emerged over the 10 ensuing conferences the 200-mile economic zone not only became respectable, but also began to represent a consensus; the idea of a 12-mile limit however, which had been largely overtaken by events, continued under its own momentum.

Today it may well be asked what advantage a coastal State would gain by extending its territorial sea (if it had not already done so) to 12 miles. There would be no gain economically, since it could claim the resources of the sea and the sea-bed up to a distance of 200 miles. A possible gain, however, would be that it could compel foreign aircraft passing its coast to keep at least 12 miles away, since the right to innocent passage through the territorial sea does not bring with it a right of overflight.

But it may be asked whether the advantages to coastal States (the majority of which have already extended their control in one form and another to 12 miles and have made the concomitant adjustments) of a universal 12-mile limit, could possibly outweigh the drawbacks. The new rule would throw a spanner in the delicately balanced works by which international law as it has evolved over the years ensures the greatest practical measure of freedom to the world's shipping in navigating through straits.

It remains to be seen whether the international community will address itself to the problems of securing passage through straits—a task which may demand not only the declaration of a new rule but many treaty adjustments and arrangements to take care of individual cases—or whether it will decide to put paid to the whole exercise and to leave territorial limits as they are.

Bibliography

Brûel, Erik. "Les Détroits Danois au Point de Vue du Droit Internationale." *Receuil des Cours de l'Academie de Droit International*, No. 55, 1936, Vol.1. Librairie Hachette, Paris.

O'Connell, D. P. *The Influence of Law on Sea Power* (esp. Chapter VIII—the Access Routes of Sea Power). Manchester University Press, 1975.

Hambro, Edward. *The Case Law of the International Court*. A.W. Sijthoff, Leyden, 1966. [Especially extracts 165-168—Corfu Channel Case (merits)]. ICJ. Reports, 1949. pp. 28-31.

Hill, Charles. "Le Régime International des Détroits Maritimes." *Receuil des Cours de l'Academie de Droit International*, 1933, Vol.III. Librairie Hachette, Paris.

International Court of Justice. *The Corfu Channel Case, 1949: Reports of Judgments, Advisory Opinions and Orders: Judgment of 9 April, 1949*. A. W. Sijthoff, Leyden.

Lapidoth, Ruth. *Les Détroits en Droit International*. Publications de la Revue Générale de Droit International Public. Nouvelle Série 17, Editions A. Pedone: Paris 1972.

Lapidoth, Ruth. *Freedom of Navigation with Special Reference to International Waterways in the Middle East*. Jerusalem Papers on Peace Problems. The Leonard Davis Institute for International Relations, The Hebrew University, 1975.

Lapidoth, Ruth. "Le Passage par le Détroit de Tiran." *Revue Générale de Droit International Public*, Janvier-Mars, 1969, No. 1. Editions A. Pedone, Paris, 1979.

Oelofsen, P. D. "Third United Nations Conference on the Law of the Sea—Passage through Straits used for International Navigation." *Comparative and International Law Journal of Southern Africa*. November 1975.

Oppenheim, Ed. Lauterpacht. *International Law*. Vol. 1: Peace. 8th edition. Longman. (Part II, Chapter I, Section VIII).

Swing, John Temple. "Who will own the Oceans?" *Foreign Affairs*, April, 1976.

United Nations. Press Release SEA/214 of 7 May 1976. pp.14 and 15.

United Nations. Document A (CONF. 62/WP.8/Rev. 1, Parts I-III (Single Negotiating Text of the 4th Session of the Third United Nations Conference on the Law of the Sea; New York, May 1976.)

Chapter Seven
The High Seas

As the name suggests, the High Seas embrace all the vast areas of sea and ocean lying beyond the limits of national jurisdiction—i.e., beyond the internal waters and territorial seas of the coastal States. (The relationship between the High Seas and the Economic Zone or Patrimonial Sea is discussed in Chapter Nine.)

It is today universally accepted that the High Seas are an area in which the ships of all nations may navigate in peace and in war and where all may enjoy the freedom of fishing and overflight.

Such limitations as the Law of Nations imposes on the freedom of the High Seas relate to rules of law which are generally accepted, such as those concerned with the suppression of the slave trade and piracy, and with the principle that no State is entitled to use the seas in such a way as to create hazards to other users or to deprive them of their rights.

So well established are these ground rules, that one is apt to forget that the High Seas have not always been free.

Before going on to sketch the chequered history of this most fundamental of the principles enshrined in the modern Law of the Sea, it may be useful to consider however briefly the regime laid down in the Geneva Convention of 1958 on the High Seas. This is the more worthwhile since it seems unlikely that any further reexamination of this topic by the Third Law of the Sea Conference, or insofar as one can see ahead, by any other international meeting, will produce any drastic change.

It is perhaps suggestive that the opening words of the Convention refer to its provisions as being "generally declaratory of established principles of international law." No such claim is made in respect of the other three Conventions of 1958 — the Territorial Sea Convention considered earlier, the Continental Shelf Convention, or the Fisheries Convention. This means that we are dealing here with the *lex lata* — a codification of settled law rather than a law-making treaty in the sense in which the term is discussed earlier on in this book.

The key article of the Convention, which more than any other gives expression to the underlying philosophy, is Article 2, which provides that "The High Seas being open for all nations, no State may validly purport to subject any part of them to its sovereignty." Freedom of the High Seas is exercised under the conditions laid down in these Articles and by the other rules of international law. It comprises, *inter-alia*, both for coastal and for non-coastal States:

(1) Freedom of navigation
(2) Freedom of fishing
(3) Freedom to lay submarine cables and pipelines
(4) Freedom to fly over the High Seas.

After stating the central idea, the Convention goes on to make provision for free access to the sea by States having no sea coast and for equal treatment for ships of such land-locked States; for the right of each State to determine how and when a ship may be granted its nationality and the right to fly its flag.

A ship may sail under the flag of one State only — on pain of being treated as stateless — and shall, when on the High Seas, be subject to its exclusive jurisdiction. Warships have complete immunity from the jurisdiction of a State other than the flag State.

The flag State shall take measures conforming with generally accepted international standards, for the safety of life at sea.

In case of collision or "any other incident of navigation," only the flag State or the State of which the master or crew member concerned is a national, shall take penal or disciplinary action against him; and only the flag State may order the arrest or detention of a ship.

The obligation is placed on the master of a ship to render assistance to persons or vessels in distress, insofar as it may be possible, and on the coastal State to establish a search and rescue service.

All States are enjoined to prevent and punish the slave trade by ships flying their flag. A slave taking refuge on any ship shall automatically be free.

There are several articles defining piracy on the high seas, and prescribing when and under what conditions pirate ships or aircraft shall be seized.

In principle, and saving treaty provisions, a warship may detain a foreign merchant ship on the high seas only under certain well defined conditions, including reasonable suspicion that it is engaged in piracy or the slave trade.

A long and fairly involved, but interesting Article deals with the doctrine of hot pursuit, the principle that the pursuit of a vessel begun within the territorial sea or the contiguous zone may be continued into the area of the high seas, provided that the pursuit is continuous (the doctrine is discussed later in this chapter).

The duty of every State to prevent pollution of the seas by oil, by activities connected with the exploration and mining of the sea-bed, and by the dumping of radio-active wastes, is spelled out.

The Convention concludes with some rules about submarine cables and pipelines—the right of States to lay them, and their responsibility in case of cables and pipelines, fishing nets and other installations belonging to other States, being damaged through their actions.

It was pointed out at the beginning of this chapter that the seas and oceans have not always been open to all. Through a long and eventful period of history, the doctrine of the freedom of the high seas was opposed by the contrary view that they were capable of being brought under the dominion of States.

Lauterpacht points out that when the modern Law of Nations was emerging during the Middle Ages it was already fairly well accepted that States could extend their dominion over the open sea:

> Thus the Republic of Venice was recognised as sovereign over the Adriatic Sea, and the Republic of Genoa as the sovereign of the Ligurian Sea. Portugal claimed sovereignty over the whole of the Indian Ocean and over the Atlantic South of Morocco, and Spain over the Pacific and the Gulf of Mexico, both basing their claims on two Papal Bulls promulgated by Alexander VI in 1493, which divided the New World between these Powers. Sweden and Denmark claimed sovereignty over the Baltic, and Great Britain over the Narrow Seas (the St. George's Channel, the Bristol Channel, the Irish Sea, and the North Channel), over the North Sea and over the Atlantic from the North Cape to Finisterre.[1]

For several hundreds of years these claims were recognised, more or less. Perhaps there was some advantage to seafaring nations in accepting them, at least by default; the States which claimed sovereignty had some kind of duty, however imperfectly exercised, to control piracy; and the duties they imposed on other States to respect their flags were in any case not too onerous. The worm turned, however, when Spain and Portugal, after the discovery of America, started to take the sovereignty which they claimed a little too seriously and sought to deny foreign vessels the right to navigate over the vast areas of ocean space which they claimed as their own. Nothing destroys the authority of a law more speedily than the inability to enforce it; and other maritime powers, like Britain, France and the Netherlands, which had trading interests in the "closed" seas, were in no mood to abide by such limitations. Lauterpacht traces the germ of the notion of freedom of the open seas to the reply which Queen Elizabeth I returned to the Spanish Ambassador in 1580, when the latter protested at Drake's epoch-making voyage to the Pacific. "Elizabeth answered that vessels of all nations could navigate on the Pacific, since the use of the sea and air is common to all and that no title to the ocean can belong to any nation, since neither nature nor regard for the public use permits any possession of the oceans."[2]

The Portuguese and Spanish claim to sovereignty over the vast area of the oceans, could not but clash with the spirit of the new Age of Discovery dawning in the world. The battle-lines were drawn for the war of words and ideas.

The first broadside was fired by the Dutch, in the person of the now famous jurist Hugo de Groot (Grotius) who in 1609 published his treatise "De Mare Liberum" in which he argued that the Sea could not be brought under the sovereignty of any State, since sovereignty depends upon effective occupation and the sea was altogether too vast for that. He also advanced the "Natural Law" argument that the sea's bounty was inexhaustible and should therefore be open to enjoyment in peace by all nations. It is a curious reflection that the doctrine of the Mare Liberum which became universally accepted was founded by Grotius on premises which might well be challenged today although its conclusion would not. It could be said that Grotius came to the right conclusion for reasons which were convincing enough at the time but which would not necessarily hold good today when the Natural Law philosophy is in decline. It requires no great perspicacity however, to see that the real motive was to propose some counter to the Portuguese claim to exclusive use of the Indian Ocean—an area which was vital to the Dutch not least because of the East Indies.

Ruth Lapidoth goes so far as to say that "the freedom of the high seas is not a self-contained legal principle, but it is ancillary to and dependent upon another norm—the right to commerce and communication." She concludes: "Whatever may be the origin of the legal principle of the freedom of the high seas, it has acquired the status of an independent binding legal norm. It has long been an obligatory rule of customary international law . . ." It would be hard to find fault with this conclusion.[3]

Grotius' tract was followed by a spate of counter attacks, in a veritable "battle of the books" in which it was sought to defend the claims of those States which had asserted their sovereignty over the seas and oceans or parts of them. Perhaps the best known is the tract "Mare Clausum, sive de Dominio Maris," published by the British jurist John Selden in 1635. The arguments may seem a little esoteric today, and there is little point in reopening them as the die has now been cast; but for those readers who may wish to have a fuller account of the legal and philosophical issues involved, Professor Lapidoth's article is rewarding.

It may be noted in passing that whereas Grotius' arguments in favour of the "Mare Liberum" were not all such as would be accepted today when the trend is away from the "Natural Law" school of jurisprudence, the arguments of Selden, which lost the day, were not all so far off the mark considered in the modern context. He rejects the "natural law" argument that since the resources of the seas are inexhaustible it therefore follows that members of the community of States have an equal right to them. Indeed he rejects the very notion that the seas are inexhaustible, and in this sense anticipates the ecologists of today.

It is also a sobering reflection that Selden fought the good fight at a time when Holland was in the ascendancy as a maritime power, but when Britain had not yet reached that stage and was worried by the incursions of foreign vessels into the fishing grounds off her coasts. Only when Britannia moved into the class where she could fairly claim to "rule the waves" did she quietly drop her insistence on the salute to her flag and other trappings of sovereignty and become the leading champion of freedom of the high seas and narrow territorial belts.

The concept of the Mare Liberum, the idea that the high seas are open to all, did not immediately take root; but many writers in many countries built on the ideas which Grotius had put forward and the doctrine gained ground. Unlike Spain and Portugal Britain had never pushed her claim to sovereignty so far as to deny other States the right to navigate her seas. The freedom of navigation—one of the key elements in the freedom of the high seas—came to be established in fact and in practice although some pockets remained where the older concepts held sway. Venice for example continued to control the Adriatic until the middle of the seventeenth century.

In the eighteenth century most writers of any consequence came out in support of the Mare Liberum doctrine—but with a difference. Side by side with the view that the high seas should be open to all, there emerged a recognition that coastal States could validly assert their dominion over a narrow maritime belt—the territorial sea which is the subject of Chapter 2.

If it be accepted that the ground rules governing man's conduct in the high seas have been set in a form which is unlikely to be changed in the foreseeable future, it remains to consider some of the main exceptions to the regime.

The High Seas Convention of 1958, the main features of which are summarised above, made special provision for two international crimes, slave trading and piracy, and had some interesting things to say about the doctrine of hot pursuit and about the special status of warships.

It may be asked why, if the high seas are open to the ships of all nations, the Law allows the arrest of pirate ships and ships engaged in the slave trade. The answer appears to be that piracy and the slave trade are recognised as crimes against the international community. Those who engage in such activities are outlaws like the highwaymen of old. Every State has the right and indeed the duty to apprehend them and bring them to justice.

The classical definition of piracy covers any unauthorised act of violence committed by a private vessel (i.e., not a warship) against another vessel with intent to plunder.

There is a large volume of international agreements and of jurisprudence on this subject, built up over the years by municipal and international courts. Much of it is concerned—since the basic rules are not in dispute—with defining what acts constitute piracy. The original concept has in effect been clarified and expanded over the years. The "intent to plunder" for example has acquired a somewhat wider meaning, so that today there are good grounds for the view that when the crew of a vessel mutinies (whether the mutiny is violent or carried out with the aid of a toy pistol) with the object of taking over the ship and its cargo, it is committing piracy; but where the mutiny is directed to getting rid of an unpopular officer rather than to robbery or plunder, the crew may become liable for murder, manslaughter, insubordination or some other heinous offence, but not necessarily for piracy. (The reader will no doubt have thought of the classic, much dramatised example of the mutiny on the *Bounty*.)

The thin red line which divides piracy from other crimes committed on the high seas is well documented in the literature and is in itself an absorbing study. For the purposes of this book, suffice it to say that piracy can be committed only on the high seas (the same act, when committed in territorial waters, comes under a different regime); that by the act of engaging in piracy, a vessel automatically forfeits the protection of the flag State and becomes an outlaw vessel under the Law of Nations; and that any vessel can arrest it and bring it into port where its master and crew can be tried, sentenced and punished by the local court according to local municipal law. The law applied by such courts may differ, but any court in a civilised country would take into account the position of pirates under the Law of Nations.

Although piracy has not yet been completely suppressed, there can be little doubt that the Law of Nations as it has developed over the last century has gone a long way in this direction. Where it does occur, in the more inaccessible areas of the world, it survives as an anomaly and an exception to the rules of civilised conduct. (It is a sad comment on our times that the international community has been so much less succesful in dealing with piracy in its modern guise of the hijacking of aircraft, a scourge which could readily be brought under control if States could agree on tough measures against it and apply them honestly and consistently.).

In contrast to the law on piracy, which can be regarded as a crime under the Law of Nations, the legal position of slavery and the slave trade is much less settled. Starting with the Congress of Vienna in 1815, which condemned the institution of slavery in rather general terms, and culminating in the Slavery Convention of the League of Nations of 1926, in which the States parties to the Convention undertook to suppress and prevent slavery *in all its forms*, a long series of international instruments were addressed to one or other aspect of slavery and the slave trade. Unfortunately, as annual reports of the United Nations attest, this loathsome institution continues to exist in certain parts of the world. One reason no doubt is that it is more difficult to detect and control. The traffic in human beings—whether war captives or children sold into slavery or prostitution by their parents—is carried on in the more inaccessible regions of the world and is deeply ingrained in the custom of some primitive societies; whereas piracy (by definition) takes place on the high seas which are subject to no nation but where only the writ of the world community runs.

A factor which throws some doubt on whether slavery can be regarded as an international crime in the narrow formal sense of the term, is the difficulty of determing exactly where slavery ends and its equally vicious offshoots begin. It is a matter of definition. If one includes under the heading of slavery any form of unpaid forced labour imposed on human beings without proper trial, for offences which would not be considered offences by civilised States, one comes to the sad conclusion that slavery flourishes in one guise or another, in all too many of the States which are most vociferous in their defence of human rights

The right of hot pursuit has an interesting legal history and there are a number of leading cases which would repay closer study by the reader with a penchant for jurisprudence. The origin of the doctrine, as it applies on land in the various municipal legal systems, is probably quite simple; when an offender is pursued by officers of the law and arrested, the arrest is deemed to have been made at the point where the chase began. This is perhaps not so necessary today, when the administration of justice is more or less centralised, but in earlier times it could determine which Court had jurisdiction to try an offender. There was an obvious advantage in the rule that the Court of the area where the offence was committed and where the evidence and witnesses could be most readily assembled, should try the case rather than the Court of the area to which the offender happened to flee.

There is some doubt as to how this doctrine which was based in the first place on common sense found its way into the Law of the Sea. O'Connell sums it up in one terse sentence:

> The doctrine has been explained as an emanation of the primordial right of self-defence, a projection of a rule of common law, a continuation of an act of jurisdiction already begun, and a delegation of jurisdiction in the interests of international order.[4]

Whatever its philosophical basis, the doctrine was well established at the time of the Codification Conference at The Hague in 1930.

It emerged from the 1958 Geneva Conference as Article 23 of the Convention on the High Seas. It will be seen that the right of hot pursuit arises when the coastal State has reason to believe that a foreign vessel has violated its laws. Pursuit may be begun when the offending vessel (or one of its boats) is in the internal waters, the territorial sea or (insofar as the more limited contiguous zone rights are involved) in the contiguous zone; it may be continued outside these areas if the pursuit has not been interrupted, into the area of the high seas. The right of hot pursuit ceases as soon as the fugitive enters its own territorial sea or the territorial sea of a third State, whose sovereignty must always be respected. The right may be exercised only by warships or military aircraft or by specially authorised Government vessels and aircraft such as those of the coastal patrol. Compensation may be payable where a ship is stopped or arrested on the high seas without justification.

It has been said earlier in this chapter that the basic rules governing man's conduct on the high seas are unlikely to be changed by the current or any foreseeable future revision of the Law of the Sea. Whatever regime is established for the exploitation of the resources of the sea-bed and ocean floor "beyond the limits of national juris-diction"—i.e., beneath the high seas—there will still be freedom of navigation and overflight, freedom to lay pipelines and cables, freedom to fish and to mine (subject to the rules of customary international law and to such limitations as States may voluntarily impose themselves by the Convention). Vessels will continue to be under the jurisdiction of their flag State alone; warships will continue to enjoy the same immunity from visit and search; pirates and slave-traders will continue to be treated as outlaws; and vessels breaking the law in the seas under the jurisdiction of coastal States (such as fishing without licenses, smuggling, violating health and sanitary and security regulations etc.,) will continue to be chased into the high seas and arrested under the law of hot pursuit.

The principles are likely to remain although their detailed appli-cation may well become more difficult, and the law more nuancé, as the area of the high seas is reduced by the encroachment of 200-mile zones, and the seabed and ocean floor beneath them is more intensively explored and exploited.

Notes

1. Oppenheim, ed. Lauterpacht. *International Law*. 8th ed. Vol. 1, p.583. Longmans, Green & Co., London, 1955.
2. Oppenheim, ed. Lauterpacht. *Op.cit*. Vol. 1, p.584.
3. Lapidoth, Ruth. "Freedom of Navigation and the New Law of the Sea." *Israel Law Review*, Vol. 10, No.4. October, 1975..
4. O'Connell, D. P. *International Law*. 2nd ed. Vol. 2., p.663. Steven and Son, London, 1970.

Bibliography

Kish, John. *The Law of International Spaces*. A. W. Sijthoff, Leyden, 1973.

Chapter Eight
The Natural Prolongation of the Land Mass—Continental Shelves

The traditional Law of the Sea was concerned primarily with the maritime interests of the major sea-faring nations. Although the living resources of the sea have been an important source of protein for mankind, there was little concern about their conservation until about 25 years ago. The mineral resources of the sea remained largely untapped until after the Second World War. Technological developments during the third decade of this century, and particularly during the Second World War, opened up the possibility of exploiting these resources in the shallower parts of the continental shelf.

The first major departure from the classical approach to the Law of the Sea — the Law of Grotius and his *Mare Liberum* — was the Truman Proclamation of 1943 in which the United States of America staked its claim to the resources of its continental shelf and in so doing, triggered off a chain reaction of claims by other nations.[1]

The nub of the Truman Proclamation is the sentence " . . .the Government of the United States regards the natural resources of the subsoil and the seabed of the continental shelf beneath the high seas but contiguous to the coast of the United States as appertaining to the United States, subject to its jurisdiction . . . the character as high seas of the waters above the continental shelf and the right to their free and unimpeded navigation are in no way thus affected."

There was no mention of a depth or distance limit to this jurisdiction, although press releases accompanying the Truman Proclamation described the continental shelf generally as being " . . .submerged land which is contiguous to the continent and which is covered by no more than 100 fathoms (600 feet) of water . . ."

83

How did the United States seek to justify this revolutionary departure from the old concept of sovereignty over a narrow belt of territorial waters (three to a maximum of 12 miles), while the rest of the seas and oceans were subject to free and unfettered use by all? The answer to this lies in the series of "whereas"-es in the Preamble to the Proclamation. This speaks of the world-wide need for petroleum and other minerals, the discovery and exploitation of which should therefore be encouraged; of the technological progress which was bringing these resources withreach of mankind; and of the view that the "exercise of jurisdiction over the natural resources of the subsoil and seabed of the continental shelf by the coastal nation is *reasonable and just* since the effectiveness of measures to utilise or conserve these resources would be contingent upon cooperation and protection from the shore, since the continental shelf may be regarded as an extension of the landmass of the coastal nation *and thus* naturally appurtement to it, since these resources frequently form a sea-ward extension of a pool or deposit lying within the territory, and since self-protection compels the coastal nation to keep close watch over activities off its shores which are of the nature necessary for the utilisation of these resources" (Italics added).

Not a model of English style, perhaps, but the reasoning emerges.

So many States followed the USA in pegging out claims, whether flimsily or soundly based, to the resources of the Shelf, that four years later the International Law Commission was charged with the task of preparing a draft treaty which might, so the Assembly hoped, bring some kind of order into an area of the Law of the Sea which was becoming increasingly chaotic. Whatever the legal reasoning behind them, unilateral claims do not favour the orderly development of international law. The legal argument tends to be rather partisan; it must, in the nature of things, proceed from premises and legal philosophies peculiar to the State advancing it.

The notion of the continental shelf as the natural prolongation of the land-mass will be readily understood after a glance at figure 2.

This does not mean, however, that the shelf always conforms in all respects to the criteria we have laid down for it. The elemental forces which shaped the dry land and the sea, in the remote beginning of the world, have not read the Convention and there are areas which do not fit as neatly into the picture as our diagram might suggest. The average depth of the continental shelf averages from about 130 metres to as much as 500 metres.

In a multilateral treaty, a definition must be more than merely descriptive. States, like individual taxpayers, will try to get away with as much as the law allows. This means that there must be firm and definite criteria. Should we adopt a depth criterion for determining what is or is not a continental shelf? Or a distance criterion? Or a geological one? If a depth criterion, what depth should be regarded as decisive? At the time of the Truman Proclamation, the United States spoke of 100 fathoms — a figure which is near enough to the 200 metres which appeared in the Convention of 1958. But this was, and remains, a rather arbitrary figure.

The principle of coastal State jurisdiction over the resources of the continental shelf was discussed for several years by the International Law Commission and was incorporated in the Continental Shelf Convention adopted by the First Law of the Sea Conference in 1958. Article I of the Convention defined the continental shelf as: "...the seabed and subsoil of the submarine areas adjacent to the coast but outside the area of the territorial sea, to a depth of 200 metres or, beyond that limit, to where the depth of the superjacent water permits of the exploitation of the natural resources of the said area."[2]

The history of the debate concerning the outer limit of coastal State jurisdiction over the resources of the continental shelf revolves around four separate textual elements of Article I.

The first element is the term "continental shelf" itself. While it can be maintained that since the term is defined it is merely an "X" quantity, the history of the debates on Article I indicates that the retention of the term was considered significant by its proponents as well as its opponents. The legal continental shelf is not necessarily restricted to the geophysical shelf, nor does it include all the geophysical shelves.

The second element is the word "adjacent." The history of Article I(a) reveals that concepts of adjacency appeared quite early in the debates of the International Law Commission and were used by proponents of nearly all formulae. It does appear to restrict the seaward distance beyond the 200 metre isobath to which a coastal State may claim jurisdiction over the resources of the seabed.

The third element is the inclusion of the 200 metre criterion. It pervades the history of both the geological and legal concepts of the shelf. The legal experts believed that the 200 metre isobath roughly approximates the depth of the outer edge of the world's continental shelves. It should be remembered that commercial exploitation of petroleum beyond that depth appeared a remote possibility in 1958. Commercial exploitation at water depths greater than 200 metres has in fact only recently taken place.

The final element is the "exploitability" criterion. Does this mean technological or commercial exploitability? Would exploitation in waters deeper than 200 metres automatically modify the 200 metre provision on a world-wide basis or only locally?

Although a great number of different interpretations of these four elements have been proposed it is clear that the Continental Shelf Convention did not establish a definite limit to the coastal State's jurisdiction over the resources adjacent to its coasts. On the other hand, the history of the debates reveals no attempt to subdivide the ocean floor between coastal States. Most experts would agree that the ultimate limit of coastal State jurisdiction in terms of the Convention would be the base of the continental margin.

However, the "open-ended" definition means that as its technology improves, a State can push further and further out to sea the area of continental shelf in which it can claim exclusive rights. Such shifting frontiers to the State's jurisdiction over the natural resources of its shelf can produce nothing but conflict. The *reductio ad absurdum* is that coastal States with an advanced technology can have exclusive control of the resources of vast and ever-increasing areas whereas those without the necessary technology must stick to the rule book. This is perhaps an over-simplification; it is doubtful whether countries without any kind of a continental shelf in the geological sense (i.e., where the water drops precipitately down from the shore to the abyssal depths of the ocean) would be able to use the exploitability criterion to back up claims to a continental shelf which they did not possess. But this is an extreme case. There are many coastal States with very extensive continental shelves by any accepted test; a few of these States are capable of working at great depths, although most are not.

The Continental Shelf Convention of 1958 was ratified by 50 States—not a great number compared with the 150 which make up the present membership of the United Nations (and there are sovereign States like Switzerland, which are not members).

It is basic to treaty law that a State can only be bound by engagements which it has freely accepted; and the reader might therefore be forgiven for drawing the common sense conclusion that only about a third of the members of the international community of

States need take heed of the Convention, since only they have elected to be bound by it. It does not work this way, however.

International treaties are law-making in two distinct and complementary ways. The first and obvious way is that they create binding obligations with immediate effect between the States parties to them; the second and more insidious, but no less important way is that conventions, and the work which went into them, and the crystallisation of thinking and of State practice which follows them, can and do develop into customary international law which the International Court and a whole network of general and special arbitral tribunals are enjoined to take into account in their decisions. An important point in this regard is that the Truman Proclamation was never challenged by any State.

A case of crucial importance, both in the context of the Law of the Sea and in the broader context of the influence of conventions on customary law, is the North Sea Continental Shelf Case, which was decided by the International Court of Justice in 1969.[3]

This was a case between the Federal Republic of Germany on one hand, and Denmark and the Netherlands on the other, concerning the delimitation of the boundaries between their respective continental shelves in the North Sea.

The details need not concern us here; what does matter is that in deciding the issue, the Court held that "the rights of the coastal State in respect of the area of the continental shelf that constitutes a natural prolongation of its land territory into and under the sea, exists *ipso facto* and *ab initio*, by virtue of its sovereignty over the land, and as an extension of it in an exercise of sovereign rights for the purpose of exploring the seabed and exploiting its natural resources. *In short there is here an inherent right*" (Italics added).

The significant thing about this judgment is that only 13 years after the Geneva Convention on the Continental Shelf the Court could find that a State (Germany) which was never a party of it could be bound not by the Convention itself, but by the customary international law which had in the meantime grown up around it. The result was much the same. The Court was not guided by the 1958 Convention—as it was at pains to explain at various points in the Judgment—but by the law which had crystallised round it.[4]

The fact remains however that in the 24 years since the Truman Proclamation, legal thinking, including that which led up to and followed the 1958 Convention, had moved inexorably towards the principles which it declares. In the light of this decision of the world's highest legal tribunal, there can be no doubt that the concept of the coastal State's jurisdiction over the resources of the continental shelf has passed into the body of the Law of Nations, and that the customary law (which in this case has solidified in record time) exists independently of and side-by-side with the conventional law created (for those who accepted it) by the 1958 Treaty.

If the legal right of coastal States to the resources of their continental shelves is not accepted, and there is an international Convention to prove it, why is the issue important to the new Law of the Sea which is emerging, and what are the legal issues which have yet to be solved?

It has been said that the fatal defect in the Continental Shelf Convention of 1958 was the open-ended definition, as it introduces the test of exploitability—a test which is altogether too uncertain, being tied as it is to the level of technological skill available to coastal States at any given time. We are back to square one and must try to work out an acceptable definition, from the point where the Commission and the 1958 Conference side-stepped the issue and went off the rails.

But what kind of test could be adopted? Distance from the baselines, or depth, or the physical conformation of the shore and the way it falls off to the abyssal depths? Or a combination of these elements? Each has merit, and all are imperfect, being either too arbitrary or too fatally vague.

In the informal single negotiating text presented by the Chairman of the 2nd Conference in the dying days of the Geneva Conference of the spring of 1975, an attempt is made to say what the continental shelf is, although the Chairman is at pains to explain that the "single text" has no status and does not profess to incorporate a consensus but is merely a procedural device to focus the argument. It is perhaps still helpful as illustrating a body of opinion which may or may not emerge as the majority view. According to this formulation, the continental shelf comprises "the seabed and subsoil of submarine areas that extend beyond its territorial sea through the natural prolongation of its land territory to the outer edge of the continental margin, or to a distance of 200 nautical miles from the baselines from which the breadth of the territorial sea is measured, where the outer edge of the continental margin does not extend to that distance."

Why 200 miles, and what has this to do with the continental shelf which is a fairly clear concept reflecting the physical shape of the sea's edge? Thereby hangs another tale which can perhaps best be unfolded in the context of the economic zone or patrimonial sea, a new concept which is superimposed, as it were, on that of the continental shelf. At this stage, it is enough to say that the continental shelf retains its importance for at least 31 States which have margins extending beyond the 200-mile limit of distance; and if these seem an insignificant minority one must not forget that there are States which have neither broad nor narrow shelves — indeed have no shelves at all since they are landlocked — and that they constitute an important "floating" vote, which could move this way or that.

It is common cause that the rights which the coastal State exercises over the resources of the continental shelf are sovereign rights, but only within certain parameters. They are rights for the purpose, and only for the purpose, of exploring the shelf and exploiting its natural resources. Such rights, as the International Court has clearly laid down, are inherent and *ipso facto*: they do not depend on occupation by the coastal State or on any express proclamation.

We have referred to "its natural resources" in relation to the shelf, and this immediately brings us up against a question mark. What are the resources of the shelf? Obviously they include mineral and non-living resources and — by an extension which has itself been the subject of some lively argument between States — living resources which are sedentary in nature, being attached to or dependent on physical contact with the seabed. Clearly, shoals of fish which breed, navigate and have their being through the waters lying above the shelf (or what the Convention refers to, poetically, as the superjacent waters) are not subject to the continental shelf regime; they are not appurtenant to the shelf. But what of the less athletic species such as oysters and lobsters which spend a large part of their lifespan attached more or less to one spot?

As far as the latter are concerned, the controversy between France and Brazil which raged in the early 'sixties, and which became known as the "Lobster War" raised some nice points of jurisprudence. Lawyers may indeed be forgiven a slight twinge of regret that the case was settled by argreement and thus never reached the International Court. There is something rather appealing about the thought of 15 learned judges wading through huge mountains of evidence and argument, and addressing their erudition to the question of whether a lobster, from the larval stage to the stage when it appears on a Parisian menu through all the vicissitudes of its conception, birth, reproduction and death, is a sedentary creature and thus an appurtenance of a continental shelf claimed by Brazil; or whether it belongs to a free-swimming species, a denizen of the superjacent waters and is therefore legitimate prey for a French fisherman operating far from his home port. As if the question were not difficult enough, we have the case of creatures which are of roving disposition during their youth, but which become singularly immobile during maturity and old age. Hence the stress in the 1958 Convention, and in the single negotiating text which it closely resembles, on the way of life of creatures "at the harvestable stage."

It is accepted law that the rights of the coastal State over the resources of its continental shelf do not affect the status of the superjacent waters or of the air space above them, and that subject to reasonable controls the coastal State may not prevent the laying of submarine cables and pipelines over its shelf.

Artificial islands, installations and platforms on the continental shelf are under the exclusive control of the coastal States; it may forbid other States to erect them or may authorize them to do so subject to pollution, safety and other controls.

Where a continental shelf is shared between opposite or adjacent States, the boundary between their respective shelves must be determined by agreement, in accordance with the principles of equidistance and the median line, or failing that by arbitration.

As far as scientific research on the continental shelf is concerned, it has been suggested that research is like motherhood — everyone is in favour of it, and it is just a question of modalities. Unfortunately the question of research is not so simple. There is a thin red line dividing research for pure-minded purposes, and sheer espionage; a State may be prepared to welcome research by other States into the problems of its shelf — particularly if they are well-equipped to carry out such research and open-handed in sharing the results with the host State. But it is all a matter of confidence. Research vessels are admirably equipped for spying; and the data turned out by the marine research teams, though in themselves innocuous, may and often do have strategic value when all the pieces are put together. It is a well-known principle of intelligence that a comprehensive picture of the enemy's dispositions and weak points may be built up by assembling the pieces of a jigsaw each individual element of which may seem insignificant.

It is a fair guess that when an agreed text of scientific research on the continental shelf is reached, it will be a wolf in sheep's clothing — an innocuous sounding formulation saying all the right things about scientific research but concealing real teeth by reserving coastal States' rights to refuse permission for scientific research by others on their shelves for reasons which seem good to them and which will not have to be explained.

How does the single negotiating text produced at the end of the Geneva session of the Conference in the Spring of 1975 and subsequently revised differ from the provisions of the Continental Shelf Convention of 1958? Hardly at all: there is only one article which is new in substance and conception, and which reflects the new emphasis on the sea as the common heritage of mankind. It provides that a coastal State having a continental shelf broader than 200 miles, should pay an as yet undetermined percentage of what it earns from exploiting its shelf beyond the 200 mile limit to the International Authority which should distribute this largesse equitably, "taking into account the interests and needs of the developing countries."

There is also in the first article of the Committee II text, containing the geological definition of the continental shelf, a reference to the 200 mile criterion which however seems to bear no relation to the descriptive criteria. There will be occasion to return to this in the chapter on the Economic Zone concept.

It must be stressed that the single negotiating text is only a beginning. But what to us is significant is that this beginning, tentative though it may be, bears a remarkably close resemblance to the end result achieved in 1958.

The emergence of a new and dynamic concept—that of the 200-mile economic zone—is discussed in chapter nine.

It might be supposed that the consensus which is emerging in favour of allowing coastal States to have exclusive control of the economic resources within a 200-mile belt off their shores would supersede the rights which they now enjoy under the 1958 Convention to exploit the resources of their continental shelves, especially as most States' continental shelves fall within the 200-mile limit. There is nevertheless an important group of coastal States having Continental shelves extending more than 200 miles from their shores. Under the 1958 Convention, they have an unchallenged right to the resources of their shelves no matter how far out they extend, provided only that they conform to the rather elastic criteria which the Convention lays down. It would be too much to expect that States in this fortunate position would settle for a regime which gave them less than they can claim under the 1958 Convention.

It is therefore a safe bet that the existing regime of the continental shelf will continue to exist side by side with the regime of the 200-mile economic zone, and that the Continental Shelf regime as laid down in 1958 will remain substantially as it is today. On this matter the Press Release (SEA/85) issued during the first part of the Seventh Session, on 19 May 1978, sounds what may be a prophetic note:

A legal definition of this geological feature (i.e., the Continental Shelf) remained beyond reach, despite the aid of a Secretariat study showing how many square miles the various definitions would cover. The Soviet Union and the Arab Group suggested new definitions while Ireland continued to press a formula it had put forward two years ago.

Notes

1. *The Truman Proclamation.* Proclamation. No. 2667, 10 Feb., Reg. 12303: Exec. Order No. 9633.
2. *Continental Shelf Convention:* Geneva, 1958. See annexure.
3. International Court of Justice: *North Sea Continental Shelf Cases.* ICJ. Reports. The Hague, 1969.
4. Foigel, Isi. "The North Sea Continental Shelf Case." Article in *Of Law and Man.* Sabra Books, New York and Tel Aviv, 1971.

Bibliography

Gaskell, T. F. *Moving into Deeper Waters: Development and Promise of Off-shore Technology.* Interregional Seminar on the Development of the Mineral Resources of the Continental Shelf. Port-of-Spain, Trinidad and Tobago, 5-16 April 1971.
Slouka, Zdenek J. *International Custom and the Continental Shelf: A Study in the Dynamics of the Customary Rules of International Law.* Martinus Nijhoff, The Hague, 1968.
United Nations Technical Papers: Doc. ST/TAO/SER, C/138. Sales No. E/F.7211-A.6.

Chapter Nine
The Economic Zone
or Patrimonial Sea

If there is one issue which highlights the difference between the "resource-orientated" thinking of today and the more traditional approach to the Law of the Sea as enshrined in the Conventions of 1958, it is the issue of an economic zone, extending 200 miles to seaward of the base-lines from which the territorial sea is measured — a zone within which the coastal State will be able to claim exclusive rights to mine the minerals of the sea-bed, to exploit the living resources of the bottom and the superjacent waters, and to limit and control the activities of other States with a view to combatting pollution and preserving the delicate ecological balance of the zone.

At the first session of the enlarged Seabeds Committee, which took place in Geneva in the Spring of 1971, the claims of a few Latin American States to a 200-mile zone — whether in the original and extreme form of a claim to territorial sea rights, or in the form of more limited rights to the economic resources of the zone, without prejudice to its use for other purposes by the international community — were regarded by many delegations as the claims of some sort of lunatic fringe, not to be taken seriously. Admittedly, they seemed to reason, the old three-mile limit to the territorial sea was out of date and could stand reexamination; and the Continental Shelf Convention with the open-ended definition discussed in the previous chapter, needed tightening up to cope with the demands of the new technology. But 200 miles? One might as well return to the old "mare clausum" concept and think in terms of partitioning the seas and oceans of the world between rival States with the lion's share going to the most fortunate in terms of their geographical inheritance.

95

Such an attitude, however, would be an over simplification. While the concept of a 200-mile zone may have seemed to some States, in 1971, to be somewhat startling, it did not arise fullgrown and comely as the Venus of legend is supposed to have arisen from the waves.

The manner in which this concept was developed over the years provides an intriguing illustration of how rules of law may emerge from the crucible of events. To any reader who is prepared to delve a little deeper—and the exercise will be rewarding—we commend a small volume by Hjertonsson entitled "The New Law of the Sea" which clearly sets forth the history and the influence of the Latin American States in this most important evolution of legal and diplomatic thought.

Two very important pointers to the direction in which international thinking was beginning to move were the Declaration of Panama of 1939, in which the American Republics proclaimed a neutrality zone of 200 miles from their coasts, and the Truman Declarations of 1945. In regard to the former, Shabtai Rosenne writes "while of itself this proclamation could not prevent belligerent actions within that zone . . . clearly the concept of an extended zone for national and possibly regional security purposes, going far beyond the traditional concept of a narrow belt of territorial sea, could no longer be dismissed."

This declaration was followed in 1945 by two proclamations of President Truman, dealing respectively with coastal fisheries and the assumption of federal jurisdiction over the continental shelf of the United States. These, to quote Shabtai Rosenne once more "are commonly taken as the points of departure for a new assertiveness by coastal States of preferential or exclusive rights over certain living and mineral resources of areas of sea beyond the three-mile limit, and standing in some relationship with their land territory."

The Proclamation dealing with fisheries claimed the right of the United States to establish conservation zones in areas of the high seas contiguous to its shores, and to regulate fisheries either alone or in concert with other countries. Here, already, was the germ of the idea that coastal States could claim exclusive or preferential rights to the fishery resources off their coasts, beyond the territorial sea and the contiguous zone, and indeed in parts of the high seas area itself.

The United States claim to the resources of its shelf was a matter of indifference to most States, which did not see it as a menace to their interests—the more so as their rights to navigate in and to overfly the waters of the shelf were not affected. Those States which were not so indifferent to the issue, saw in the United States action an invitation to follow suit by staking their claim to resources of real and potential value off their coasts. Some 40 States followed, in rapid succession, in proclaiming their jurisdiction over off-shore areas beyond the territorial sea.

Amongst the claims which were staked out following the Truman Declarations of 1945, were those of Mexico and Panama—with this difference however, that they sought to extend their jurisdiction not merely to the resources of the shelf, but to the whole shelf itself. In October 1946 Argentine claimed the shelf and the "epicontinental sea" above it.

China and Peru, in 1947, and Ecuador in 1950, claimed sovereignty over a 200-mile zone. All three have vital fishing interests in the rich waters of the Humboldt Current, which coincides more or less with the 200-mile belt off their shores, and it requires no great imagination to see that their interest, then as now, was to protect their fishing grounds, which are the richest in the world, from the depredations of foreign fishing fleets operating far from their homebases. The fact that Chile and Peru have virtually no continental shelves and Ecuador only a modest one, lends credibility to this view.

Unlike the claims to the continental shelf (with or without super-jacent waters) which followed the Truman Proclamation and which provoked little reaction, the claims of Chile, Peru and Ecuador on the west coast of South America were condemned by a number of States as a derogation from the freedom of the high seas. The Argentine claim to an epicontinental sea met with a similar response.

It would be a mistake to assume that the claims of Chile, Peru and Ecuador, which which were later to be defended with such skill in the Seabeds Committee, were initially based on any valid legal principle. Hjertonsson describes the legal position which prevailed in regard to the initial claims of these three States, as one of "total confusion."

Even in the first session of the Enlarged Seabeds Committee in 1971, when the position of these and other Latin American States were beginning to crystallize, their delegates were hard put to it to give an account of just what would be entailed in the "sovereignty" which they claimed to exercise in the 200-mile belt. It seemed however, that what they desired was something less than the full sovereignty which States exercise in the territorial sea under the classical doctrine; it was jurisdiction for certain purposes only—i.e., mostly for the purpose of enjoying exclusive control of their fisheries.

The slow growth of a body of international law on any given matter has occasioned some comment in previous chapters. The main reason for this inertia is that there is nothing on the international plane to match the legislature which, in a single State, lays down the rules and is backed up by the machinery of state which sees to their implementation.

Occasionally, however, one comes across the exception to the rule that customary law is born of the slow accretion of state practice. This may occur when the unilateral action of a State is met with little or no opposition from the rest of the community, and when the example it sets is even followed by other States until, in a relatively short time, it becomes the accepted norm.

As the International Court remarked in its advisory opinion in the North Sea Continental Shelf Cases, the general legal regime of the continental shelf "furnishes an example of a legal theory derived from a particular source that has secured a general following." As the Court recalled, "...it was the Truman Proclamation of 28 September 1945 which was at the origin of the theory, whose special features reflect that origin."

It is indeed remarkable that between 1945 and 1958 — a spell of only 13 years — a unilateral assertion by the United States for which there was no discernable foundation in law, could have gained such wide acceptance that it came to be enshrined in the 1958 Geneva Convention on the Continental Shelf.

The moral, surprisingly enough, seems to be that unilateral actions can in certain cases give rise to rules of customary international law. Clearly unilateral action, or even action by a substantial number of States, does not set a legal precedent if it is contrary to accepted norms; but it can and very occasionally does set in train a series of events and generate a series of pressures which can lead to the norm itself being modified. In a situation where customary and conventional international law has allowed a vacuum to arise, the creation of "facts on the ground" can influence the development of new law.

Such, undoubtedly, is the case with the economic zone or patrimonial sea concept.

The idea that coastal States should be entitled to the exclusive use of the resources of the seabed and ocean floor, and of the waters which lie above them, up to a distance of 200 miles from their shores, is a new and revolutionary one. Only seven years ago the claims of the Latin Amerian States to which reference has been made, to the exclusive use of their 200-mile belt, were treated in the Seabeds Committee with a measure of polite incredulity. In debate the maritime countries, including the super powers, let it be known that that never, but never, would such claims be entertained; and off the record, weary delegates could be heard to condemn those who put forward such egregious demands. Today there are few States if any—and this goes for the superpowers as well as for those smaller countries which nevertheless have important shipping interests—who would oppose the idea of a 200-mile economic zone. After seven years of debate, in which the fortunes of war ebbed and flowed like the tides themselves, the international community has come to accept the idea of the economic zone.

This result was perhaps not entirely unexpected, and it had indeed been foreseen by some of the more perceptive delegates to the first meeting of the Enlarged Seabeds Committee in the spring of 1971.

It was the Latin Americans who made all the running at that Conference. They were clear about what they wanted and about how they would attain their ends. While some of the western delegations floundered, addressing themselves to nitpicking arguments conceived within the framework of a classical Law of the Sea which was losing its relevance, the Latin Americans concentrated on representatives of the Third World, the developing countries. They were largely uncommitted and some of them even confessed, privately, that they did not know where their own best interests lay. The Latin Americans were out to enlighten them, and they did so to such good effect that within a few sessions a new line-up emerged, to the dismay of some of the maritime powers. Credit must be given to the former for their skilled generalship, and to the latter for their wisdom and restraint in abandoning, bit by bit, some of the cherished principles by which they had been wont to justify their stand on the freedom of the high seas and the narrowest possible limits to coastal State jurisdiction. It could not have been easy for them.

It has been said that the 200-mile economic zone is a revolutionary concept. But it is no more revolutionary than Pardo's suggestion that the resources of the seabed and ocean floor, beyond the limits of national jurisdiction, should be exploited cooperatively as the common heritage of mankind. On the basis that the child is father to the man, the enunciation of the "Pardo Principle" could only elicit one response— the economic zone concept, or something very like it. For in accepting the novel idea that the resources of the seabed and ocean floor beyond the limits of national jurisdiction should be reserved to all mankind, States not unnaturally took a hard second look at where the limits of national jurisdiction might come to be fixed, and began to be attracted to a doctrine which promised to fix those limits as far as possible away from their shores.

The options come into sharp relief if one imagines oneself to be in the position of a policy planner of a coastal State having no continental shelf, or very little. Under the old dispensation vast areas of the seabed and ocean floor, with living resources and possible mineral wealth, would be outside its reach because with no shelf it would have nothing on which to base its claim to exclusive or preferential rights. Small wonder then that such a State would find in the new doctrine of the economic zone or patrimonial sea the answer to its most vital needs.

States having little or no continental shelves, include States heavily dependent on fishing resources, most of which are found within the 200-mile belt. It is no coincidence that these countries have been the strongest protagonists of the 200-mile economic zone. This is not to say that States putting forward the concept of the 200-mile economic zone were only concerned with fishing interests. The rights envisaged for the zone go much further. But there is little doubt that the desire to secure wide-ranging control of living resources off their coasts, was a powerful motive.

It is of some interest that the case for reserving to coastal States the enjoyment of the living and non-living resources in a 200-mile belt off their coasts rests more on political and economic arguments than it does on any clearly understood legal principle. Even today, when the merits of the 200-mile zone are widely conceded, there is no agreement on the legal regime which would be applicable to the waters of the zone. There is still some confusion as to what the 200-milers are claiming. The hard-liners still speak of "sovereignty" over the economic zone, which implies territorial sea rights subject only to the international servitude of innocent passage. The suspicion arises that States claiming territorial seas of 200 miles were holding out for the maximum not in the hope that it would be granted, but in order to have a bargaining position from which they could fall back. Some delegates indeed admitted, in private, that this was the case; others endeavoured to soften the impact of claims to an extensive territorial belt by explaining that what coastal States sought to exercise in the 200-mile belt was modified sovereignty, for certain purposes only.

Gidel solved the problem of the contiguous zone described in chapter three, by postulating that States were exercising in it not sovereign rights, but only certain limited rights which the community allowed them to enjoy in what had been, remained and always would be, an area of the high seas. Perhaps the same solution could best be applied to the economic zone, which would then be seen as an area of the high seas in which States could be allowed, by international agreement as enshrined in the Convention, to enjoy carefully circumscribed but nevertheless important and exclusive rights to the economic resources of the area.

However difficult its resolution may be, the dichotomy may be stated in simple terms. On the one hand there are the States which claim whether seriously or for tactical reasons to exercise complete sovereign rights over the 200-mile zone analogous to those which they enjoy in the territorial sea; at the other extreme are those who aver that the zone will be part of the high seas, in which coastal States will enjoy certain rights not because of their sovereignty, but by grace and favour of the international community, expressing its will through a Convention.

By the end of the sixth session of the Conference in the summer of 1977, there was no solution in sight and at least one of the superpowers, having concluded that there was no prospect of bringing the two sides together, indicated that they were prepared to consider a new and special "sui generis" status for the waters of the zone.

The situation today must therefore be regarded as somewhat obscure legally, although it is clear in broad terms that the international community has accepted the 200-mile economic zone and it will undoubtedly form part of the new dispensation—whether that dispensation comes to be enshrined in a convention, or whether it is spawned by the slower and untidier process of an accretion of customary international law—as positions are taken up and tested in practice.

It has been said that most of the living resources of the sea are to be found within 200 miles off-shore. Valuable species may be found further out, especially over the continental shelves which stretch beyond the 200-mile limit. But by and large, the deep and distant oceans are like the deserts on land—there is not much life in them.,

Clearly, the "common heritage" is beginning to look less valuable than it did at its conception. Not only does it now exclude most of the living resources of the sea which fall in the 200-mile economic zones of coastal States, but in terms of area it remains poorly defined. States will retain the rights to their continental shelves which the 1958 Convention allows them; but since the Convention contains an open-ended definition of the limit, it is not yet clear where the area of national jurisdiction ends and where the seabeds which are reserved as the common heritage of mankind, begin. There is a substantial number of States which have continental shelves extending far beyond the 200-mile limit of the economic zone or patrimonial sea.

Despite everything that has been said about the uncertainties surrounding the 200-mile economic zone as a legal concept, the last few years have seen a virtual scramble by coastal States to extend their fishing limits to 200 miles, without prejudice to their claims to the mineral and seabed resources of their future economic zones. By 8 November 1977 no less than 53 States had claimed exclusive fishing rights in a zone extending 200 miles from their shores.

The dynamics of such a movement can be easily understood. As the distant-waters fishing fleets were excluded from one rich fishing ground after the other, they turned their attention to the areas which remained. The result could only be that more and more fishing fleets were concentrated in fewer fishing grounds. Coastal States were faced with serious overfishing which could only lead to the depletion, or even the extinction, of fish stocks off their shores; and in self defence they hastened to extend their own limits.

These extended limits which, in a sense, anticipate the Convention, are here to stay at least as far as fisheries are concerned.

Bibliography

Fernandez, Javier Illanes. "El Derecho del Mar e Sus Problemas Actuales,"
     .   Friedman, Wolfgang. *The Future of the Oceans*. George Braziller Inc.,
          New York, 1971.
Editorial Universitoria de Buenos Aires, 1974.
Hjertonsson, Karin. *The New Law of the Sea: Influence of the Latin American
          States on Recent Developments of the Law of the Sea*. A.W. Sijthoff.
          Leyden, 1973.
Mexico y el Régimen Del mar. Secretaría de Relaciones Exteriores Tlateloko,
          Mexico, 1974.
Oelofsen, P. D. "Some Observations on the Concept of the Exclusive Economic
          Zone".*South African Yearbook of International Law*, 1975, vol. 1.
Rao, P. Streenivasa. *The Public Order of Ocean Resources: A Critique of the
          Contemporary Law of the Sea*. The MIT Press, 1975.
Rosenne, Shabtai. "The Third United Nations Conference on the Law of the
          Sea." *Israel Law Review*.
Swing, John Temple. "Who will own the Oceans?" *Foreign Affairs*, vol. 54, no.
          3, April 1976.
"The North Sea Continental Shelf Cases." *I.C.J.*, 1968
Truman Proclamations. See notes on Chapter Eight
United Nations Legislative Series. *National Legislation and Treaties Relating
          to the Law of the Sea*. ST/LEG/SER. B/16, B/18.

Chapter Ten

The Common Heritage
of Mankind

Following Ambassador Pardo's dramatic introduction of a resolution to
the General Assembly of the United Nations in 1967, in which he
proposed that "the sea-bed and the ocean floor beyond the limits of
national jurisdiction are the common heritage of mankind and the
resources of this area should be used for peaceful purposes only and in
the interest of all mankind", an *ad hoc* committee of 35 members (later
changed to a standing committee) was established to:

(a) Elaborate legal principles and norms which would promote inter-
    national co-operation in the exploration and use of the sea-bed and
    ocean floor;
(b) Study ways of promoting the exploration and use of the area's
    resources;
(c) Review studies concerned with exploration and research and
(d) Examine proposed measures of co-operation aimed at preventing
    marine pollution which might result from the exploration of the
    resources of the sea. (Resolution 2457 A (XXIII)).

During 1970, the General Assembly passed Resolutions 2749
(XXV) and 2750 (XXV) which respectively proclaimed general principles on the Law of the Sea and conferred a new mandate on the Sea-
beds Committee, and increased its membership to 86 States.

Still later, during December 1971, in accordance with Resolution
2881 (XXVI) of the General Assembly, the membership of the Committee
was further expanded to 91 States.

The new mandate conferred on the Sea-beds Committee in effect changed the Committee into a preparatory committee for a Third Law of the Sea Conference, then envisaged to take place during 1973.

One may well ask why there was a necessity for a new conference on the Law of the Sea a mere twelve years after the successful conclusion of the 1958 Geneva Conventions. That the developed countries asked themselves exactly this question is clear from their initial reactions in this regard. When Ambassador Pardo raised the question of the legal status of the sea-bed beyond national jurisdiction, the immediate reaction of the developed nations was to restrict any future conferences to a discussion of those subjects which remained unsolved at the 1958 Geneva Conference, including the legal status of the sea-bed and related matters as envisaged by Ambassador Pardo. At that time, and to some extent this remains true today, the existing law as codified in the Geneva Conventions suited the needs and interests of the developed countries.

The 1958 regime granted them freedom over the largest possible area of the seas for purposes of navigation, fishing and strategic uses. Even more important, it granted them freedom in principle to exploit the vast virgin area of the deep sea-bed with all its mineral resources.

The developing countries, on the other hand, grabbed the opportunity offered them by Ambassador Pardo with both hands and for a variety of reasons insisted on a complete reexamination of the entire Law of the Sea.

Their demands to rewrite the Law of the Sea must be viewed against the background of developments which has taken place since 1958. The most important was probably the rapid advance of sub-sea technology, which rendered obsolete the 1958 Convention on the Continental Shelf with its open-ended definition of the shelf. The exploitability of deep-sea minerals and hydrocarbons was no longer a mere possibility but within reach of the few technologically highly advanced nations. Add furthermore the resentment of those States which were still dependent territories during the 1958 conference on the Law of the Sea against a regime which, according to them, was created by and for the developed States of the world, and the scene was set for an important clash between the maritime interests of the developed countries and the marine resource interests of developing countries.

However, to ascribe all differences of opinion on the Law of the Sea to such a simple dichotomy would be misleading. There are also countries with both marine resource and maritime interests, and others who have neither. Many other issues are also at stake.

Whether or not Ambassador Pardo appreciated it at the time, the fact is that the most significant resources on the deep sea-bed are the so called manganese nodules which had been discovered more than 100 years earlier. If the scientists aboard HMS *Challenger* had realized that it was their discovery which would precipitate the Third Law of the Sea Conference with all the agonizing deliberations attendant on it, they might well have been tempted to drop the strange, potato-like objects right back into the sea.

Characteristics of Manganese Nodules and their Deposits

Manganese nodules have received a considerable amount of publicity in the past few years as a potential source of nickel, copper, cobalt, manganese and other materials. Yet for more than 80 years after their discovery on the ocean floor in the 1870s the nodules were regarded as a scientific curiosity of no economic significance. Since the detailed description of marine minerals by Mero in 1965,[1] interest in the nodules has increased and substantial commercial preparation has been made towards their exploitation.

Ocean manganese nodules vary considerably in size, shape, texture and colour, but the typical material of current economic interest is spheroidal, brown to black, with a diameter of 2-5 cm. and a concentric, onion-like structure. It is friable and porous (with a water content up to one third of its total weight), and has a density of 2-3 g/cm.[3] Some variations in these properties include the fact that nodules as small as 0.5 cm. or as large as 25 cm. in diameter, as well as large agglomerate slabs of nodules, grains or micronodules, impregnations of manganese oxides in porous materials and encrustations of manganese oxides on rocks are all found on the ocean floor. Nodules high in calcium carbonate are relatively hard and compact and iron-rich nodules are generally reddish-brown in colour.[1] It has been observed that the highest concentrations of nickel and copper occur in nodules 2-3 cm. in diameter.[2]

The most common manganese minerals in the nodules are todo-rokite, rancieite, and birnessite[3] but a number of other manganese minerals have been mentioned[4] and the nomenclature of hydrated manganese oxide minerals has not been well-defined. The iron occurs as hydrogoethite, hydrohematite and other hydrated ferric oxides.[5]

Other minerals present, mainly detrital, are quartz, feldspars, olivine, pyroxene, zeolites and clays, together with small amounts of rutile, barite, or apatite.[6]

The nodules contain different microscopically visible zones. Some of the valuable constituents tend to concentrate in certain of these zones, but this differentiation is not distinct enough, nor are the zones easily enough separable for this factor to serve as a basis for physical concentration of the valuable constituents.[3] In other words, normal ore-dressing techniques cannot be used to concentrate the valuable metal constituents of the nodules.

There are various theories on the origin and genesis of ferro-manganese nodules. Bonatti[7] divided ferromanganese deposits into four classes:

(a) Hydrogenous deposits formed by slow precipitation of manganese and iron from sea-water.
(b) Hydrothermal deposits in which the material was obtained through volcanic activity.
(c) Halmyrolytic deposits resulting from submarine weathering.
(d) Diagenetic deposits arising from the movement of manganese from a reducing to an oxidizing environment.

However, Bonatti intended his classification to indicate only the main types. There are also combined and transitional types of deposits.

Manganese nodules are still continually being formed. A rate of formation of 10 million tons per annum in the Pacific[8] has been given, which is higher than the expected mining rate during the first few years of operation. However, there is no evidence that these newly-formed accretions are concentrated in potential mine sites. Therefore the nodules should not be considered as a renewable resource.

Occurrence of Manganese Nodules

Nodules have been found in shallow water, even at a depth of two metres but a strong correlation has been found between nickel and copper contents and the depth of the water in which the nodules occur.[9]

Despite the fact that manganese nodules occur on the floors of all the oceans[10] and that there is probably no extensive area at a distance of more than 300 kilometres from continental land masses in which manganese concretions in one form or another cannot be found,[8] the densities of coverate vary considerably. The occurrence of manganese nodules can be correlated with the physiography of submarine floor.[11]

The major ocean basins, which comprise some 42 percent of the total under-sea area, have the densest deposits of manganese nodules. It should be stressed that the nodules are the only known mineral resource in these regions. Manganese nodules also occur on the mid-ocean rise, on volcanic ridges and on the continental slopes, but they are not as abundant as on the abyssal plains and they contain lower contents of the valuable metals — copper and nickel.

The best deposits of nodules are usually 800 to 1000 miles from the nearest land,[12] and manganese nodules do not represent viable economic deposits within the coastal limits of at least 120 countries[13] However, our knowledge about the location of nodules should not be overrated. It has been estimated[15] that only about three percent of the sea-floor has been extensively surveyed. The most complete published survey of the distribution of nodules on the ocean floor is probably that by Ewing, et. al.[16] prepared from 50,000 bottom photographs from 3,000 camera stations.

Grade of Manganese Nodules

The components most likely to be of economic value are nickel, copper, cobalt, and possibly manganese. The highest concentrations of individual elements reported are nickel 2.46 percent,[17] copper, 2.5 percent,[18] cobalt, 2.6 percent, and manganese, 55 percent.[19] But such concentrations of all four elements are not known to occur together. Average contents of nodules in all the oceans and in different oceans have been published[6] but because concentrations of the elements in nodules vary widely between oceans (Table 1), between different regions of an ocean (Tables 1 and 2), over distances of a few kilometres and even within the same nodule, these averages are useful for scientific rather than economic purposes.

It should also be stressed that most available information on the occurrence, grade, and distribution of manganese nodules was obtained by private mining companies who treat this information as proprietary and confidential. As somebody once put it to the authors: "The only way in which any person could obtain the true picture about the value of ocean manganese nodules is by using a few sticks of dynamite on the safes of the major companies engaged in their exploration."

Table 1

**Average Concentrations of Metals in Ferromanganese
Nodules and Crusts in Different Oceans
(After Horn, Horn, and Delach)[10]**

| | Metal concentration, % | | | | |
	Ni	Cu	Co	Mn	Ca
North Atlantic					
Kelvin Seamounts	0.11	0.04	0.04	1.80	
Blake Plateau	0.52	0.08	0.42	14.7	10.2
Abyssal Hills	0.41	0.29	0.40	14.9	
Mid-Atlantic Ridge	0.18	0.12	0.3	10.4	
South-Atlantic					
Rio Grande Rise and					
adjacent plain	0.14	0.09	0.05	7.2	
Agulhas Plateau	0.83	0.15	0.36	17.1	1.2
Adjacent deep	0.67	0.16	0.18	13.0	
Indian Ocean					
Madagascar Basin	0.24	0.12	0.25	11.0	
Kerguelen-Gaussberg					
Ridge	0.34	0.05	0.04	2.3	
Crozet Basin	0.42	0.12	0.14	12.4	
South Pacific					
Deep	0.13	0.10	0.31	11.36	
Manihiki Plateau	0.30	0.17	0.51	16.9	

With these reservations in mind, Table 2 shows that the highest manganese (and lowest iron) concentrations occur in nodules off Baja, California, but their concentrations of nickel, copper, and cobalt are low.

Nodules high in cobalt are found in areas of the western and southern Pacific Ocean, but their nickel and copper concentrations are low.

Horn[10] has delineated an east to west band in the North Pacific between 6° and 20°N, and 110° and 180° W, as containing the most extensive deposits of ferromanganese nodules, where the nodules are very abundant and are rich in copper and nickel—their elements of major economic interest. Nodules with contents of at least one percent of nickel and one percent of copper are apparently restricted to regions

Table 2

Average Composition Of Surface Nodules From Different Areas Within the Pacific Ocean (After Cronan)[9]

	1	2	3	4	5	6	7	8	9
Mn	15.85	33.98	22.33	19.81	15.71	16.61	16.87	13.96	12.29
Fe	12.22	1.62	9.44	10.20	9.06	13.92	13.30	13.10	12.00
Ni	0.348	0.097	1.080	0.961	0.956	0.433	0.564	0.393	0.422
Co	0.514	0.00075	0.192	0.164	0.213	0.595	0.395	1.127	0.144
Cu	0.077	0.065	0.627	0.311	0.711	0.185	0.393	0.061	0.294
Pb	0.085	0,006	0.028	0.030	0.049	0.073	0.034	0.174	0.015
Ba	0.306	0.171	0.381	0.145	0.155	0.230	0.152	0.274	0.196
Mo	0.040	0.072	0.047	0.037	0.041	0.035	0.037	0.042	0.018
V	0.065	0.031	0.041	0.031	0.036	0.050	0.044	0.054	0.037
Cr	0.0051	0.0019	0.0007	0.0005	0.0012	0.0007	0.0007	0.0011	0 004
Ti	0.489	0.060	0.425	0.467	0.561	1.007	0.810	0.773	0.634
L.O.I.†	24.78	21.96	24.75	27.21	22.12	28.73	25.50	30.87	22.52
Depth, m.	1146	3003	4537	4324	5049	3539	5001	1757	4990

1. Southern Borderland Seamount Province
2. Continental Borderland off Baja Calilfornia
3. North-east Pacific
4. South-east Pacific
9. North Pacific

5. Central Pacific
6. South Pacific
7. West Pacific
8. Mid-Pacific Mountains
† Loss on ignition

of siliceous sediments which form only part of this band. They identified the region from 8°30′ N, 150° W to 10° N, 131°30′ W south-east of Hawaii, as offering the highest potential for mining.

The average values from these siliceous deposits have been reported[13] as nickel (1.28 percent), copper (1.16 percent), manganese (24.6 percent) and cobalt (0.23 percent). Although it has been claimed that several potentially mineable nodule deposits have been discovered in the Indian and South Pacific Oceans, Horn[10] rules out all regions other than the North Pacific because of low metal values and often low densities of coverage or unsuitable ocean-bottom topology.

Nearly all the chemical elements have been detected in ocean manganese nodules. Some elements other than nickel, copper, cobalt, and manganese have been mentioned as being of possible economic value. Some nodules, especially from the Blake Plateau in the North Atlantic, have high calcium values that restrict the use of several processes to treat these nodules. The iron content of nodules in some potential mine sites is between 5 and 12 percent.[12] The average silica content of ocean manganese nodule is around 19 percent.[14]

However, it should once more be stressed that these conclusions are based on published information relating to only about 800 analyses of some 1,205 samples of nodules recovered by oceanographic research vessels. Commercial companies have very many more analyses at their disposal. It does appear, however, from summaries published from commercial sources,[2] that they do not contradict the above conclusions.

McKelvey[20] has warned that published averages should not be taken as characteristic of the regions from which the samples were taken because collection of samples is difficult and the reasons for variations in the distribution and contents of nodules not well understood.

Density of Coverage

The terms density, coverage, population, abundance, and concentration apply to various aspects of the amount of nodules present in a given area. Population is defined as the areal percentage of the sediment surface occupied by visible nodules.[12] The term concentration refers to the weight of nodules per unit area, and is usually calculated on a wet weight basis. Concentration is a function of nodule population, size, and specific gravity.

There is little agreement on the reasons for variations in the abundance and grade of nodules. Differences in the type of volcanism, rates of precipitation, degree of diagenetic remobilization patterns of sedimentation, variations of mineral phases in the nodules, the proportion of different elements supplied to the nodule deposits, and various other factors are mentioned in this regard.

There are also different views regarding the occurrence of nodules below the sediment—water interface. It has been reported that there are as many nodules in the first two to five metres of sediment as there are at the surface, but in some areas this is certainly not the case.

Exploitation of Manganese Nodules

It should be stressed that despite all the statements made about the vast riches of the deep sea-floor—and most of these statements refer to manganese nodules—there is at this point in time not a single commercial operation anywhere in the world which is based on the exploitation of these nodules.

Nearly all the available information about the occurrence of ocean manganese nodules has been obtained with optical or television cameras or acoustic scanners,[21] but these devices are limited by the speed of ground coverage that they can attain. Metal concentrations of nodules and sediments and other information on their properties have to be obtained by the examination of dredge and core samples in the laboratory. A seabed nuclear probe for in-place analysis of nodule composition is being developed but has not yet been used on site.

It should also be pointed out that many of the analyses reported in the literature are regarded as suspect because of possible analytical or sampling errors.

Reserves

The total amount of ferromanganese nodules on the ocean floor is huge. Mero[19] has estimated that there are 1.5×10^{12} tonnes in the Pacific Ocean alone. One report is of the opinion that the recovery of nodules would be like taking oxygen from the air. However, any reference to these total figures as reserves is completely misleading because only a very small fraction of them can be considered as suitable for recovery within the foreseeable future.

The nearest figure that can be estimated for reserves of nodules is that based on the extent of Horn's preferred area[10] and its nodule contents. This area, from 8°30'N to 10°N and from 131°30'W to 150° W. covers an area of about 300,000 km.[2] If the average nodule concentration is taken as 9.76 kg/m² (wet),[12] this area contains about 2000 million dry tonnes of nodules. With an average grade for this area of 1.28 percent nickel, 1.16 percent copper and 0.23 percent cobalt,[13] the region would contain about 26 million tonnes of nickel, 22 million tonnes of copper, and 4.6 million tonnes of cobalt.

These figures are still impressive because they work out for example at about one-third of the world's land-based reserves (in 1970) of nickel. There may be a much larger amount of high-grade nodules in the North Pacific because the siliceous sediment region which contains the highest-grade nodules covers about 40 percent of the band delineated by Horn[10] at 6°N, 110°W to 20°N, 180°W. The siliceous sediment region covers an area about 10 times as large as the preferred region of high mining potential. However, because only the preferred area has been intensively explored, its nodule contents come nearest to the term "reserves." There are also bound to be parts of this preferred region that are not mineable because of the topology of the sea floor and sub-grade values. Even in a good mining site, it has been estimated[12] that the combination of inaccessible area, dredge efficiency, sweep efficiency, and cut-off grade would lower the overall efficiency of nodule collection to about 20 percent.

Although other regions of the ocean contain very large amounts of nodules, they can be regarded at best as resources rather than reserves, especially in view of their low metal contents.[10] The possibility that nodule mining and processing may become much cheaper than expected in the future, thus allowing the recovery of low-grade nodules, or that rich new deposits may be found, must be regarded as speculative at this stage.[32]

Mining Systems

A mining system for operation at below 4000 metres has to fulfil more stringent requirements than do present offshore systems which usually operate relatively close to shore at depths of less than 40 metres. Nevertheless, the knowledge gained from such operations as offshore dredging for diamonds and other minerals, the offshore petroleum industry, and deep-ocean geological exploration has been used to design systems for deep-ocean nodule mining.

The systems that have been developed for the mining of nodules are of two types, namely, hydraulic and mechanical. Hydraulic systems (see Figure 1) are based on a continuous pipe suspended from the mining ship or barge to a dredge head on the ocean floor and compressed air from a supplementary pipe is used to propel the nodules upwards through the collection pipe. A hydraulic system with a capacity of 10 to 60 tonnes of nodules per hour was tested in 760 metres of water on the Blake Plateau. Summa Corporation has built a mining ship, Hughes' *Glomar Explorer*, and a submersible barge large enough for full-scale hydraulic mining operations.

The only mechanical system which has been used at depth is the continuous-line bucket (CLB) system developed by Masuda.[23] It consists of a continuous loop of rope to which collecting buckets are attached at regular intervals. The CLB system has been tested in the South Pacific in 3760 metres of water,[23] using buckets of about one-hundredth of the full-scale size required. this system is claimed[24] to have large advantages over hydraulic systems and to be considerably cheaper, but it has difficulties of its own, not the least of which is the problem of entanglement between the two sides of the line. Plans were made to build a modified two-ship CLB system in France to be ready for testing in late 1975.[15]

Many other systems have been proposed for the mining of ocean nodules, including the descent of 30 ton vehicles to the ocean floor, but it is believed that none of these have been tested on nodule deposits.

Since operations of this kind are radically different from any comparable regular operations and great difficulties have been experienced with dredging at a depth of less than 100 metres, and since no report has been received of full-scale operations at the required depth, it is difficult to understand the confidence with which spokesmen in industry have claimed that the required technology is available.[25] Nevertheless, the large investments that have been made for nodule mining indicate that the claim is not an idle one.

Figure 1
Nodule Mining By Airlift System
(Adapted from a pamphlet, "Raw Materials from the Sea" by A. M. R.)

1. *Mining station*   2. *Compressed air*
3. *Mixer nozzles*   4. *Hauling pipe*
                5. *Collector*

Extraction Processes

Processes for the physical concentration of the valuable constituents of the nodules are not available, mainly because of the complex mineralogical structure[3] of the nodules. The use of pyrometallurgy is made more difficult by the lack of a suitable method for physical concentration and by the high water content of the nodules. Therefore, although pyrometallurgical extraction and thermal upgrading have been studied,[26] it is most likely that hydrometallurgy will be the basis of extraction techniques.

These hydrometallurgical techniques vary in the degree of dissolution at which they aim. At one extreme is a differential leaching method by which copper, nickel and cobalt are leached from the ore by dilute sulphuric acid. Recoveries tend to be low with this method. High temperatures or low pH values improve recoveries but also increase the dissolution of manganese and iron. However, autoclave leaching with sulphuric acid can increase the rate of reaction at the same time as it lowers the dissolution of iron and manganese.[27]

At the other extreme there is a hydrochlorination process developed by Deepsea Ventures Inc., in which manganese is also dissolved, after which the valuable constituents are separated by solvent extraction or ion exchange (see Figure 2). Recoveries with this method tend to be high (93 percent for manganese, 96 percent for nickel, 94 percent for copper and 96 percent for cobalt), but capital and operating costs can also be expected to be high, especially because of the highly corrosive conditions prevailing. The hydrochlorination technique would be most applicable in cases where the chlorine produced could be used, for example in conjunction with an adjacent plant which produced chlorinated hydrocarbons. This hydrochlorination technique would produce manganese metal as well as copper, nickel, and cobalt, whereas the differential leaching process would not produce manganese.

A number of other extraction techniques have been studied. Most of these are variations of processes using ammonia or sulphur dioxide. ammoniacal leaching[28] also aims to recover only the copper, nickel, cobalt and by-products. Either the use of high pressures and temperatures, or the use of manganous salts is necessary in order to achieve good recoveries. Calcareous nodules require an alkaline leaching method in order to avoid high consumption of reagents (particularly acids).

Figure 2
**Flowsheet for the Deepsea Ventures Inc.
Hydrochlorination Method**
(Adapted from N. R. Lammartina. "Metals from Nodules"
Chemical Engineering. (Albany, 25th Nov. 1974, pp. 52-53)[32]

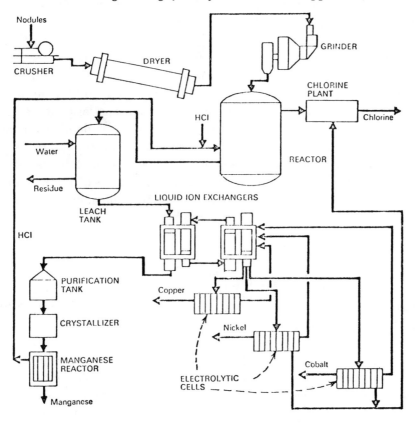

Sulphation roasting or leaching with sulphurous acid dissolves iron and manganese, as well as cobalt, nickel, and copper, after which the manganese can be recovered as a metal. For those who are interested, more detailed reviews of the extractive metallurgy of nodules are given by Hubred,[27] Cardwell[28] and others.

Several hydrochlorination pilot plants treating a tonne of nodules per day have been operated by Deepsea Ventures Incorporated.[30] Kennecott Copper Corporation has also operated a pilot plant of similar size,[27] but its choice of process has not been publicised.

Some mention has been made of the location of plants on floating sites that could be relocated at will, and which would reduce the transportation costs of the ore. It has even been suggested that some processing will be done under water. However, the cost of transport of reagents and the problems of waste disposal are likely to prevent extractive processing at sea, and it seems rather likely that the only things that are being considered for under-water processing are screening and possibly crushing.

The nodules have also been considered for uses other than as a source of metals. The high surface area of nodules[4] suggests their use for catalytic applications. They are more active than commercial catalysts for the oxidation of hydrocarbons and could therefore be used for the removal of some automobile exhaust gases. The use of nsutite, which is said to be present in nodules, as a depolarizer for batteries has been noted,[3] but there is no indication that the battery-active part of the nodule can be extracted. Manganese nodules can also be used to remove sulphur dioxide from the stack gases of sulphide ore smelters. The sulphur would be converted to manganous sulphate, which could subsequently be recovered by a process of leaching with water.[31]

Environmental Factors

Ocean mining has been attacked as a potential cause of damage to the marine environment. These attacks generally centre on the possibility that marine life will be disturbed, or that harmful effluents will be emitted. However it is considered that nodule mining in the deep ocean is unlikely to harm marine life because of the low biomass at the probable depths of operation. On the contrary, it is possible that bottom water which is rich in inorganic nutrients could generate phytoplankton when brought to the surface by an air-lift mining operation.[32] On the other hand it is not known what magnitude of effect would be caused by mining as compared to natural upwelling processes.

Environmental damage is more likely to occur as a result of marine mining near to the coast than of deep-ocean mining. The marine life that occurs in the region of phosophorite deposits on the continental shelf may be disturbed by operations to recover this material but the extent of the potential effect is not known.

Commercial Activities

The claim that a significant amount of commercial activity has taken place towards the mining of nodules is supported by the fact that large sums have been invested in the development of mining and processing systems. The total investment was estimated as 300 million dollars by 1973.

The company reputed to be farthest advanced with regard to the mining of the nodules is Summa Corporation, previously owned by Howard Hughes. This company built and launched a 26,000-ton prototype ocean-mining ship, the Hughes' *Glomar Explorer* and a submersible barge 90 metres by 30 metres to which a 15 metre-wide dredge head is to be attached.[33] The barge and ship were tested early in 1974 off California,[34] but no reports have been received regarding the success of these tests. Although there have been reports that this ship and barge were intended for the recovery of a sunken submarine,[35] descriptions of their construction indicate that they may still be suitable for nodule mining.

A number of other companies and groups of companies, some of which have spent or committed large amounts of money, are involved in developments towards nodule mining. A consortium to study mining and extraction over a five-year, 50-million dollar programme has been organized with the participation of Kennecott (50 percent), Rio Tinto (20 percent), and Consolidated Gold Fields, Mitsubishi, and Noranda (10 percent each). Kennecott is operating a large research programme in mining and processing at San Diego, through which the programme of the consortium is to be coordinated. A spokesman for the company said in 1973 that deep-sea nodules could be processed on a commercial scale within 30 months if a crash programme were undertaken.[36]

Deepsea Ventures Inc. is the company that has released the most information about its own activities, possibly in an attempt to find partners and raise money. The demonstration of the hydraulic dredge on the Blake Plateau was operated by this company.[37] Deepsea Ventures and Kennecott were reported to have dredged 150 and 200 tons of nodules respectively for use in extraction pilot plants. Deepsea Ventures has requested the U.S. Secretary of State for diplomatic protection for a claim of exclusive mining rights over an area of about 60,000 km., centering on 15° N, 126° W. This area is about 2000 km. west of the southern tip of Baja California and about 4000 km. east of Hawaii. It lies on the northern edge of the siliceous ooze region described by Horn, but about 700 km. north-east of the region that is recommended as having the greatest mining potential.

A joint company, Ocean Mining Associates, has been formed to perfect recovery methods initially and thereafter to consider commercial exploitation of nodules. Besides Deepsea Ventures, this consortium includes Union Miniere, Nichimen Co., Itoh and Co., Kanematsu-Gosho Ltd., and U.S. Steel.[39] A joint association of German companies (A.M.R.) has conducted exploration and surveys of nodule deposits in the Pacific, using the exploration ship R/V *Valdivia*. Other organizations actively involved in aspects of nodule mining include the French companies CNEXO and Le Nickel, the International Nickel Company,[40] a large number of Japanese companies and groups and the U.S.S.R.

Recent press accounts indicate that the above list is by no means complete. The latest news in this regard is that a U.S. Congressional Committee, meeting in secret session, has taken the first step to offer military protection to four U.S. mining consortiums that are ready to exploit the nodules of the deep-sea.

The recent trend towards establishment of mineral-producer cartels (such as OPEC) gave impetus to this development. The issue was laid before the House Oceanography Subcommittee on 15 March 1976. Behind closed doors, chairman John Murphy of New York State described the "awesome" mineral wealth that lies on the stygian bottoms of the world.

> If the United States prepares now to recover these minerals, we can become virtually independent of foreign imports of manganese by the early 1990s and in terms of nickel, copper and cobalt, we would be totally independent.

He also claimed that the Group of 77 at the U.N. were plotting to establish cartels for these minerals under U.N. auspices:

> They insist upon complete and effective control of mineral recovery operations and the right to discriminate against our ocean miners. There is a world wide cartel in the making. The cartel even has a proposed headquarters — Jamaica, the location of the international bauxite producers' organization.

The Group of 77 has (according to this report) accused the industrialized lands of trying to steal minerals that are the "common heritage of mankind" and speaking of the Group of 77, a spokesman from the industrialized countries said: "It would be easier to reach compromise with Attila the Hun."[41]

The available information therefore indicates that while a number of companies and consortia from the industrialized countries are actively investigating the feasibility of exploiting ocean manganese nodules, and some are even seeking legal security of tenure from their governments, these moves are being vigorously opposed by the developing countries who, though probably lacking the technological and financial resources to undertake the exploitation of the nodules by themselves, nevertheless favour a system under which the right of exploitation and the major share of any revenues derived therefrom would be in the hands of an international authority.

Economic Aspects

Profitability of Nodule Mining
It has been claimed that nodule mining will be so profitable that land-based mines for base minerals will be closed,[42] and ocean nodules are still being described as a "treasure trove" awaiting exploitation.[43] Other views have been expressed that nodule mining is not likely to be profitable.[44]

The range of cost estimates used to support these views is shown by Tables 3 and 4. It is difficult to judge the reliability of the various

Table 3

Estimated Costs of CLB Method and Differential Leaching Recovery of One Million Short Tons of Nodules Per Annum (Mero[19])

	Capital costs $ million	Operating cost $ million p.a.
Preliminary investigations	0.1	
Investigation of nodule deposits	0.3	0.3
Mining system	2.0	2.0
Processing system	10.0	10.0
Transport of nodules	—	4.0
Operating capital and miscellaneous costs	7.6	2.0
Total	20.0	18.3

Table 4

**Estimated Cost of Hydraulic Dredging and Differential Leaching
for the Recovery of 1.8 Million Short Tons of Nodules Per Annum
(Sorensen and Mead[44])**

	Capital costs $ million	Operating cost $ million p.a.*
Dredging	150	16.5
Transport	15	10.5
Processing	50	45
Total	215	72

*These are direct costs, including insurance.

cost estimates published, because there are no projects in operation
from which realistic data can be obtained.

The cost of nodule mining is expected to depend heavily on the
scale of operation, and the optimum size of individual projects depends
not only on the ability of the market to absorb the products but also
on the availability of resources, especially capital and equipment.
According to Mero, a project using the CLB mining method and
differential leaching would be profitable at a production rate of
300,000 tonnes of nodules per annum.

However, the general opinion seems to be that the minimum size
for a first generation project for profitability would be three million dry
tonnes of nodules per annum, if the three major metals produced were
nickel, copper and cobalt. If manganese metal were also produced, a
production rate of one million tonnes of nodules per annum would be
sufficient.

From a number of cost estimates published, Rothstein and Kaufman[30] selected five that range from "optimistic" to "pessimistic." The
estimates of capital cost based on the recovery of one million short tons
of nodules per year, ranged from 20 million to 227 million dollars. The
main reason for the variation is that the estimates are based on the use
of different mining and processing systems, and that the products and
the degree of detail considered in the estimates differ. After adding an
allowance to compensate for the factors not considered in each
estimate, Rothstein and Kaufman narrowed the range of capital cost
estimates to 130 to 180 million dollars. The resultant range of operating
cost was between 55 and 75 dollars per short ton of nodules, including

marine-based and land-based costs. No indication was given whether these operating costs included depreciation.

A recent detailed analysis by Moncrieff[45] of the economics of ocean mining (Table 5) gives estimates which are similar to those of Rothstein and Kaufman. Moncrieff's estimates refer to an operation producing nickel, copper, cobalt, and some minor metals, but leaving manganese in the residue. The medium recoveries assumed were 90 percent for nickel and copper and 55 percent for cobalt. Some systems can recover much more cobalt from the nodules but the belief is that technically it is not necessary to do so.

A report of the U.N. Secretary-General[15] quotes an official of Kennecott Copper Inc. as estimating (in September 1973) considerably lower costs for a similar system. The operating costs for nodule recovery, transportation, and metallurgical processing were quoted as 20 to 30 dollars per ton, and the total investments to bring a three million ton operation on stream was quoted as 250 to 280 million dollars.

Table 5

**Costs for an Operation to Recover
Three Million Dry Tonnes of Nodules Per Annum[45]**

	Low	Medium	High
Exploration and R. & D	60	80	150
Capital costs:			
Plant, equipment, land tailings dam,			
offices, engineering, design, and erection	250	300	400
Commissioning	10	30	50
Working capital	30	40	50
Total investment	**350**	**450**	**650**
Annual operating costs	90	105	130
Depreciation averaged at 10% per annum	25	30	40
Total cost of production	**115**	**135**	**170**
Major replacements, redeployment of			
mining units, and other annual costs			
of a capital nature, average per annum	10	15	30

Costs are in U.S. $ million (in mid-1974 dollar values except for some research and development costs).

Direct operating costs include chartering vessels for transportation of nodules to port, handling and stockpiling of nodules, selling expenses and overheads.

Table 6

Revenues for a Three Million Tonne-Per-Annum Operation
(Moncrieff[45] medium estimate)

	Grade	Recovery	Price	Annual revenue
	%	%	$ per lb	$ million
Nickel	1.3	90	1.75	135.4
Copper	1.1	90	0.80	52.4
Cobalt	0.2	55	3.00	21.8
Other metals				2.0
Total				211.6

Estimates of profitability for nodule mining vary even more widely, than cost estimates, because profitability depends also on revenues. Some indication of the expected initial profitability can be obtained from Moncrieff's estimates of costs (Table 5) and from his medium estimates for revenues (Table 6). Combined with the medium estimate of an investment of 450 million dollars and of annual operating costs (excluding depreciation) of 120 million dollars, the internal rate of return over 10 years (the period estimated by that author) would be 15.6 percent before tax.

It has often been assumed that Rothstein and Kaufman's estimates apply to a process of producing manganese metal as well as nickel, copper, and cobalt. Calculations made on this basis give much higher estimates of profitability. Because of the large number of technological problems, nodule mining involves a large degree of financial risk. Therefore, the rate of return calculated earlier does not appear excessive when compared with conventional land-based mining. (The average return on investment in mining in the United States of America in 1972 was reported as being 10.4 percent.) It appears even less so when it is considered that revenues could be considerably lower than those estimated in Table 6. Some recent South African price forecasts for 1980 support Moncrieff's low estimate for revenues (150 million dollars per annum), which would give a negative internal rate of return over 10 years on the basis of the above cost estimates.

However, there are factors which make nodule mining a more attractive proposition than it might otherwise appear. The life of a project is likely to be considerably longer than the 10 years normally assumed. For example, reserves in Horn's preferred area are large enough to assure operation for 40 years for about four projects recovering three million tonnes per annum of dry nodules each at 24 percent overall collection efficiency. The need for some countries to ensure mineral supplies could cause them to subsidize nodule mining either by direct grants or indirectly, for example in the form of low tax rates. Some governments have already been involved in direct or indirect subsidization of nodule mining. For further estimates of the costs of ocean nodule mining, see Mero[19] and Swan.[46]

Of course it should be pointed out that some proponents of ocean nodule mining hold far more optimistic views than those stated above. Mero, one of the pioneers of manganese nodule research, has suggested in a number of papers that the exploitation of these nodules will be so profitable that even established land-based producers of copper, nickel and cobalt will be hard pressed to compete with this new resource.

Again, one is faced with the problem that there is at present no commercial production of these metals from ocean mining operations, most of the feasibility studies that have been undertaken are company-confidential, and the mining and processing operations have yet to be proved on a commercial scale. One is therefore left with a feeling of ignorance about the true profitability potential of such operations, and with an incomplete understanding of the extent to which direct or indirect government subsidies, preferential tax agreements or perhaps the incentives granted by an international authority might contribute to their profitability.

Influence on Metal Markets

The fear that nodule mining will decrease the prices of copper, nickel, cobalt and manganese is one of the major factors determining the attitude of some countries towards international agreement on the legal regime for ocean mining. One estimate[47] gives the decrease in export earnings of developing States in 1980 which would result from "a very modest volume" of sea-bed output, as 360 million dollars.

Actually, South Africa should take part of the blame for this interest in the effect of ocean manganese mining on metal markets and on the economies of present producers of copper, nickel, cobalt and manganese from land-based deposits. After Pardo's resolution on "the common heritage of mankind" the Secretary-General of the United Nations asked member States for suggestions for the list of subjects and issues to be discussed. South Africa suggested that the effect of nodule mining on the markets for nickel, copper, cobalt and manganese, and on the economies of present producers of these metals should be considered. Despite the general hostility towards South Africa at the United Nations, this suggestion was, for obvious reasons, warmly supported by other producers of these metals .

The actual effects of manganese nodule mining will depend mainly on the scale and timing of nodule mining operations. These will in turn depend on factors like the profitability of nodule production relative to that of land-based production, the availability of capital and of nodule reserves, the technological problems of recovery and extraction, the legal regime controlling access to nodule deposits, the demand for these products, the level of taxation and of concessions afforded to those who produce metals from nodules. Because a large number of these factors will remain unknown until the commercial recovery of nodules begins, any estimate of the rate of expansion of nodule mining must be speculative. At this stage most estimates of the beginning of commercial sales of metals from nodules concentrate around 1980. On the basis of the time needed for exploration, process development, development of equipment and plant construction, and taking into account developments which have already occurred, Rothstein and Kaufman estimated that eight million tons of nodules would be recovered in that year. However their paper has also been interpreted as predicting a recovery of 15 million tons of nodules in 1985.

Sisselman[48] estimated that by 1985 production from nodules would account for six percent of the world's manganese demand, 18 percent of its nickel, 1.3 percent of its copper, and 50 percent of its cobalt. He also suggested that this would represent 13 percent of the imports of manganese by the industrialized countries, 26 percent of their nickel, and 5.5 percent of their copper.

The impact of nodule mining on market prices is often considered in terms of the potential penetration of nodule products into the relevant material markets. It is recognized that this approach is inaccurate, and that a large range of factors affecting demand, supply and price should be taken into account. However, where the market penetration is expected to be small, the simplified approach may be acceptable. For example, even at a projected production of 15 million tons of nodules in 1985, production from nodules is expected to have a very limited effect on copper markets at that time, provided that normal supply-demand relationships prevail.

It would appear on the basis of the estimates of market penetration that for the most part traditional producers of nickel are not likely to be seriously affected.

Production of cobalt from nodules was predicted to be 50 percent of world consumption in 1985, and is expected to cause the cobalt price to fall to two dollars per pound. Cobalt is probably the product most likely to be affected by nodule mining, but the short-term effect is moderated mainly by the probability that nodule mining may not expand as rapidly as the U.N. would assume and that cobalt recovery may in fact be low, especially for the early projects. An official of Kennecott Copper Corporation has stated in a private communication that cobalt need not be recovered at all. In the longer term if cobalt continues to be used only for its present purposes a significant fall in the cobalt price would undoubtedly result from nodule mining.

It has been suggested that cobalt could replace nickel in its major metallurgical uses, and that the price of cobalt would therefore not fall below that of nickel. Cobalt could be used as a substitute for nickel in electroplating.[49] Its abililty to replace nickel in stainless steel, the major use of that metal, has not been adequately tested, but there are indications that cobalt does not adversely affect the properties of stainless steels, and may even be beneficial.[50]

New uses of cobalt should be stimulated if cobalt becomes more readily available and cheaper than it is at present. The only country whose cobalt exports are significant to its economy is Zaire.

U.N. estimates indicate that the markets for manganese ore or ferromanganese are not likely to be affected by nodule mining until 1985. In terms of manganese exports of developing countries to the industrial countries, this U.N. analysis considered the potential effect to be more than twice as great. However, such an approach neglects the possibility that production of manganese from nodules would replace land-based manganese operations in the industrial countries rather than in the developing countries, and it also neglects the manganese needs of the developing countries which are growing at a respectable rate.

This estimate of manganese production from nodules could be high. In fact it is possible that no manganese at all will be produced from ocean nodules for a long time. Nodules may be too low grade a source of manganese to be sold as such or to serve for the production of ferromanganese, and their impurities are likely to be too high for the latter purpose. Production of manganese metal from nodules has been demonstrated by Deepsea Ventures, but the costs of their process may prove too high for it to compete with other nodule processes. Pure manganese metal has a limited market at present and it is not known to what extent the pure metal can economically replace ferromanganese for steelmaking.

However, it should be appreciated that the major steel producing countries (except for the U.S.S.R.) lack domestic reserves of manganese. Therefore it is possible that such countries might stockpile tailings from nodule operations after the extraction of copper, nickel and cobalt, to serve as a source of manganese which would prevent the undue escalation of manganese prices.

It now appears that there has been some modification to previous predictions of disaster to mineral exporters from the developing countries as a result of the exploitation of nodules and that there is a growing appreciation of the fact that these nodules from a purely economic and technological point of view, merely represent an additional low grade source of supply of the four major metals they contain.

However, one should not ignore the increasing concern of the industrial countries with security of supply of raw materials in preference to cost aspects. Direct or indirect subsidies of nodule operations by these nations in the interest of security of supplies could have a material effect on the viability of nodule mining operations and on the markets for the metals thus produced.

Legal and Political Aspects

If the technology for the exploitation of ocean manganese nodules is available and this exploitation were profitable, the major factor holding up development is the lack of security of tenure over deposits. This security is necessary for most companies if they are to be able to raise the finance necessary for development.

The Geneva Convention on the Continental Shelf, adopted in 1958, recognized the rights of coastal States to exploit the natural resources of the adjacent continental shelf to a depth of 200 metres or, beyond that limit to where the depth of the superjacent waters admits of the exploitation of the natural resources of said areas.[51]

At that time, commercial exploitation of resources beyond this point appeared to be a remote possibility but now it seems likely that such exploitation will occur. Thus, technology has overtaken legal definitions and the legal status of the sea-bed beyond the limits of national jurisdiction is a matter of contention.

As discussed in Chapter Three, it appears that consensus on a 200-mile economic zone, in which the coastal State will have exclusive rights to the exploitation of sea-bed resources, is likely to be reached. However, the present "Single Negotiating Text" prepared at the Caracas Session of the Third Law of the Sea Conference indicates that coastal State jurisdiction over mineral resources will be dealt with under the regime of the continental shelf and not under that of the economic zone.[52] There are however certain States which strongly advocate that the doctrine of the continental shelf should be subsumed within the economic zone.[52] At the end of the Caracas Conference the Chairman of the Second Committee stated that the concept of the economic zone was the keystone of the compromise solution favoured by the majority of participating States, although acceptance depended on the satisfactory solution of other issues.[53] It would therefore appear that the coastal State enjoys sovereign rights over the mineral resources of its continental shelf, slope and rise in terms of the Geneva Convention of the Continental Shelf and that these rights are likely to be confirmed and even expanded in terms of the proposed economic zone.

However, most manganese nodule deposits—and certainly the economically more promising ones—occur at depths and distances beyond any area covered by the Continental Shelf Convention or the proposed economic zone. Who therefore owns these resources, and who has the right to mine them?

Following Ambassador Pardo's proposal in December 1967, there is now fairly common agreement that the status of the deep sea-bed is neither *res communis* nor *res nullens* but that it represents the "common heritage of mankind." This latter concept is new to international law and still needs to be defined.

Although the 1958 Geneva Convention on the High Seas which enshrines the long established principles of freedom of the high seas, makes no express reference to resources of the sea-bed, clearly States have the right under existing law to exploit these resources but not to acquire exclusive rights to do so in any particular area[54]—a system of law to make any mining man cringe!

The High Seas Convention provides that no State may assume sovereignty over areas of the high seas and that reasonable regard must be paid to other users, which includes such activities as the laying of submarine cables and pipelines.

It is widely accepted that an international authority will be established to supervise the mineral resources of the sea-bed beyond the limits of national jurisdiction. The First Committee of the Third Law of the Sea Conference proposed various regimes to ensure that these were exploited for the benefit of mankind as a whole — ranging from one by which the authority would issue exclusive licences to States or to companies and would benefit financially by royalties or other arrangements, to providing the authority with the right to exploit the area exclusively by establishing its own mining enterprise. At the Geneva Session of the Third Law of the Sea Conference (in 1975), the possibility of the Convention enabling the authority to enter into either contractual or equity joint ventures with States and other entities was discussed.[54] A more detailed discussion of the composition, powers and limits of jurisdiction of the proposed International Sea Resources Authority may be found in Chapter Eight. However this Authority has not been established and attempts have been made by both the developing countries and the industrial nations to propose interim arrangements and thus to some extent preempt the decisions of the Law of the Sea Conference.

The developing countries proposed a "moratorium resolution" which declared any marine exploration and exploitation illegal until a corresponding convention had been reached. This resolution, though adopted by a substantial majority, was opposed by most of the industrialized nations. The opinion has been expressed that this resolution has no binding force in view of the Charter of the United Nations. "Hence ocean mining, especially the exploitation of manganese nodules, may be regarded as legal in terms of international law."[55] However it is not at all clear what limits are to be respected regarding the safety zones around ocean mining installations, or whether those engaging in ocean mining would be allowed to reserve a certain region for exclusive exploitation and what the maximum area of such a region would be.

Meanwhile in the United States companies concerned with exploration of the deep sea-bed prepared a "Draft Deep Seabed Hard Minerals Act," presented to the House of Representatives and the Senate as HR13076 and as S2801 respectively in 1972.

The President of Tenneco testified as follows before the House Merchant Marine and Fisheries Sub-Committee on Oceanography on this draft bill:

> I feel it necessary to reiterate that Tenneco has, by supporting the ocean mining programme of Deepsea Ventures, sought to corporate objectives further and to strengthen the resource base of the nation in a responsible and orderly manner . . . .
>
> It now asks that government assume its share of responsibility by taking the steps necessary to assure the orderly development of ocean resources and the protection of investment made by U.S. private enterprise in that development. Your constructive consideration of HR 13904 (HR 13076) will be the first step in that process whereby government may discharge its duty to assure secure and diverse supplies of vital metals for the benefit of the American people.

These draft bills enjoyed strong support from the American Mining Congress, the National Petroleum Council and sections of the U.S. Executive Branch. They were however opposed by the State and Defense Departments.

The bills were reintroduced at subsequent sessions of Congress under different numbers. In a surprise move in 1975 the Secretary of the Interior proposed to begin issuing permits for ocean nodule mining to U.S. companies if the United Nations failed to wrap up a Law of the Sea treaty by 31 January 1976. The United States also established an Ocean Mining Administration charged with the responsibility of developing a policy for ocean mining to oversee the technical programmes of all elements in the Department of the Interior having programmes relating to ocean mining.

The director of the OMA commented as follows on the objectives of the developing countries regarding ocean nodule mining:

> Their object in limiting deep ocean mining is to obtain sufficient control over seabed minerals so as to ensure that this new source of raw materials can be managed in accordance with the new objectives of the Third World—to transfer wealth from rich to poor nations and to protect land-based producers from competition with seabed producers by stabilizing seabed mineral prices at potentially articifical levels. In order to do so, they would deny or severely limit the access of the United States to the copper, nickel, cobalt, manganese and other minerals of the seabed. That result would be an unacceptable compromise of the national interest in assuring supplies.

On the chances of reaching an acceptable compromise regarding establishment of an international regime for ocean mining, he said:

> As long as industrialized countries heavily dependent on raw materials are expected to rely for their access to the vast resources of the seabed on the generosity of an international organization whose decision making apparatus is effectively in the hands of a large group of countries who have made it clear that they wish to limit access to raw material lifelines, we cannot be hopeful. When there is a clear political understanding that an accommodation in the Law of the Sea depends on recognition in a treaty that sovereign States and their nationals will have direct access to resources of the seabed, subject to regulation and supervision by an international body without artificially-imposed limits on their productive capacity, then and only then will the treaty we have been seeking for almost ten years begin to take shape and give us cause for optimism.[56]

These statements reflect a growing impatience in the Executive Branch of the U.S. Government with the delaying tactics of the developing countries at the Law of the Sea negotiations.

Equally significant is the growing disenchantment of mining companies from the industrial nations with the lack of support from their own governments and particularly with the "unreasonable" attitude of the developing countries. On this issue John Flipse, President of Deepsea Ventures, has said:

> Cartel, fever, mob rule, and the extension of the Law of the Sea Conference into 1976 do not encourage us to seek a solution through the U.N. effort. The ocean mining bills will be reintroduced in the U.S. Congress. There should be a sense in the Congress that we are not going to place ourselves at the mercy of others in regard to essential metals for U.S. industrial production. The same principles govern our partners. The fundamental trade-off will be this—a good law on the books of the United States under which a joint venture such as ours can operate with enough protection and enough incentives to offset the taxes and the restrictions, including environment restrictions, found in the United States or foreign domestication. Otherwise we *will* go foreign. If there is any message I can bring you, it is that there are

foreign nations that will welcome this kind of business activity. Will their incentives be any better than those in the United States? We have not yet seen *any* in the United States.[57]

At the latest hearings on S713 (the most recent version of the "Draft Deepsea Hard Minerals Act") the Senate Subcommittee on Minerals was told that the French, British and West German governments were either participating directly in ocean mining investigations or were providing financial support to their companies in such work,[58] whereas the U.S. State Department had not even recognized the claim filed by Deepsea Ventures for a nodule mining site in the Pacific Ocean.

The conclusion drawn from all this is clearly that the international mining consortia and many industrialized countries of the west have lost patience with the intractable stand of the developing nations at the Law of the Sea Conference. Even within the Executive Branch of the U.S. Government there is a move towards support for unilateral action such as the proposed Deepsea Hard Minerals Act. If the U.S. does not provide mining companies with the necessary legal security of tenure for the exploitation of nodules, some other nations will.

The developing countries have probably over estimated their bargaining powers and may soon be faced with a fait accompli. The resource hungry nations of the West are badly in need of the metals that can be extracted from ocean manganese nodules.

References

1. Mero, J. L. "Mineral Resources of the Sea." *Australian*, Elsevier, 1965.

2. Friedrich, G. H. W. et al. "Ship-bone geochemical investigations of deep-sea deposits in the Pacific using a radio isotope energy dispersive X-ray system," *Journal of Geochemical Exploration*, Vol. 3, 1974, pp 303-317. (See also n. 12.)

3. Sorem, R. K. and Foster, A. R. "Internal structure of manganese nodules and implications in beneficiation." Papers from a conference on ferromanganese deposits on the ocean floor. Palisades, N.Y. 20-22 Jan., 1972. Horn, D. R. Washington, National Science Foundation, 1972, pp 167-182.

4. Fuersterau, D. W., Herring, A. P. and Hoover, M. "Characterization and extraction of metals from sea floor manganese nodules." Transactions of the Society of Mining Engineers. *AIME*, Vol. 254; September 1973, pp. 205-211.

5. Burns, R. G. and Brown, A. B. "Nucleation and mineralogical controls on the composition of manganese nodules." Papers from a conference on ferromanganese deposits on the ocean floor. Palisades, N.Y. 20-22 Jan., 1972. Horn, D. R. Washington, National Science Foundation, 1972, pp 51-66.

6. Willis, J. P. "Investigation on the composition of manganese nodules with particular reference to certain trace elements." M.Sc. Thesis, University of Cape Town, June 1970.

7. Bonatti, E., Kraemer, T., and Rydill, H. "Classification and genesis of submarine iron-manganese deposits." Papers from a conference on ferromanganese deposits on the ocean floor. Palisades, N.Y. 20-22 Jan., 1972. Horn, D. R. Washington National Science Foundation, 1972, pp 149-166.

8. U. N. Economic and Social Council. *Mineral Resources of the Sea*. United Nations. Report of the Secretary-General, E/4680, 2 June, 1969.

9. Cronan, D.S. "Regional geochemistry of ferromanganese nodules in the world ocean. Papers from a conference on ferromanganese nodules on the ocean floor. Palisades, N.Y. 20-22 Jan., 1972. Horn, D. R. Washington, National Science Foundation, 1972. pp 19-30.

10. Horn, D. R., Horn, B. M., and Delach, M. N. *Ocean manganese nodules—metal values and mining sites*. Washington, National Science Foundation, Technical Report No. 4, Grant GX33616, 1973.

11. James, H. L. "Mineral resource potential of the deep oceans." Proceedings of a symposium on mineral resources of the World ocean. Newport, Rhode Island, 11-12 July, 1968. Occasional Publication No. 4. Newport, University of Rhode Island.

12. Flipse, J. E., Dubs, M. A., and Greenwald, R. J. "Preproduction manganese nodule mining activities and requirements." Hearings before the Subcommittee on Minerals, Materials and Fuels of the Committee on Interior and Insular Affairs. First Session on S1134, May/June, 1973.

13. United Nations. *Economic significance, in terms of sea-bed mineral resources, of the various limits proposed for national jurisdiction*. United

Nations, Report of the Secretary-General, A/AC138/87, 4 June 1973. (See also n. 14)

14. Albers, J. P., et al. *Summary petroleum and selected mineral statistics for 120 countries, including off-shore areas.* U.S. Geological Survey, Professional Paper 817, 1973.

15. United Nations. Third Law of the Sea Conference. *Economic implications of sea-bed mineral development in the international area.* Report of the Secretary-General, A/CONF. 62/25, 22 May 1974.

16. Ewing, M., et al. "Photographing manganese nodules on the ocean floor." *Oceanology,* Vol 6, Dec 1971, pp. 26-32.

17. Frazer, J. Z., and Arrhenius, G. *World-wide distribution of ferromanganese nodules and element concentrations in selected Pacific Ocean nodules.* Washington, National Science Foundation, Report No. 2, Grant GX 34659, 1972.

18. South Africa, Department of Planning. *Atlas of Marine Resources.* Pretoria, 1974 (confidential).

19. Mero, J. L. "Potential economic value of ocean-floor manganese nodule deposits." Papers from a conference on ferromanganese deposits of the ocean floor. Palisades, N.Y. 20-22 Jan., 1972. Horn, D. R. Washington, National Science Foundation, 1972. pp. 191-204.

20. McKelvey, V. E., Wang, F. F. H. *World sub-sea mineral resources.* U. S. Geological Survey, Miscellaneous Geological Investigations, 1969.

21. Schatz, C. E. Obervations of sampling and occurrence of manganese nodules. Third annual offshore technology conference, Houston, April 1971. (See also n. 22)

22. Hering, N. "New knowledge on prospecting and exploration of ore nodule deposits." *Meerestechnik,* Mt 4, Nr 1, Feb. 1973, pp 1-11.

23. Masudu, Y. "Development work to deep sea resources of manganese nodules using continuous line bucket system (ChB) by Japanese group and its future." 2nd. International Ocean Development Conference 1972. Preprints, Vol. 2, pp 1913-1924.

24. Mero, J. L. "Recent concepts in undersea mining." *Mining Congress Journal* Vol. 58, May 1972, pp 43-48, 54.

25. Ary, T. S. Letter to Senator Lee Metcalf, 7th June, 1973.

26. Hoover, M. P. Studies on the dissolution of copper, nickel and cobalt from oceanic manganese nodules. M.Sc. Thesis, Berkeley, University of California, 1966.

27. Hubred, G. "Deep-sea manganese nodules: a review of the literature." *Minerals Science Engineering.* Vol. 7, No. 1, 1975, pp 71-85.

28. Skarbo, R.R. *Extraction of copper and nickel from manganese nodules.* U.S. Pat 3723095, 27th March, 1973.

29. Cardwell, P. H." Extractive metallurgy of ocean nodules." *Mining Congress Journal,* Nov. 1973, pp 38-43.

30. Rothstein A. J., and Kaufman, R. The approaching maturity of deep-ocean mining — the pace quickens. 5th Offshore Technology Conference. Houston, 1973.

31. Zimmerley, S. R. *Use of deep-sea nodules for removing sulphurs from gases.* U.S. Pat 3330096.

32. Granville, A. "The recovery of deep-sea minerals: problems and prospects." *Minerals Science and Engineering,* July 1975, pp 170-187.

33. Newman, B. "The sea — mysterious nodules at bottom of oceans may yield a treasure." *Wall Street Journal,* May 1973.

34. Poole, R. "The sea-bed power struggle." *Mineral Engineering,* Sept. 1974, pp 42-48.

35. Alpern, D. M. et al. "CIA's mission impossible." *Newsweek,* 31 March, 1975.

36. *Ocean Science News,* 18 May, 1973.

37. Lamotte, C. "Deepsea Ventures' pilot run is successful." *Ocean Industry,* Oct. 1970. pp. 7-13.

38. *Ocean Science News,* 15 Nov. 1974.

39. "U.S. steel forges onward in the manganese nodule-mining regatta." *Chemical Engineering* (Albany), 25 Nov. 1974, p. 35. (See also n. 42)

40. "Law of the Sea Conference decisive for ocean mining." *Northern Miner,* 29 Nov. 1973.

41. Anderson, J. and Whitten, L. "U.S. to harvest ocean minerals." *The Standard-Star,* 30 March 1976.

42. "The oceans: wild west scramble for control." *Time Magazine,* 29 July 1974, p. 37.

43. Ali, M. "All eyes on earth's east treasure chest." Johannesburg, *The Star,* 24 February 1975.

44. Sorensen, P. E., and Mead, W. J. "A cost-benefit analysis of ocean resource development: the case of manganese nodules." *American Journal of Agricultural Economics* Vol. 50, 1968, pp. 1611-1620.

45. Moncrieff, A. G. and Small-Adams, K. B. The economics of first generation manganese nodules. American Mining Congress, 10 October 1974

6. Swan, D. A. "The potential of manganese nodules as a future mineral resource." *SNAME, Marine Technology,* 1974, pp 9-18.

47. United Nations. Third Law of the Sea Conference. Note by the Chairman of the First Committee, A/CONF. 62/C1/L.2. 26 July 1974.

48. Sisselman, H. "Ocean miners take soundings on legal problems, development alternatives." *Engineering and Mining Journal,* Vol. 176, No. 14, April 1975, pp. 75-86.

49. "Cobalt — an understudy for metal plating." *Metals Week,* 30 March 1970.

50. American Society for Testing Materials. *Effects of residual elements on properties of austenitic stainless steels.* The Society, Special Technical Publication 418, 1967.

51. United Nations. Document A/CONF. 13/L55.

52. Oelofsen, P. D. Some observations on the concept of the exclusive Economic Zone. Unpublished paper, 1976.

53. Stevenson, J. R. *Statement before the Senate Foreign Relations Com-*

mittee hearings on S1988. United Nations source documents on sea-bed mining. Washington, Nautilus Press, 5 Sept. 1974,pp. 373-391.

54. Archer, A. A. The prospects for the exploitation of manganese nodules: the main technical, economic and legal problems. Unpublished paper, 1975.

55. Rieger, H. "Ocean mining — a new legal field." Metallgesellschaft A.G. Review of the Activities, Edition 18, 1975, Manganese Nodules — Metals from the Sea.

56. Ratiner, L. S. Law of the sea and U.S. legislation: government perspective. Department of the Interior. Mining Convention of the American Mining Congress, San Francisco, California, 28 September 1975.

57. Flipse, J. E. "Deep ocean mining technology and its impact on the law of the sea." *Proceedings of the Law of the Sea Institute*, 9th Annual Conference, 6-9 Jan. 1975. Chapter 12, pp 325-332.

58. "Special report on the present state of deep-sea mining." *Ocean Science News*. Vol. 17, No. 48, 28 November 1975.

Chapter Eleven
The International
Sea-Beds Authority

In accordance with the mandate of the Seabeds Committee as defined in General Assembly Resolution 2750 C (XXV), the following subjects and functions were allocated to Subcommittee I:

> To prepare draft Treaty articles embodying the International Regime—including an international machinery—for the area and the resources of the seabed and the ocean floor, and the subsoil thereof, beyond the limits of national jurisdiction, taking into account the equitable sharing by all states in the benefits to be derived therefrom, bearing in mind the special interests and needs of developing countries, whether coastal or landlocked, on the basis of the Declaration of Principles Governing the Sea-Bed and the Ocean Floor and the Subsoil Thereof Beyond the Limits of National Jurisdiction, economic implications resulting from the exploitation of the resources of the area, as well as the particular needs and problems of landlocked countries.

It soon became clear that the issues were complex, that there was a great diversity of interests and opinions, and that many of the delegations did not really know where their real interests lay with regard to the regime. Only at its 33rd meeting, on 6 March 1972, did Subcommittee I adopt its programme of work. This programme was:

1. Status, scope and basic provisions of the regime.
2. Status, scope, functions and powers of the international machinery in relation to:

139

a. organs of the international machinery, including composition, procedures and dispute settlement;

b. rules and practices relating to activities for the exploration, exploitation and management of the resources of the area, as well as those relating to the preservation of the marine environment and scientific research, including technical assistance to developing countries;

c. the equitable sharing in the benefits to be derived from the area, bearing in mind the special interests and needs of developing countries, whether coastal or landlocked;

d. the economic considerations and implications relating to the exploitation of the resources of the area, including their processing and marketing;

e. the particular needs and problems of landlocked countries, and

f. the relationship of the international machinery to the United Nations system.

At the 44th meeting on 27 March 1972, it was agreed to establish a Working Group of the whole of the Subcommittee with a mandate to draw up in the first instance a working paper showing areas of agreement and disagreement on the various issues before the subcommittee. The Working Group was supposed thereafter to attempt to negotiate questions of substance on the points where no agreement existed. The idea was to produce as far as possible a set of agreed texts on the various issues.

During the July/August 1972 session, the Working Group had before it an informal working paper which had been prepared as a preliminary attempt to reflect within a single paper, areas of agreement and disagreement on matters relating to the status, scope and basic provisions of the regime as indicated in the debates in the Committee and in Subcommittee I. This paper contained 21 texts covering a variety of relevant aspects.

As a result of the first reading of the text, completed on 28 July 1972, the working paper was revised to take account of the opinions expressed. During a second reading, an attempt was made to narrow the areas of disagreement as far as possible and to merge alternative texts where there was no fundamental difference of approach.

Draft articles relating to the status, scope and basic provision of the international regime were prepared. These general principles, with several alternative texts, covered the following subjects:

Limits of the area;

Common heritage of mankind;

Activities regarding exploration nd exploitation;

Non-appropriation and no claim rights in the area;

Use of the area by all States without discrimination;

General conduct in the area and in relation to the area;

Benefit of mankind as a whole;

Reservation of the area exclusively for peaceful purposes;

Who may exploit the area;

General norms regarding exploitation;

Scientific research;

Transfer of technology;

Protection of the marine environment;

Protection of human life;

Due regard to the rights of coastal States;

Legal status of water superjacent to the area;

Accomodation of activities in the marine environment and in the area;

Responsibility to ensure observance of the international regime and liability for damages;

Access to and from the area;

Archaeological and historical objects;

Settlement of disputes.

After numerous sessions—most of them closed—a single negotiating text was prepared. This text indicates the areas where strong differences of opinion still exist. In fact it is clear that very little compromise has taken place on matters of substance relating to the international regime and to its various proposed organs. On the contrary, it appears that there has been a hardening of attitudes and a growing dichotomy between the developed and developing nations.

At this point in time there is no generally accepted regime for more than half the earth's surface, namely the seafloor and the subsoil beyond the limits of national jurisdiction. Indeed it is not even clear what the limits of this area are. The only consensus in this regard is that "there is an area beyond the limits of national jurisdiction." These differences of opinion are so serious that there can be no customary international law on many of these issues.

• • • •

The International Machinery

The Authority: an international organization (provisionally called "The Authority" or "The International Sea-Bed Authority") is to be established. It will be responsible for the international sea-bed area and its resources.

No agreement has been reached on the powers and functions of the Authority, that is whether it should be a "weak'" or a "strong" organization, and whether it should have the sole right to exploit the international seabed area or whether it should function merely as a licensing body or be involved in joint ventures with States or mining companies.

The developed maritime States which possess an underwater technology, are in favour of a weak regime which would act simply as a registry for claims and as an agency which would collect royalties on exploitation. Most of the countries of the Third World favour a strong regime and many of them would like to give the regime the sole right to exploit the resources of the area. Some of the mineral producing developing countries believe that a strong regime would be so cumbersome and riddled with bureaucracy that it would never operate in practice. They therefore support such a regime, hoping that this will be the most effective means of protection for their land-based mining operations. A number of Latin American countries support a strong regime because they see this as an emotionally appealing institution for most Third World countries. Their support for a strong Authority is in exchange for the support of these countries for the 200 mile economic zone.

Draft articles have been discussed on the following aspects relating to the Authority:

> Establishment of International Machinery;
> Nature of the Authority;
> Status of the Authority;
> Operation of vessels and emplacement of installations by the Authority;
> Installations and other facilities for the exploration of the area and the exploitation of its resources;
> Privileges and immunities;
> Relationship with other organizations;
> Fundamental principles of the functioning of the Authority, and Purposes of the Authority.

Insufficient attention has been devoted to the problem of financing the Authority. A delegate from one of the developing States proposed in all seriousness that the Authority should be financed by member States in proportion to their contributions to the United Nations Organization and that the benefits derived from the exploitation of the resources of the area should be distributed in inverse proportion.

The Assembly: The question as to whether there should be a strong or a weak Assembly is one of the crucial issues to be decided by the Third Law of the Sea Conference.

The developing countries are only interested in a strong Assembly where they intend, through their majority in it to impose their will not only on the management of the Authority, but also on all its organs. It is their view that the Assembly should be the supreme body which should hold all the power.

This type of hierarchy is not acceptable to the Soviet Union and to the western countries who have indicated with equal forcefulness to those holding the opposing view, that it would be both illogical and impractical to vest all the power in an Assembly meeting once a year, or even less according to some alternative proposals, when *inter alia* urgent decisions involving vast sums of money would be required. Such functions could be entrusted only to a Council in permanent session.

One fundamental area of disagreement concerns the question of who should frame policy in respect of resource management. It is clear that major powers such as the United States would not allow the Assembly as an organ of the proposed International Sea-Beds Authority to dictate power concerning resource management policy. This provision would have to be contained in a treaty to satisfy the United States and other countries who intend to exploit the sea-bed on their own.

The developing countries insist that the Assembly, with each country having one vote (thus giving them a built-in majority), should also have the powers and functions of such organs.

The developed States are equally as adamant that a weak Assembly is all that is required and that the other organs, as indeed the Assembly, should be created by the treaty, which would itself, or in its annexures, spell out in detail their powers and functions.

Suspension of membership is one of the matters on which the Assembly would probably have the final say. As the power to deprive or suspend rights of membership is of such a serious nature, it is to be hoped that the procedure relating to such cases will be carefully circumscribed in the treaty and not left to the Assembly to decide.

The Council: Generally speaking, States are still divided into two camps as far as the powers and functions of both the Council and the Assembly are concerned. The developing States are in favour of a strong Assembly and a weak Council, whereas the major powers, and especially those who intend to explore and exploit the sea-bed, want the reverse—a weak Assembly and a strong Council.

The latter States argue that billions of dollars will be involved in exploiting the deep sea-bed. Decisions will often have to be taken with the minimum of delay and Assembly procedure would prove too cumbersome and time consuming.

The composition of the Council and other issues relating to its procedure have been discussed but are still in need of much clarification. Proposals regarding the size of the Council range from 18 to 54 members and cover both geographical and interest groupings.

Numerous draft sub-articles, with a range of alternatives have been prepared dealing with the powers and the functions of the Council. The two main trends running through the draft and subarticles are:

- that the Council should perform the functions delegated to it by the Assembly and would be responsible to the Assembly for the prompt and effective execution of its directions and recommendations, i.e., the so called weak Council.
- that the Council should be the executive organ of the Authority and primarily responsible for the implementation of its suggested powers and functions, i.e., the so called strong Council.

The System of Settlement of Disputes: The system of settlement of disputes (including the Tribunal proposed by the United States) is another very important item which runs right through to the core of the whole Law of the Sea settlement. It is estimated that U.S. $ 250–400 million will be required to exploit one single deep-sea mine site and up to 90 such mine sites are envisaged.

A speedy and non-political system for the settlement of disputes which could involve hundred of millions of dollars is therefore of vital importance. Uruguay was the only country which mentioned the International Court of Justice as a possible tribunal. The final outcome with regard to this issue, as will be the case in respect of many other issues as well, will depend to a large extent on the system of exploitation which will finally be adopted in respect of the deep sea-bed.

This matter has not received sufficient attention to date and the draft articles which have been prepared can be considered only a loose framework. Some delegations have indicated that their governments would not be prepared to sign any Law of the Sea Treaty which did not include clear provisions relating to the system of settlement of disputes, with the rules and regulations of the Tribunal, or whatever system is decided upon, included in the Treaty as an annexure.

It is interesting that there has been scant support for the International Court of Justice as the organ which would deal with the settlement of disputes. It would appear that most countries appreciate that experts on the Law of the Sea and not political appointees are required on the Tribunal. Far too much money will be at stake to allow for political decisions.

The Enterprise and the Licensing Commissions: As in the case of the powers and functions of the Assembly and the Council, there are amongst States two basic schools of thought concerning both the exploration and exploitation of the deep sea-bed.

Thirteen Latin American States have sponsored a proposal which is supported by most of the developing States that an organ of the Authority be created which should be called the Enterprise, and which should be responsible for carrying out all technical, industrial and commercial activities relating to the exploration of the international sea-bed area and the exploitation of its resources, whether on its own account or under contracts of operation or association, or in joint ventures with juridical persons.

The majority of the developed States, on the other hand, do not see any necessity for an organ such as the Enterprise and maintain that all that is required is one or other type of licensing system which would ensure that licences could be issued either to a State or to a group of States, or to natural or juridical persons possibly under the sponsorship of one or more countries, under certain clearly defined terms and conditions.

The following six types of licensing systems have been proposed by different countries as alternatives to the Enterprise system:

The Operations Commission — sponsored by the United States, would allow exploration and exploitation by a State party to the Treaty, groups of States, or natural or juridical persons sponsored by a State or States.

The Permanent Board — sponsored by France, would allocate blocks, being specific areas of the international deep sea-bed, after examining applications received by members or groups of the Authority.

The Management and Development Commission — sponsored by Malta, makes provision for the exploitation of the non-living resources of the international deep sea-bed by the Authority itself, or by means of service contracts, joint ventures or through a system of licensing.

The International Sea-Bed Operations Organization — sponsored by Australia, makes provision for the exploration and exploitation of the resources of the area by the organization itself, or by entering into licensing and other contract arrangements with States subject to the approval of the Council.

The Exploration and Production Agency — sponsored by Canada, makes provision, subject to approval by the Council, for exploration and exploitation directly through its own resources, or through joint ventures, service contracts, production sharing schemes or other legal arrangements, or by issuing licences to contracting parties or to national or juridical persons sponsored by contracting parties.

The Exploitation Commission — sponsored by the Soviet Union, will permit the Commission to make recommendations to the Council on the issuance of licences to any contracting party or group of contracting parties for the exploration of the area and the exploitation of its resources.

Although there is a clear divergence of views between States favouring one or other of the licensing systems, the two basic systems are actually not that far apart. What is really involved is *permission to operate on the sea-bed.* However it is equally clear that there has been a hardening of stands on both sides.

The system of distribution of revenue benefits accruing from the exploitation of the area which one would expect to be equitable is still clouded in vagueness and will require more precise definition. Most of the developing States consider that they are the only ones entitled to benefit from such revenues which should be considered as compensation for the loss of their riches of which they were "robbed" during the colonial era. The greediness and arrogance of the developing States may still prove to be the rock on which the Third Law of the Sea Conference will founder.

The advanced developed States on other hand, are becoming increasingly concerned about the depletion of their own resources and the growing problems in securing reliable sources of supply of these materials at a time of growing nationalism in most mineral-producing States. They see the deep sea-bed as the last frontier of mineral supplies.

Additional Organs of the Sea-Bed Regime: Additional organs of the regime have been proposed by a number of countries. It is not yet clear whether all or any of them will require definition in the Treaty or whether this function will be allocated to the Assembly or the Council.

The Secretariat will comprise a secretary-general and such staff as the Authority may require, including an inspectorate.

The Rules and Recommended Practices Commission, which the United States proposed, is to consider and recommend rules for the exploration of the area and for the exploitation of its resources.

The Planning and Price Stabilization Commission is to investigate or review the current trends of supply and demand and the prices of raw materials obtained from the area. It will also make recommendations regarding the price rates at which any raw materials obtained from the area may be sold and the quantities of such materials that may be made available at any given time, balancing the need of the world community for raw materials and the need for stability of the economies of the producers of land minerals.

The Scientific and Technological Commission's powers and functions have not been specified in concrete terms.

The Legal Commission shall promote the harmonization of national maritime laws and the development of international law relating to ocean space and in particular to the international sea-bed area.

The International Sea-Bed Boundary Review Commission shall review the delineation of boundaries submitted by contracting parties to ensure that they conform with the provisions of the Treaty, negotiate any differences with contracting parties and if necessary, initiate proceedings before the Tribunal or upon request render advice on any boundary question.

The Inspection and Conservation Commission shall be responsible for reviewing, approving and inspecting all work programmes carried out in the area under exploration and exploitation licences, or other arrangements authorized by the Exploration and Production Agency.

The Area of International Jurisdiction

When Ambassador Pardo introduced his resolution to the General Assembly, his proposal was that the sea-bed and the ocean floor beyond national jurisdiction should be used and exploited for the benefit of "all mankind." At that time (1967) however, there was no certainty as to what part of the area of the sea-bed and ocean floor would fall within the ambit of Pardo's proposal. The term "outside the limits of national jurisdiction" did not mean much in the sense that there was uncertainty as to the limits of "national jurisdiction" over submarine areas.

In this regard the 1958 and 1960 Geneva Conferences failed to reach agreement on the breadth of the territorial sea. Even more important—bearing in mind that Pardo's proposal related to the sea-bed and the ocean floor—the definition of the continental shelf, as it appears in the 1958 Convention on the Continental Shelf, was completely outdated by the time Pardo introduced his resolution. In this Convention the continental shelf, as the area of the sea-bed over which coastal States exercise sovereignty, was defined in an open-ended manner and was referred to as the submarine area adjacent to coasts to a depth of 200 metres or beyond that limit "to where the superjacent waters admits of the exploitation of the natural resources of the said areas." In 1967 exploitation beyond the 200 metre depth was no longer a mere possibility.

The question of limits gained added importance when the entire Law of the Sea as codified in the 1958 Conventions was added to the already complex problem.

The question of limits has now manifested itself in the concept of the Exclusive Economic Zone or Patrimonial Sea which has grown in popularity among States, including some that had been initially strongly opposed to this concept. To complicate matters further, there are some States with continental margins extending beyond the 200 mile limit.

It is clear from all this that the exact limits of the International Area beyond those of national jurisdiction have not been adequately defined.

The Likely Outcome

It now appears that the developing States have overplayed their hand with regard to the International Sea-Beds Authority. At a time of rampant inflation and recession in the wake of much higher oil prices, there is little enthusiasm for the creation of another large international bureaucracy. The developed nations are not in favour of forming such an institution and in their concern for securing reliable sources of supply of minerals, are finding the deep sea-bed increasingly attractive.

They do not want this area controlled by an automatic majority of developing States and they certainly would not want to rely on supplies of vital strategic minerals from an international Enterprise controlled by developing States. The delaying tactics of these nations, and their unwillingness to compromise on a more reasonable and equitable regime for the deep sea-bed, which would allow the developed nations free access to the resources of the area, has led to a situation in which it appears certain that the industrialized nations will simply go ahead and mine the deep sea-bed.

The mountain that was the International Deep Sea-Bed Regime has brought forth a mouse.

Chapter Twelve
The Riches of the Continental Margin

The oceans comprise about three-quarters of the area of the earth. The continental margins constitute more than 20 percent of the world's total marine area. This largely unexplored area represents a potentially very important source of a variety of minerals of importance to industry. Although popularly referred to as the "last frontier," the marine environment has a long history of mineral production—salt from evaporation of sea water and the recovery of fresh water from submarine sources going back to ancient times. Sub-sea mining of coal and several other minerals from extensions of land deposits took place 300 years ago, and in recent years sulphur, sand, gravel, lime, coral, tin, diamonds, gold, platinum group metals, and titanium minerals have been recovered from relatively shallow waters. The chances of finding additional supplies of these minerals on the continental shelves are favourable.

The mineral resources of the deep-sea and offshore oil and gas are discussed elsewhere in this book. In this chapter the non-fuel mineral resources of the ocean, which in terms of the 1958 Convention on the Continental Shelf fall under the jurisdiction of coastal States, are discussed.

The continental margins represent the submerged parts of continental land masses. This area includes the continental shelf and slope, and in many areas the continental rise where a thick apron of sediments spreads over the contact between the continental and

151

oceanic crusts. The continental shelf is a relatively flat area of the sea-floor between the low-water mark where the change in the inclination of the sea-floor marks the shelf edge, and the beginning of the continental slope. Although the Geneva Convention on the Continental Shelf was based on the concept that this change in inclination occurs at an average depth of 200 metres, the usual depth is between 130 and 200 metres, and in exceptional cases is even as shallow as 50 or as deep as 500 metres. The width of the shelf varies tremendously in different parts of the world, ranging from less than one to more than 800 miles. The inclination of the continental slope varies from less than three degrees along coasts with large rivers and deltas, to over 45 degrees of faulted coasts but the inclination is usually about five degrees.[1]

Although the continental margins contain several types of igneous rocks, they generally consist of granitic rocks, which are richer in silica and alkalis, and poorer in iron and magnesia than the oceanic crust. The continental margins are generally overlain by sediments up to several miles thick. Water depths at the landward edge of continental rises vary from about 1,500 to 3,500, and depths at their seaward edge from 3500 to 5500 metres. The widths of continental rises vary from 60 miles to about 600 miles. Sediments of the continental rises may be deposited along the border of both the great and small ocean basins. They are particularly well developed off stable coasts having huge supplies of sediments opposite the deltas of the world's giant rivers, and around some of the semi-enclosed small ocean basins.

The continental shelves, slopes, and rises, and small ocean basins probably contain the greatest proportion of sub-sea mineral resources, both in terms of the variety of minerals and the value of those likely to be recovered in the next 20 to 30 years.[1] In 1972 the world production of non-fuel minerals from the sea-floor and rocks beneath the ocean floor amounted to about $740 million—only about two percent of land-based production of these minerals. However it is expected that this proportion will increase considerably. This is likely to result from the greater development of minerals in short supply (such as diamonds, gold, platinum, nickel, and phosphorites), the availability of large, high-grade offshore deposits of tin off the coasts of Malaysia, Indonesia and Thailand and the need for bulk materials (such as sand and gravel) which are in short supply locally. The economic conditions prevailing in individual countries would also encourage them to exploit certain offshore deposits in order to earn foreign exchange, increase security of supplies and conserve their land-based resources.

Apart from these considerations, many countries may initiate offshore mineral ventures to enhance their prestige, stake their claims to jurisdiction adjacent marine areas resources (fearing changes in the established legal regime of the continental shelf), and improve the security of supply of important raw materials.

However, a realistic assessment of the mineral potential of the continental margins must take into account the cost of exploiting minerals from this area. As a result of the strange and hostile environment and the availability of adequate land-based resources of most minerals, indications are that greatly expanded effort in exploitation of the non-fuel mineral resources of the continental margins will not be stimulated by purely economic considerations, but rather by changing national mineral policies based on greater concern about security of supply, a fear that their rights to exploit these minerals in terms of the Geneva Convention on the Continental Shelf may be eroded, or by special local considerations.

Mineral Resources of the Continental Margins

1.   *Minerals Extractable by Bore-hole Extraction Methods.* A large proportion of the world's resources of salt, anhydrite, potash and gypsum were deposited in the past by evaporation of sea water and brines in sedimentary basins. Substantial deposits of sources of magnesium and magnesite were also formed in similar environments, and deposits of native sulphur formed in such areas by biological processes involving the transformation of anhydrite. Recent oceanographic research projects have uncovered a number of new deposits of this type. Some offshore sedimentary basins contain enormous amounts of salt, gypsum, potash, magnesia, and other minerals of saline origin.

An important proportion of the world's sulphur production comes from marine deposits in bedded deposits or in salt domes. Recent scientific investigations have indicated that sub-sea salt domes may contain very extensive deposits of native sulphur.[2]

2.   *Heavy Mineral and other Surficial Deposits extractable by Conventional Dredging Methods.* A number of minerals can be recovered economically by dredging methods from the marine environment at depths of less than 40 metres of water and within a few miles from shore. These include tin, precious coral, lime, sand and gravel rutile and ilmenite, aircen, monazite, barite, and magnetite. Most of these so-called offshore placer deposits were formed during relatively recent Ice

Ages when the sea level was as much as 160 metres lower than at present.[3] The offshore placer deposits are generally restricted to shelf areas, either adjacent to the primary source rocks or to areas in the shallower or landward portions of the shelf. Very special conditions are required for their development and their offshore potential is therefore unlikely to rival that of similar deposits on land.

The exploitation of many of these deposits started early this century. Despite the glamour of offshore dredging operations for diamonds off South West Africa (Namibia), tin in South East Asia, and attempts at the recovery of platinum in North American waters, it is likely that sand and gravel will remain the most important products of this type of offshore mining for the foreseeable future. They are already by far the most important surficial deposits exploited on the sea-floor both in terms of value and of volume.

3.   *Submarine Phosphorite Deposits.* After a period of declining prices of phosphates from the end of World War II to the mid-1970s, there was a flurry of excitement when Morocco, the world's major exporter of phosphates, increased the price of her phosphates by more than 385 percent in 1975. Although this caught farmers and laymen by surprise, fertilizer manufacturers in Europe were aware of the fact that the so-called "Holy War" against the Spanish Sahara in which Morocco, Algeria and Mauritania were the major contenders against Spain's belated colonial exploits, had a commercial, rather than a religious or moralistic overtone. Morocco saw an opportunity, through control over the rich phosphate deposits of the Spanish Sahara, to secure an almost unassailable position as a dominant exporter of phosphates — an essential ingredient of fertilizers. Despite the fact that this attempt at the establishment of a phosphate export monopoly failed, as is witnessed by the subsequent depressed prices of phosphates and phosphatic fertilizers, this development served to focus renewed interest in submarine phosphorite deposits.

Phosphorite of marine origin has long been used as a source of phosphate for fertilizers and chemicals. Submarine phosphorite was first discovered on the Agulhas Plateau off South Africa by the Challenger Expedition in 1873.[4] Just before World War II phosphorite nodules were discovered off southern California, and subsequent oceanographic expeditions have discovered phosphorite nodules off the coasts of North and South America, Africa, Australia and New Zealand. Most of these deposits occur in the outer shelf and upper slope areas and on the tops and sides of submarine banks and seamounts. The deposits occur near the shore and as far as 180 miles offshore, and in water depths ranging from 20 metres to more than 3000 metres. However, there has been no commercial production to date of offshore phosphorite deposits.

Generally speaking, marine phosphorite deposits appear to be lower in grade than their counterparts on land (about 27 percent P_2O_5, as against 35 percent P_2O_5). This lower grade, together with a more difficult mining environment, has militated against commercial exploitation. However it should be appreciated that special types of phosphate deposits, containing less than 10 percent P_2O_5, are being commercially exploited from land-based deposits in countries with a fairly advanced mining and processing technology, such as the U.S.S.R. and South Africa. This indicates that given special considerations such as security of supply or foreign exchange considerations, marine phosphorites could become economically exploitable in the foreseeable future.

4.   *Sub-Seafloor Deposits Exploitable by Underground Mining.* The technological problems of sinking sea shafts and maintaining them have not yet been overcome. Extensions of mineral deposits discovered on land, which extend to the submerged portions of the continents are therefore exploited from land or from artificial islands. McKelvey and Wang state that more than 100 sub-sea underground mines with shaft entry from land, islands or artificial islands have recovered minerals such as coal, iron ore, nickel-copper ores, tin, gold, copper and mercury off the coasts of a large number of countries.[1] The maximum depth below sea-level is about 2,400 metres, maximum water cover 120 metres and maximum distance from the shore, about five miles. The most important mineral exploited in this manner has traditionally been coal, and it can confidently be expected that in the wake of the energy crisis this trend will continue.

It should be clear from the above that deposits under the ocean floor which are exploited from land, islands or artificial islands generally represent extensions of land-based deposits.

5.   *Offshore Sediments and Brines.* Highly saline and abnormally hot brines with a rich metallic content have been discovered near the central rift valley of the Red Sea at depths of about 2,000 metres.[5] In some of these deep basins, metal-enriched sediments which occur on the sea-floor are probably associated with the overlying hot brines. The salt content of these brines is about ten times that of normal sea-water, and they contain iron, manganese, zinc, lead, copper, silver, and gold in concentrations very much higher than that of normal seawater.

Metal-enriched sediments similar to those in the Red Sea are present in certain areas at the crest of the East Pacific Rise,[8] and adjacent to the Bann Wuho volcano off Indonesia.[9]

6.   *Mineral Resources in Bedrock Under the Deep-sea Floor.* The bedrock beneath the great oceanic basins is composed of oceanic-type basalt with a remarkably uniform composition over large areas which, apart from technological and cost considerations, has been considered to have little potential for metal resources.

However, more recent evidence suggests that selected areas of the deep sea-bed could have a substantial potential for the exploitation of non-ferrous metals (such as copper, lead and zinc), precious metals (such as gold, silver and platinum group metals), and ferrous metals (such as molybdenum, chromium and. nickel). Most of these new discoveries were made during the Deep Sea Drilling Project of the *Glomar Challenger.* It appears that much of this mineralization is associated with the oceanic rifts as for example along the mid-Atlantic Ridge. The origin of this mineralization has been discussed exhaustively by numerous authors, and requires no further elaboration in this book.

7.   *Minerals Dissolved in Seawater.* The world's oceans contain more than 1300 million cubic kilometers of sea-water, and each cubic kilometer holds about 40 million tons of dissolved solids. This ancient solution which has evolved since the Creation contains elements in almost every conceivable chemical form, from simple ions to complex molecules, dissolved gases and a wide variety of organic compounds.

Water in the open sea is relatively uniform in composition as far as the major and minor elements are concerned. Trace elements can show wide variations, particularly in coastal waters.

McKelvey and Wang reported that in 1972 there were more than 300 near-shore operations in 60 countries which recovered sea-water constituents with an annual value of about $ 415 million. The materials which are at present commercially extracted from sea-water include salt, magnesium metal, magnesium compounds, bromine, heavy water and fresh water. Small amounts of potassium and calcium compounds are produced as by-products of salt. At one stage much publicity was given to the possibility of extracting uranium from seawater but no commercial operations have been established despite the dramatic increase in the price of uranium since 1973.

The oceans are destined to become an increasingly important source of the world's fresh water needs. There are already several hundred desalination plants located throughout the world and it was estimated that by 1978 production of fresh water from the ocean would reach four million cubic metres per day, with a value of over $ 250 million per annum.

Conclusions

It is clear that the continental margins show promise as an important future source of industrial metals and minerals. The growth of the offshore mining industry will require scientific research aimed at the development of better methods to find, mine and beneficiate these minerals in a strange and hostile environment. A balance will have to be found between the resource interests of coastal States and the maritime interests of other nations. Security of tenure of the coastal States over the resources of the continental shelf are covered by the 1958 Geneva Convention on the Continental Shelf which, by the end of 1976 had been ratified by 53 nations. Any revision of the Law of the Sea will have to take this fact into account, since coastal States will not be prepared to accept an erosion of their jurisdiction over sea-bed resources in any new legislation. However, the open-ended nature of the definition of the continental shelf (as discussed earlier in this book) raises some question about the outer limit of coastal State jurisdiction over the deeper portions of the continental margins, such as the slope and rise. It is now generally accepted that this jurisdiction over the resources of the seabed must have a limit, but no unanimity on what it should be or whether a depth or distance criterion should be used in setting it.

The potential values of the non-fuel mineral resources of the continental margins are large but they are dwarfed by the enormous potential of the oil and gas resources of this area. The effects these resources will have on the attitudes of nations to the issues at stake in the Law of the Sea are discussed in the next chapter.

References

1.   U.N. Economic and Social Council. Mineral resources of the sea. United Nations, Report of the Secretary-General, E/4608, June 2, 1969.

2.   United Nations. Economic significance, in terms of sea-bed mineral resources, of the various limits proposed for national jurisdiction. United Nations, Report of the Secretary-General, A/AC 138/87, June 4, 1973.

3.   Albers, J.P., et al. Summary petroleum and selected mineral statistics for 120 countries, including off-shore areas. U.S. Geol. Surv., Professional Paper 817, 1973.

4.   South Africa, Department of Planning. Atlas of Marine Resources. Pretoria, 1974 (confidential).

5.   McKelvey, V. E. and Wang, F. F. H. World subsea mineral resources. U.S. Geol. Surv., Miscellaneous Geological Investigations, 1969.

6.   Mero, J. L. Recent concepts in undersea mining. Mining Congress Journal, Vol. 58, May 1972, pp. 43-48 and 54.

7.   Poole, R. The seabed power struggle. Min. Engng., Sept. 1974, pp. 42-48.

8.   Anderson, J. and Whitten, L. U.S. to harvest ocean minerals. The Standard-Star, March 30, 1976.

9.   Anon. The oceans: wild west scramble for control. Time Magazine, 29th July, 1974, p. 37.

10.   Ali, M. All eyes on earth's east treasure chest. Johannesburg, The Star, 24th February, 1975.

11.   Sisselman, H. Ocean Miners take soundings on legal problems, development alternatives. E and MJ., Vol. 176, No. 14, April 1975, pp. 75-86.

12.   Stevenson, J. R. Statement before the Senate Foreign Relations Committee hearings on S1988. United Nations source documents on sea-bed mining. Washington, Nautilus Press, Sept. 5, 1974, pp. 373-391.

13.   Rieger, H. Ocean mining — a new legal field. Metallgesellschaft A.G. Review of the Activities, Edition 18, 1975, Manganese Nodules — Metals from the Sea.

14.   Ratiner, L. S. Law of the Sea and U.S. Legislation; Government Perspective, Department of the Interior. Mining Convention of the American Mining Congress, San Francisco, California, September 28, 1975.

15.   Anon. Special report on the present state of deepsea mining. Ocean Science News. Vol. 17, No. 48, November 28, 1975.

Chapter Thirteen
Energy From The Oceans
Oil And Gas

A healthy, hard working person can produce sufficient energy to keep a 100 watt light glowing.[1] In the distant past muscle power was man's most important source of energy, and most of it was expended in acquiring food. Gradually man's own power was supplemented by that of wives, children, slaves and animals. Eventually other sources of energy such as wind, water, and steam were developed, and later internal combustion motors, electricity, and nuclear power.

Other sources of energy are now more important that muscle power in every walk of life from recreation to the production of materials and goods and transportation. This may be compared to a team of silent slaves that toil ceaselessly to feed, clothe, and keep us. This energy is derived mainly from fossil fuels such as oil, gas and coal and each person on earth has energy slaves that work for him.[1] In India each man, woman, and child has about 15 energy slaves, in South America 30, Russia 120, Europe 150, and in the United States a massive 350.

Our modern industrial civilization is completely dependent on adequate supplies of fossil fuels. With the development of the internal combustion engine, oil became increasingly popular as a primary source of energy. The first successful oil well was completed in 1857.[2] Since then the supply has generally exceeded the demand. Consequently prices were low, conversion and refining relatively simple, and handling and transportation convenient, since crude oil is a liquid.

161

The development of giant oil fields, first in Texas and then in the Middle East, caused an acceleration in the substitution of oil for coal. In most of the industrial nations of the West, oil became the most important source of energy. The prosperity which the West enjoyed in the two decades after World War II was based on a geological freak—the giant oil fields of the Middle East. It does not appear likely that any other occurrences of this magnitude occur on earth.

Natural gas occurs with oil or in separate fields. For many years this clean source of energy was flared or wasted because it could not be economically transported to suitable markets. The development of pipelines and of techniques to liquefy natural gas led to huge increases in the consumption of this source of energy, particularly in the United States, and to a lesser extent in Western Europe.

Over the past few years unconventional sources of energy, such as solar, tidal, wind and geothermal energy, have received much publicity. However, it should be appreciated that these sources of energy are not sufficiently concentrated and that the technology for their large scale utilization is not sufficiently advanced for them to make a significant contribution to world energy supplies before the end of this century.

For the rest of this century we have to face the facts and take effective steps to reduce energy wastage. Everything possible has to be done to ensure that our economically available sources of energy are exploited, converted, and utilized as efficiently as possible, taking into account the environmental, political and social implications which this will have. Even if this is done, several reputable studies[3] indicate that the world will be facing a real shortage of oil somewhere between 1985 and 1995.

Some two-thirds of the world's reserves of oil are in the Middle East. Apart from natural depletion, the political unrest in that part of the world, and in particular the recent events in Iran, are causing grave concern over future oil supplies.

There were four main phases in the development of the energy policies of Western nations. During the first phase these countries concentrated on the development of domestic coal resources. In the second phase governments and multi-national corporations competed for oil concessions in foreign countries. The third phase[4] started between World War I and World War II. It was characterized by the emergence of national oil companies which attempted to develop a national involvement in the supply of a critically important commodity and to counter the British-American domination of the industry. With

the increasing influence of the governments of the producer countries
the consumer nations were forced to take steps to ensure adequate oil
supplies for the future. The producer countries began to appreciate the
political power of oil, as they showed during the Yom Kippur War of
October 1973, when they unilaterally quadrupled the price of oil.

The fourth phase of energy policy formulation followed. This
phase is characterized by much greater concern about the security of
energy supply than over prices, whereas in the previous three phases
excessive emphasis was placed on cheap energy supplies. After OPEC
placed an embargo on oil exports to the United States in October
1973 the American government reacted heatedly. In the first instance
the over hasty and poorly conceived "Project Independence" was
proposed. The stated purpose of this project was to make the United
States independent of foreign energy supplies by 1980. Serious attempts
were also made to obtain international cooperation amongst consumer
nations, for instance through the International Energy Agency.

The cruel facts are that most Western industrial nations will
remain critically dependent on Middle East oil supplies for at least the
next decade or two, that only five giant oil fields have been discovered
outside the Middle East in the past four decades, that it takes about ten
years to develop such an oil field and that no Western nation has
developed a comprehensive energy policy or strategy.

There is growing fear in most Western countries that capital
generation will not take place rapidly and efficiently enough to
develop sufficient new oil or gas fields, or other sources of energy. It is
clearly becoming more difficult and expensive to develop new primary
energy sources and many scientists and engineers no longer share the
public's optimism that technology will come to our aid.

It is against this background of fear and despondency that nations
and corporations are looking to the oceans as the last remaining
frontiers for oil and gas exploration. Exploration for oil is now taking
place off the shores of more than 75 countries. Offshore oil and gas
already supply a significant proportion of world oil and gas production.
However our knowledge of the extent of these resources is still very
incomplete and as we move into deeper waters off the edges of the
continental shelves, new geological and engineering problems are
encountered, and the costs of production become astronomical.

The growing demand for offshore oil and gas at ever increasing
prices on world markets and the desire of many nations to become
more self-sufficient in the supply of oil have spurred these efforts, and

have led to the establishment of new alliances based on the need for capital and technology to develop these resources.

A growing appreciation of the potential of offshore oil and gas has prompted coastal States to reassert their rights to the mineral resources in and under their continental margins in terms of the Continental Shelf Convention of 1958 and through the new concept of the exclusive economic zone.

Offshore Oil and Gas

There is a sound geological basis for turning to the continental shelves and slopes in search of oil. Favourable sediments and structures exist beneath the seas in geological settings that have proven highly productive onshore. Sub-sea geological basins, having sediments considered favourable for petroleum deposits, total about six million square miles to a water depth of 1000 feet, or about 57 percent of the world's total continental shelf. This is equivalent to about one-third of the favourable areas on land. World proven reserves amount to about 640 billion barrels of oil, of which some 18 percent is located offshore. About ten percent of the proven gas reserves are also located offshore. Offshore production now accounts for about six percent of world oil and 4.5 percent of natural gas, despite the fact that only about two percent of the continental shelf has been properly explored.

Virtually all of the world's continental shelves have received some geological investigation. Detailed exploration is planned or under way in the North Sea, the English Channel off France, the Red Sea bordering Egypt, the northwest shelf and south of Australia, off Sumatra, the Gulf coast and east, west, and northwest of the continental United States, off the west coast of Alaska, in the Persian Gulf, off Mexico, off the east and west coasts of South America, off Nigeria and North Africa, in the Caspian and Baltic Seas, the Gulf of Thailand, the Irish Sea, the Arctic ocean, the South China Sea and off Antarctica.

The price of success in offshore drilling is staggering in terms of capital requirements, risk and the time required to achieve a break-even point. The cost of exploration onshore used to amount to about 0.5 cents per barrel. However, one well of 4000 metres depth in 200 metres of water costs more than $5 million. The rules are such that a company may be forced to drill four or five obligation wells in a small block. In the North Sea the success rate is about one in ten.

The total cost of exploring one relatively small block in the North Sea could amount to $50 million over two to three years. In addition there are growing political risks in many offshore areas.

In offshore production platform systems to reduce oil pressure and gas separators have to be installed. While it is relatively easy to drill for oil offshore — particularly in shallow waters — it is much more difficult to produce, particularly when gas is present. Production platforms in the North Sea cost $600 to $1000 million. Offshore fields each have to contain at least 200 million barrels of oil if they are to be economically exploitable. Beyond 300 metres water depth the minimum size of an economic oil field is one billion barrels.

In 1977, with a total fleet of 4322 operating units world-wide, offshore drilling costs were estimated at about $7 billion per annum. At that rate the industry could drill about 1200 holes per year.

Until early 1975 most of the offshore rigs were employed in drilling on the outer continental shelf of the United States. The position has since changed dramatically with more than 75 percent of the offshore drilling being conducted in other areas.

There have been spectacular developments in offshore drilling technology. More than 125 companies in the United States devote a major share of their efforts to the development and manufacture of material and devices in support of offshore oil and gas. Plans for platforms in 1000 feet of water have been announced for the Gulf of Mexico and sea-bottom completions which require men or robots to make the necessary connections will soon follow. Miniature submarines have already taken their place in exploration and completion work.

It is therefore clear that the oil industry is determined to move further and further offshore. The technological problems are daunting but do not appear to be insurmountable. The costs will be much higher than for onshore oil and gas and many boundary disputes and other political problems will have to be overcome. For these reasons it would be unrealistic to predict — as some have done — a very rapid growth in the production of offshore oil and gas. A more realistic scenario is that of steady growth in production with steadily rising costs.

Offshore Rights to Oil and Gas

Offshore mineral rights, including the right to exploit oil and gas resources, are recognized in international law in terms of the Geneva Convention on the Continental Shelf of 1958. These rights are discussed

in Chapter Eight in which it is pointed out that some problems still
need to be resolved regarding the outer limit of national jurisdiction
over the resources of the continental shelf. The open-ended definition
of this limit in Article 1 of the Convention was of academic interest in
1958 but has now become very pertinent. The adjacency criterion and
the delineation of the shelf between neighbouring States may also
present problems in the future. However it is unlikely that States will
give up any rights which they enjoy in terms of the Continental Shelf
Convention in any new Law of the Sea.

In countries with a federal system of government, there have been
heated disputes between individual States or provinces and the central
government regarding the jurisdiction over the resources of this area.
This has been the case in Australia, the United States and Canada. In
the United States this matter was finally resolved by granting States
jurisdiction over these resources within the three-mile territorial sea,
while the Federal Government enjoys jurisdiction beyond that on
the so-called Outer Continental Shelf. If the United States accepts
the new proposal of a 12-mile territorial sea, individual coastal States
such as Texas, Louisiana, and California might well open this dispute
again.

In Canada, on 7 November 1967, the Supreme Court handed down
its opinion of the dispute between the Federal and Provincial Governments regarding the ownership of offshore mineral rights. At stake
were potential millions of dollars in royalties from oil discoveries
under the sea. British Columbia, supported by Ontario, Nova Scotia,
New Brunswick, and Newfoundland, argued that provincial property
rights extend into the explorable sea-bed.

Quebec remained aloof from the test case, contending that ownership of offshore mineral rights was a political decision, and not one for
the court. The other provinces based their case on the contention that
they had inherited under-sea property rights from British colonial
times. In December 1966 the British Columbia cabinet passed an order
declaring provincial ownership over the Pacific continental shelf.

In the opinion handed down by the court the Chief Justice dealt
separately with the territorial sea and the continental shelf. It said that
jurisdiction over the territorial sea was originally held by the British
Crown on behalf of Canada, and that Canada clearly acquired this jurisdiction from Britain in 1928 when the Canadian parliament passed
fishing legislation, referring for the first time to the territorial waters of
Canada.

International law recognized the Federal Government's control over territorial waters and this control had been exercised in a series of legislative actions. The court contended that there were two reasons why British Columbia lacked the right to resources of the continental shelf. First, the continental shelf was outside the boundaries of the province. Second, Canada was the sovereign State recognized by international law as having rights on the shelf, and it was Canada which would have to answer claims of other countries for breaches of obligations and responsibilities imposed by international convention.

The Atlantic provinces stated that the British Columbia precedent did not apply to them as Nova Scotia for instance had been collecting royalties with no federal challenge for well over 100 years on coal mines that run six miles out under the sea from its coast.

This example clearly illustrates what importance nations—and even provinces—attach to offshore oil and gas.

Conclusions

For the rest of this century at least offshore oil and gas unquestionably represent the most important of all marine resources. World-wide the value of this production will amount to billions of dollars annually. In a world with an insatiable appetite for oil and with dwindling onshore reserves, offshore oil and gas will assume ever increasing strategic importance.

Although our geological knowledge of the extent and location of offshore oil is still very incomplete, it appears that an appreciable part of the continental shelves have a favourable potential for oil. There is a growing conviction that the continental slopes may also contain substantial amounts of oil in suitable structures and in deposits large enough to justify the immense cost of exploitation. Farther into the future we may see the exploitation of oil in much deeper waters in the continental rise and in small ocean basins.

A new Law of the Sea would have to take this potential into account. Unfortunately it appears that few of the delegates to the Third Law of the Sea Conference have a realistic appreciation of the scientific, technological and economic aspects of offshore oil and gas.

References

1. Skinner, B. J. *Earth Resources*. Prentice-Hall, Englewood Cliffs, New Jersey, 1976.

2. Cook, E. F. "The Flow of Energy through Technological Society" in *Resources and the Environment*. Blackie, Glasgow and London, 1975.

3. Wilson, C. L. *Energy: Global Prospects 1985-2000*. McGraw-Hill, New York, 1977.

4. Corant, M. A. *Geopolitics of energy*. Committee on Interior and Insular Affairs, U. S. Senate, Energy Publication No. 95-1.

Chapter Fourteen
The Living Resources of the Sea

The concept of the exclusive economic zone was undoubtedly formulated in order to harmonize coastal State jurisdiction over the living
resources off their coasts with the jurisdiction over non-living resources.
The overriding importance of the problems posed by regulation,
conservation and utilization of the living resources of the sea cannot be
over-emphasized. The vast body of documentation on this aspect, as
well as the time allocated and spent discussing these problems amply
support such a contention.

As far as ocean fisheries are concerned, three major interest groups
(with sub-groups) can be identified. These are coastal States supporting
a 200-mile economic zone with coastal State jurisdiction over fishing,
coastal States supporting more than a 200-mile coastal State zone of
jurisdiction over fishing and distant water fishing nations which
strongly object to the concept of coastal State jurisdiction outside the
12-mile territorial sea.

Supporters of the economic zone concept are basically those States
which envisage coastal State jurisdiction within this 200-mile zone
over fishing resources. It is contended by all these States that a coastal
State has a special interest in maintaining the productivity of the living
resources of this area of the sea adjacent to its coast. For this reason
they believe that these resources should fall under the sovereignty or
jurisdiction of the coastal State for purposes of conservation and
national utilization. The coastal State, because of the sovereign rights it
possesses over these resources, may reserve to itself or its nationals the
sole right of exploitation.

171

Within this group there is little if any disagreement, and their ranks have been growing. Although a variety of terms are used to indicate the exact right or rights the coastal State should enjoy, like sovereignty, jurisdiction, exclusive jurisdiction or exclusive rights, the basic idea is the same — the coastal State will have, within this 200-mile zone, exclusive control and the right exclusively to harvest to the maximum of her ability, the living resources of the sea. Only with the permission of the coastal State will other States be allowed to enter this zone for purposes of fishing. No recognition of the existing, established or any other kind of rights of other States was acknowledged but during the past few sessions, as reflected in the draft treaty, they have had to compromise on this issue with neighbouring land-locked States, by granting them certain rights of exploitation in this zone in order to obtain their support for the concept of the exclusive economic zone.

The "plus 200-milers" led by Canada, Kenya and India is in complete agreement with the 200-milers; but they go one step further. According to them a coastal State "has a special interest in the maintenance of the productivity of the living resources of the area of the sea adjacent to the exclusive fishery zone (which is the same as the economic zone) and may take appropriate measures to protect this interest."[1]

Whereas these States claim sovereign rights for the coastal State for purposes of exploration, exploitation, conservation and management over the living resources including fisheries within the 200-mile zone, they claim outside this zone preferential rights and the authority for the coastal State to "reserve for its nationals a portion of the allowable catch of these resources corresponding to its harvesting capacity."[1] The underlying idea is coastal State authority to regulate and exploit on a preferential basis, the living resources outside the 200-mile zone. This idea was sharply criticized and it is doubtful whether its proponents will receive significant support.

The distant water fishing nations strongly oppose coastal State claims over fisheries within a 200-mile zone. However they are aware of the realities, and have seen the writing on the wall. It is probably only a matter of time, provided some recognition of their interests is accorded, before they bow to the inevitable. Their position has been further weakened by the defection from their ranks of countries who have come to place national interests before lofty international ideals. At the early stages of the negotiations there were three sub-groups amongst these nations.

The first, led by the United States was prepared to recognize exclusive coastal State rights over fisheries within the 200-mile zone provided that the coastal States guarantee that the optimum sustainable yield within their zones will be harvested. If the coastal State is not in a position to take this upon herself she must allow third parties, by way of licences or otherwise, to fish to such an extent as to ensure that the allowable catch is taken.

The second, led by the U.S.S.R. flatly refused even to consider the concept of a 200-mile zone with coastal State rights over the living resources. Russia advocated however "that in the areas of the high seas directly adjacent to its territorial sea or fishery zone (not exceeding 12 miles), a *developing coastal State* may annually reserve to itself such part of the allowable catch of fish as can be taken by vessels navigating under its flag."[2] She went one step further and acknowledged that "with the growing fishing fleet of the developing coastal State the above-mentioned part of the allowable catch of fish reserved by that State may increase accordingly."[2]

From this it is clear that the attitude of the U.S.S.R. and her allies did not differ materially from that of the United States. The reason why the Soviet Union did not recognize the economic zone is to be found in other interests, and not because she refused to recognize coastal State interests in this area. Depending on a satisfactory solution of the straits issue, the U.S.S.R. will most likely accept the economic zone, probably on the same basis as the United States has recently done.

Thirdly, Japan, Norway and Poland emphasized the recognition of established rights. Evidently they were prepared to grant coastal States all the jurisdiction claimed, provided that these States recognized such established rights. Whether the coastal State is in a position to take the optimum sustainable yield herself they regard as immaterial. How the established right came about is also of no consequence — whether by way of bilateral or multilateral treaty or by way of long and historic usage, they should be honoured by the coastal State. In this regard it may be argued that the many signatories of various regional fisheries conventions have in fact, by ratifying such treaties, recognized the established fishing rights of other States.

Highly migratory species pose a particular problem which require the formulation of special rules and regulations. Proposals regarding the conservation and utilization of these species originally fell into two categories. Some States maintained that the coastal State should regulate and have preferential rights to all coastal living resources to the limits of their migratory range. The coastal State, it was said, in whose fresh or estuarine waters anadromous resources spawn, should have authority to regulate and have preferential rights to such resources beyond the territorial sea throughout their migratory range on the high seas. In cases where anadromous resources are located in, or migrate through waters adjacent to more than one coastal State, they should be regulated by agreement among such States.

As far as catadromous fish is concerned, the coastal State in whose waters these fish spend the greater part of their life cycle should have the responsibility for management of such stocks and maintenance at optimum level. Such States should also have preferential rights in respect of the total harvest of the catadromous stocks. In circumstances where catadromous fish migrate through the economic zones of other States, the management of such fisheries, including harvesting, should be regulated by agreement between the States concerned.

On the other hand, the distant water fishing nations, led in this respect by the U.S.S.R., the United Kingdom and Japan, argued that no special status should be granted to the coastal States with regard to the conservation of resources of highly migratory species. Furthermore, such States should not be granted any preferential rights in this regard. The conservation and regulation of such stocks should be carried out pursuant to international consultation or agreement in which all interested States should have the right to participate, or through existing international or regional fishery organizations.

Nowhere in the negotiations at the Third Law of the Sea Conference did our natural human greed and the self-interest of nations emerge more clearly than in the fisheries issue. In a world experiencing a population explosion, and rising aspirations amongst the poor, the need to augment, often very selfishly, declining supplies of protein from the sea was an overriding concern among many nations.

World Marine Food Resources

The world harvest of aquatic animals and fish was estimated at 72 million tons in 1976 by the United Nations Food and Agriculture Organization (FAO). This consisted of hundreds of different species of fish, crustaceans, mussels, oysters and other moluscan shell-fish, squid and octopus, several kinds of seaweeds, and some marine mammals.

As more and more countries adopt the 200-mile economic zone, they will have to relate the conditions of stocks to fishing efficiencies and to the demand for fish. For example, both Canada and the United States used to watch distant water fleets of large high-capacity factory and freezing stern trawlers fish into stocks of cod, haddock, redfish, herrings and mackerel off their coasts in the high seas beyond the twelve-mile limit. One stock after another was fished down. The usual pattern began with an explosive increase in fishing effort by overseas fleets, resulting first in a rapid increase in catch but followed by a drastic decline. The fishing fleets then shifted their attention to other fish, working their way through traditional species to previously untouched stocks.

Canada initially attempted to promote the conservation of these stocks through the International Commission for North Atlantic Fisheries (ICNAF). However she saw the total catch decline from a peak of 4.6 million tons in 1968 to 3.8 million tons in 1975. As a result Canada became an ardent convert to the 200-mile limit as a means of obtaining protective control of these resources. But at the first session of the Third Law of the Sea Conference it became clear that it would take a long time to obtain a consensus on this issue from the more than 140 participating States.

Chile, Peru and Ecuador claimed 200-mile fishing limits in 1952 and were followed by a number of other Latin American countries. Later Iceland claimed a 50-mile limit which was vigorously opposed by British trawlers. From the beginning of 1976 it became clear that a general consensus in favour of the 200-mile fishing limit of economic zone was emerging, and Canada, the European Economic Community countries, Norway, India, the United States and the U.S.S.R. followed suit. They were followed by South Africa, Australia and New Zealand. Countries along the northwest coast of Africa also became concerned about the increasing extent of foreign fishing outside their existing fishing limits.

Meanwhile the distant water fishing nations were trying to counter this trend by improving the efficiency and sophistication of their fleets and by intensifying research and development work on aquaculture. In addition, a number of developing Asian States, including South Korea and Thailand, were developing distant water fishing fleets.

At present the world catch provides some 45 to 50 millions tons of fish for direct human consumption but demand projections based on forecasts of population and income indicate that the demand will reach 110 million tons by the year 2000. The FAO estimates a possible supply by then of 100 million tons, based on stocks presently exploited plus a whole range of species not traditionally harvested but within reach of exploitation. Beyond that it is considered that a large potential exists for the exploitation of small mesopelagic fish in deep waters, giant squid also in deepwaters, and Krill in the Arctic waters. Much more attention could be devoted to a variety of aquaculture ventures.

To predict future harvests in the oceans three general methods are used, namely the extrapolation of present trends in total harvests, the extrapolation of resource estimates from a known area to less well known areas and by estimating primary production and each successive stage in the food chain. None of these methods yields entirely satisfactory results. The experience of the past decade has shown that there is a real danger of over-fishing and has illustrated the need to make more efficient use of the fish that we do catch.

If the oceans are going to make a substantial contribution to the growing world need for protein, then conservation, the exploitation of new species and aquaculture will all have to be pursued more vigorously.

International Management

Where fishermen of two or more nations are harvesting stocks of fish jointly various international arrangements have been developed to deal with mutual problems. The 1958 Geneva Convention on Fishing and Conservation of the Living Resources of the High Seas provides general guidelines for international fishing activities, but developments in the 1970s have made this Convention obsolete.

The Food and Agricultural Organization of the United Nations through its Department of Fisheries has established a number of regional fishery councils and commissions. Several international fishery conventions have been negotiated to deal with single joint fishery agreements or special fishery problems. Some involve only two nations, such as the International Pacific Salmon Fisheries Convention between the United States and Canada. Others have many members, such as the International Convention for the Regulation of Whaling, which has 15.[3]

The Informal Composite Negotiating Text reflects the measure of agreement which has been reached with regard to fisheries.[4] Article 61 specifies that the coastal State shall determine the allowable catch in its exclusive economic zone and shall ensure that over-exploitation shall not take place. Such measures shall also be designed to maintain or restore populations of harvested species at levels which can produce the maximum sustainable yield. The coastal State should take into account the effects on species associated with or dependent upon harvested species. Available scientific information, catch and fishing statistics, and other data relevant to the conservation of fish stocks should be exchanged on a regular basis through regional and global organizations.

Article 62 requires the coastal State to promote the objective of optimum utilization of the living resources of the exclusive economic zone. Where the coastal State does not have the capacity to harvest the entire allowable catch it shall, through agreements, give other States access to the surplus of the allowable catch. However nationals of other States fishing in the exclusive economic zone shall comply with the conservation measures and with other terms and conditions established by the coastal State. Such regulations may relate to the licensing of fishermen, vessels and equipment, including payment of fees, determining the species which may be caught, regulating seasons and areas of fishing, fixing the age and size of species that may be caught, requiring the conduct of specified fisheries research programmes, placing observers or trainees on board such vessels, the landing of all or any part of the catch in the ports of the coastal State, requirements for training personnel and transfer of fisheries technology to the coastal State, and enforcement procedures.

Where the same stock or stocks of associated species occur within the exclusive economic zones of two or more coastal States, they are enjoined by Article 63 to seek, either directly or through appropriate regional organizations, agreement upon the measures necessary to coordinate and ensure the conservation and development of such stocks. They are also required to cooperate in adopting measures necessary for the conservation of these stocks in the area adjacent to the exclusive economic zone — a victory for the "plus 200-milers."

According to Article 64 the coastal State and other States whose nationals fish in the region shall cooperate with a view of ensuring the conservation and optimum utilization of such species both within and beyond the exclusive economic zone.

Article 65 states that nothing in the Convention restricts the right of a coastal State or international organization to prohibit, regulate and limit the exploitation of marine mammals.

Article 66 deals with anadromous species — those that spawn in fresh water, such as salmon. It specifies that States in whose rivers such stocks originate shall have the primary interest in and responsibility for these stocks. Their conservation should be ensured by the establishment of appropriate regulatory measures for fishing in all waters landward of the outer limits of the coastal State's exclusive economic zone. Fishing for anadromous species shall be conducted only in the waters landward of the outer limits of exclusive economic zones, except in cases where this provision would result in economic dislocation for a State other than the State of origin—a rather vague phrase, to say the least.

Enforcement of regulations regarding anadromous species beyond the exclusive economic zone shall be by agreement between the State of origin and other States concerned.

Catadromous species are covered by Article 67, which specifies that a coastal State in whose waters such stocks spend the greater part of their life shall have the resonsibility for the management of these species and shall ensure the ingress and egress of migrating fish. Harvesting of catadromous species shall be conducted only in waters in respect of which the responsible State exercises sovereign rights over the living resources. In cases where catadromous fish migrate through the waters of another State, whether as juvenile or maturing fish, the management of such stocks shall be regulated by agreement between the State in which they spend the greater part of their life and the other State concerned.

Article 69 reflects on the one hand an attempt to placate the developing land-locked States, and on the other a blatant political power play by the so-called Group of 77. This article states that land-locked States shall have the right to participate in the exploitation of the living resources of the exclusive economic zones of adjoining coastal States on an equitable basis. The terms and conditions of such participation shall be determined by the States concerned through bilateral, subregional or regional agreements. Developed land-locked States shall however be entitled to exercise their rights only within the exclusive conomic zones of adjoining *developed* coastal States.

Article 70 goes even further in providing that developing coastal States situated in a region whose geographical peculiarities make them particularly dependent for the nutritional needs of their populations upon the exploitation of the living resources in the exclusive economic zones of their neighbouring States, and developing coastal States which can claim no exclusive economic zones of their own, shall have the right to participate in the exploitation of living resources in the exclusive economic zones of other States in the region.

At the early stages of the negotiations some of the developing coastal States objected to this and pointed out that they were as entitled to claim the right to participate in the exploitation of the land-based resources of land-locked States as these States were to participate in the exploitation of the ocean resources of coastal States.

At the 7th session of the Third Law of the Sea Conference from March to May 1978 an attempt was made to redraft articles 69 and 70 in order to obtain greater consensus. Several delegations expressed reservations about the definition in these articles of terms such as "rights" and "surplus."

Although most of the living resources of the sea are present in areas which would be included in the exclusive economic zones of coastal States, provisions have been made for the management and conservation of the living resources of the high seas. Articles 116 to 120 deal with this issue. According to these articles, all States have the right for their nationals to engage in fishing on the high seas, subject to their treaty obligations and the rights and duties as well as the interests of coastal States, as provided for *inter alia* in articles 63 and 64 to 67. All States have the duty to adopt, or to cooperate with other States in adopting such measures for their respective nationals as may be necessary for the conservation of the living resources of the high seas.

In determining the allowable catch and establishing other conservation measures, States are required to adopt measures which are designed to maintain and restore populations of harvested species at levels which can produce the maximum sustainable yield. They are also enjoined to contribute and exchange available scientific information, catch and fishing effort statistics and other data relevant to the conservation of the fish stocks of the high seas.

The Significance of the Draft Treaty

The Informal Composite Negotiating Text certainly does not constitute a new Law of the Sea, and there is little chance that a new comprehensive treaty will be adopted within the next few years. Nevertheless, this text does represent a measure of consensus and reflects the success of the proponents of the exclusive economic zone in making this concept palatable to nations which initially regarded the idea with outright scorn.

The articles dealing with fisheries reflect a victory for the coastal States, for though they do contain certain provisions which appear to protect the rights of other States, these clauses are so vague as to make them meaningless. The emerging Law of the Sea spells the doom of the distant water fishing fleets, unless they can manage to survive at the mercy of and under the complete control of coastal States.

The general tone of the articles dealing with fishing is vague, except where they treat the protection of the rights of coastal States. Compromise over more than a decade has produced a text that makes the purist shudder but nevertheless the end result proclaims a new wave for the future — the exclusive economic zone.

References

1.   United Nations. Document A/AC. 138/S C II/L. 38, Article 8, 1973.

2.   United Nations. Conference Room Paper No. 22, Seabeds Committee, 1973.

3.   Rothschild, B. *World Fishery Policy: Multidisciplinary Views*.

4.   United Nations. "Informal Composite Negotiating Text." Third Law of the Sea Conference, Doc. A/CONF. 62/WP. 10, 1977.

Chapter Fifteen
Pollution of the Marine Environment

In 1962, Rachel Carson's book *Silent Spring*[1] was published and became an immediate bestseller. It is perhaps somewhat ironic that a popular book on a minor branch of the biological sciences — ecology — should have had such a profound effect on social attitudes in general and on public attitudes towards the preservation of the environment in particular.[2]

The increasing world-wide concern about environmental conservation has resulted in an insistence by many coastal States that they should have the right to take strong measures to protect their coasts from the ravages of marine pollution. The first active step in this regard was the establishment by Canada of a 100-mile pollution control zone in her Arctic waters. This initiative was received sympathetically by many other coastal States, and led to an insistence that the coastal State should have the right to control the conservation of the marine environment within the 200-mile economic zone.

This trend has caused grave concern among the maritime States who fear that strong coastal State control of marine pollution in such a wide zone would interfere with the traditional freedom of navigation on the high seas. Some delegations expressed the view that these demands by the coastal States would give them greater power to interfere with navigation in a 200-mile zone off their coasts than they enjoyed even in the territorial sea under the regime of innocent passage. The fear of the maritime States is that a multiplicity of pollution control regimes, in terms of which certain States would even specify ship design, navigational equipment and practices, would seriously interfere with maritime interests and would inhibit international trade.

The maritime States, while recognizing the need to protect the marine environment, insist on internationally agreed marine pollution control standards. They also favour flag State and international enforcement of these standards. In this regard they see an important role for the Intergovernmental Maritime Consultative Organization (IMCO). This organization is basically concerned with maritime affairs, and has a strong flag State bias. To this end an IMCO sponsored conference of Plenipotentiaries took place in London in October, 1973. Some States suspected that this conference was deliberately scheduled to take place before the first meeting of the Third Law of the Sea Conference in order to prejudge some of the issues, and to place the stamp of a flag State bias on the control of marine pollution.

The non-maritime coastal States also favour internationally agreed marine pollution control standards but they insist on enforcement by the coastal State, which should also have residual rights to impose measures stronger than the internationally agreed standards in cases of emergency.

It is clear that this issue has become one of the most important and contentious of the Third Law of the Sea Conference. There is a distinct danger that the insistence by certain coastal States on strong pollution control measures within the proposed economic zone could lead to increasing opposition to this concept by the powerful maritime States, which in turn could lead to the failure of this concept to receive the support necessary for its adoption.

At its first session in 1978, a negotiating group reported that clauses favouring ship routing systems designed to avoid collisions and highlighting the need to warn coastal States of the danger of oil spills from marine accidents were tentatively agreed on for inclusion in the negotiating text. Delegates were reported close to agreement on other provisions, including one that would permit coastal States to arrest foreign ships whose violation of an international pollution control standard caused or threatened "major damage" to that State's marine environment.

The new provisions on compulsory conciliation are part of a draft article listing various limitations on the principle set out in the negotiating text, that disputes over the interpretation or application of the convention must be settled by resort to an international tribunal chosen by the parties concerned. The discussions at the 1978 session were clearly influenced by the *Amoco Cadiz* disaster which increased the awareness of and concern over the magnitude of possible hazards and emphasized the need to improve preventive measures by strengthening both the standard-setting procedure and the enforcement measures.[3]

It is clear that the main concern at the various sessions of the Third Law of the Sea Conference has been with oil pollution. Clearly however, in our complex modern society, other forms of pollution of the marine environment will also have to be considered.

Oil Polllution

A series of mishaps, causing the spillage of many thousands of tons of oil from stranded tankers and the pollution of large areas of the coast has focussed the importance of this issue on the public mind.

Superships, many needing depths more than double those of almost all ports, are here. Some are loaded with up to 475,000 tons of crude oil. Others carry up to 125,000 cubic metres of liquefied natural gas at 162°C. Until 1973 it appeared that this trend towards supertankers would continue, and predictions of one million tonner supertankers appeared in the press.

The environmental considerations in the use of supertankers are great. The frightening spectre of the *Torrey Canyon* is frequently invoked and is brought to mind by a succession of later disasters. There are also warnings of ecological disturbances from harbour dredging, port construction and movement of tankers in harbours, bays and estuaries.[4]

Industry and governments have promised to spend millions of dollars on the prevention of disasters and ecological disturbances but the public remains sceptical. In fact a great deal has been done to reduce the risk of such accidents. Better ship design, improved navigational equipment, better routing practices in crowded shipping lanes and improved methods of confining and collecting oil are just a few of these. Yet the tonnage of oil transported by sea has reached enormous proportions and it appears that tanker disasters cannot be completely averted.

In addition to oil pollution from stranded tankers it is estimated that the amount of oil reaching the oceans from land-based sources, such as refineries sited on rivers or estuaries, from tankers at sea voiding their bilges, from port installations where transshipment takes place and from carelessly sealed underwater oil wells, may amount to 5 million tons a year.[5] Oil is also known to well up along fault lines, and an unmeasured precipitation which is first blown into the air from the exhausts of millions of automobiles is then dropped back into the oceans. Some scientists have estimated that the total amount of oil pollution in the oceans may be approaching 100 million tons per annum.

All crude oils and all oil fractions except highly purified materials are poisonous to marine organisms.[6] Principally responsible for this toxicity are three complex fractions. The low boiling saturated hydrocarbons have, until quite recently, been considered harmless to the marine environment. However it has since been discovered that this fraction may cause death in a variety of lower animals. The low boiling aromatic hydrocarbons are the most immediately toxic fraction. Benzene, toluene and xylene are acute poisons for man and other organisms. Phenanthrene and naphthalene are even more toxic to fishes. Olefinic hydrocarbons are absent in crude oil but occur in refined products.

Numerous other components of crude oil are also toxic and it has been claimed that some crude oils contain carcinogens. To make matters worse, it appears that hydrocarbons are among the most persistent organic chemicals in the marine environment.

Preliminary Rules for the Protection and Preservation of the Marine Environment

After years of negotiation, several draft articles on the protection of the marine environment, and the prevention of marine pollution have been prepared by committees, working groups and negotiating groups of the Third Law of the Sea Conference. Part XII (articles 193 to 238) deals specifically with this subject. In addition, a number of other draft articles of the Informal Composite Negotiating Text[7] make some reference to the rights and duties of States in this regard.

Section 1 of Part XII deals with general provisions regarding the prevention and control of marine pollution. Article 193 points out that all States have an obligation to protect and preserve the marine environment. However, article 194 recognizes the sovereign right of all States to exploit their natural resources "pursuant to their environmental policies and in accordance with their duty to protect and preserve the marine environment."[7] A too literal interpretation of the concept of preservation is clearly not intended.

Article 195 requires States to take all necessary measures, consistent with the draft Convention, to prevent, reduce and control marine pollution using the best means at their disposal and in accordance with their capabilities. It also enjoins them to "harmonize" their policies in this regard. States are required to conduct activities under their jurisdiction in such a manner that they do not cause pollution to the environment of other states. These measures deal with all sources of pollution and should minimize to the fullest extent possible the release of toxic, harmful and noxious substances from land-based sources, from or through the atmosphere or by dumping. Also included are pollution from vessels, installations and devices used in the exploration or exploitation of the natural resources of the sea-bed and all other installations and devices operating in the marine environment.

In taking measures to prevent, reduce or control marine pollution, States shall refrain from unjustifiable interference with activities in pursuance of the rights and duties of other States and they are expected not to act so as to transfer damage from one area to another, or to transform one type of pollution into another (article 196.)

The fears of the new technologies of the developing countries are reflected in article 197 which requires that States take all necessary measures to prevent, reduce and control marine pollution resulting from the use of technologies under their jurisdiction, or the intentional or accidental introduction of species which may cause significant and harmful changes to a marine environment.

Section 2 of Part XII of the Composite Negotiating Text deals with global and regional cooperation. This requires States to cooperate on a global basis and, as appropriate, on a regional basis directly or through competent international organizations, in formulating and elaborating international rules, standards and recommended practices and procedures for the protection and preservation of the marine environment, taking into account characteristic regional features (article 198). This reflects on the one hand the maritime States' concern that a multiplicity of pollution control regulations would seriously interfere with navigation and international trade, and on the other, the desire of the developing countries to share in the expertise of the industrial nations.

Article 199 places an obligation on a State, which becomes aware of an event in which the marine environment is in imminent danger of being damaged, to notify immediately other States which may be affected by such damage, as well as competent international organizations. Article 200 requires that States in an affected area shall cooperate in eliminating the effects of such polution and in preventing or reducing damage. They are also supposed to promote and develop contingency plans for responding to pollution incidents. They are encouraged to promote studies and to undertake scientific research on marine pollution (article 201), and to establish appropriate scientific criteria for the formulation of rules, standards and practices for the prevention of marine pollution (article 202).

Section 3 of part XII covers technical assistance to developing States in the prevention of marine pollution and in the preservation of the marine environment. It enjoins States (presumably developed nations) to promote programmes of scientific, educational, technical and other assistance to developing States, to provide assistance for the minimization of the effects of major incidents, and to assist in the preparation of environmental assessments (article 203). This obviously reflects the voting power of the developing States, and their continuous efforts to obtain more than an equitable share of the spoils of the Third Law of the Sea Conference. Article 204 goes even further in specifying that developing States shall, for the purposes of the prevention of pollution of the marine environment, be granted preferential treatment in the allocation of appropriate funds and technical facilities of international organizations, and in the utilization of their specialized services.

Section 4 of Part XII sets out rules and obligations for the monitoring and evaluation of the risks and effects of marine pollution. States are required to publish reports on the results of such work, or to provide reports to the appropriate international organizations which should make them available to all States. They are also required to assess the potential effects of any planned activities under their jurisdiction which may cause marine pollution and to communicate the results in the manner specified in article 206.

Section 5 specifies that States shall establish national laws and regulations to prevent, reduce or control pollution of the marine environment from land-based sources. They are urged to establish global or regional rules, standards and practices in this regard, designed to reduce as far as possible the release of toxic, harmful and noxious substances (article 208). Similar provisions for the control of pollution resulting from sea-bed activities are contained in article 209.

International rules, standards and recommended practices and procedures are to be established to prevent and control marine pollution from activities in the area beyond national jurisdiction, according to article 210. In terms of this article, States are accorded the right to establish national laws and regulations to prevent and control pollution in this area, provided that the requirements of such rules are no less effective than the international rules.

The prevention, reduction and control of dumping in the marine environment is covered by article 211, which forbids dumping within the territorial sea and the exclusive economic zone, and onto the continental shelf without the express prior approval of the coastal State.

Article 212, which deals with pollution from vessels, specifies that States, through a competent international organization or general diplomatic conference, shall establish international rules and standards for the prevention, reduction and control of marine pollution from vessels. States are required to establish such laws for vessels flying their flag or vessels of their registry. Coastal States may establish national laws and regulations for the prevention and control of pollution from vessels sailing within their territorial sea, provided that such measures do not hamper the innocent passage of foreign vessels. In the economic zone they may establish similar rules and regulations, provided that these are in accordance with accepted international rules and standards. This proviso is obviously intended to reduce the risk of a multiplicity of pollution control regulations in the economic zones which could seriously impede navigation. However, paragraph 5 of article 212 specifies that where international rules are inadequate to meet special circumstances and where coastal States have reasonable grounds for believing that a particular, clearly defined area of their economic zone is an area where for recognized technical reasons the adoption of special mandatory methods for the prevention of pollution is required, they may, after appropriate consultation with the competent international organization, submit scientific and technical evidence in support of such special measures. This organization shall, within twelve months of receiving such a communication, determine whether the coastal State may establish such special measures. Such additional laws and regulations may relate to discharges or navigational practices but shall not require foreign vessels to observe design, construction, manning, or equipment standards other than generally accepted international rules and standards.

Pollution of the marine environment from or through the atmosphere is covered by article 213, which requires that States adopt, within their air space or with regard to vessels or aircraft flying their flag, laws and regulations to prevent, reduce and control pollution, taking into account internationally agreed rules and practices. States are enjoined to establish global and regional rules, standards, recommended practices, and procedures in this regard.

Section 6 of Part XII covers the enforcement of marine pollution regulations with regard to land-based sources, from sea-bed activities, from activities in the area beyond national jurisdiction, and with respect to dumping (articles 214 to 217). The rights and obligations of the flag State are specified in article 218, those of the port State in article 219, and enforcement by the coastal State in article 221. From these articles it is clear that the coastal States would, subject to certain safeguards, have substantial powers for the prevention of marine pollution both in the territorial sea and in the exclusive economic zone, whereas flag States would have more responsibilities than rights.

Article 222 goes even further in specifying that "nothing in this Chapter shall affect the right of States to take measures, in accordance with international law, beyond the limits of the territorial sea for the protection of coastlines or related interests, including fishing, from grave and imminent danger from pollution or threat of pollution following upon a maritime casualty or acts related to such a casualty."[7]

The enforcement of laws with respect to pollution from or through the atmosphere is dealt with in article 223.

Section 7 of Part XII does however provide certain safeguards to the flag States and to ship owners. This section reflects an attempt by the maritime States to protect their interests. It covers measures to facilitate proceedings, rules for the exercise of the powers of enforcement, the duty to avoid adverse consequences in the exercise of the powers of enforcement, rules for the investigation of foreign vessels and provisions for non-discrimination against foreign vessels (articles 224 to 228).

Article 229 deals with the suspension and restrictions on the institution of proceedings against foreign vessels or their flag States, and sets a statute of limitation of three years on such proceedings. However, article 230 specifies that "nothing in the present Convention shall affect the institution of civil proceedings in respect of any claim for loss or damage resulting from pollution of the marine environment."

Articles 231 to 234 specify the monetary penalties which may be imposed for damage resulting from marine pollution and protects the rights of the accused. An obligation is also placed on the coastal State to notify the flag State and other States concerned of any measures taken pursuant to provisions of this Convention. Provision is also made for the liability of coastal States in cases of unlawful or unreasonable penalties.

Finally, one of the vital interests of the major maritime powers — navigation through straits used for international passage — is protected by article 234 of the Composite Negotiating Text. The relevant part of this article states that "nothing in Sections 5, 6 and 7 of this part of the Convention shall affect the legal regime of straits used for international navigation."

Canada managed to cloak in respectability a unilateral act of establishing a 100-mile pollution control zone in her Arctic waters by having article 235 inserted into the Composite Negotiating Text. This specifies that coastal States have the right to establish and enforce non-discriminatory laws and regulations for the prevention, reduction, and control of marine pollution in ice-covered areas within the limits of the exclusive economic zone.

Section 9 of part XII deals with responsibility and liability. Article 236 specifies that States are responsible for the fulfilment of their international obligations concerning the protection of the marine environment, and that they are liable for damage attributable to them. However, Section 10 (article 237) states that the provisions of this Convention regarding pollution of the marine environment shall not apply to any warship, naval auxiliary, other vessels, or aircraft owned or operated by a State and used only on governmental, non-commercial service. This article clearly reflects the vital strategic interests of the maritime powers.

Section 11 (article 238) states that the provisions of this part of the Convention shall be without prejudice to obligations assumed by States under special conventions and agreements concluded previously, but requires that specific obligations assumed by them, with respect to the protection and preservation of the marine environment, should be applied in a manner consistent with the general principles and objectives of this Convention.

• • • •

Discussion

The draft articles dealing with marine pollution and the preservation of the marine environment reflect the extent to which States had to compromise on these issues, while still protecting conflicting national interests. There is a clear dichotomy in this regard between the interests of the coastal States who are gravely concerned about the increasing pollution of the marine environment particularly by oil, and the fears of the maritime States that pollution control measures may be used to interfere unduly with passage and as a means of "creeping jurisdiction" by the coastal States. There is also a legitimate concern that pollution control measures may be used as a pretext by coastal States to increase the extent of their jurisdiction in the exclusive economic zone.

Many of the draft articles appear vague and even contradictory, and some are open to widely divergent interpretations. A number of key concepts such as "protection," "preservation," "grave damage," "non-discriminatory," etc., are not defined in qualitative, let alone quantitative, terms. A distinct lack of scientific and technical guidance is a feature of the drafting. It appears that this lack of clarity in the provisions of the articles dealing with marine pollution and the protection of the marine environment will, upon its adoption, lead to excessive litigation in terms of the Convention.

The emotional tone of the text testifies to a strong influence by environmental movements, some of which are close to the lunatic fringe.

References

1.   Carson, R. *Silent Spring*. Fawcett Publications, Inc., Greenwich, Conn., 1962. 304 p.

2.   Van Rensburg, W. C. J. and Bambrick, S. *Economics of the World's Mineral Industries*. McGraw-Hill Publishing Company, 1978. p. 366.

3.   United Nations. Reports of the Committees and Negotiating Groups on Negotiations at the Seventh Session. U.N., Geneva, 28 March to 19 May 1978.

4.   Frye, J. "Oil, Superships and the Oceans." *Oceans Magazine*, Vol. 7 (1), 1974, pp. 48-55.

5.   Ward, B. "Mankind's New Target: The Vulnerable Oceans." *Living Wilderness*, Vol. 38 (127), 1974, pp. 7-15.

6.   Blumer, M. "Scientific Aspects of the Oil Spill Problem." *Environmental Affairs*, Vol. 1 (1), 1971, pp. 54-73.

7.   United Nations. Informal Composite Negotiating Text. U.N. Third Law of the Sea Conference, Doc. No. A/CONF. 62/WP. 10.

Chapter Sixteen
The Search for Knowledge Scientific Research or Espionage?

Man has always been fascinated by the oceans which cover more than 70 percent of the earth's surface. Modern scientific research in the marine environment started with the famous voyage of HMS *Challenger* more than 100 years ago. In the past decade marine scientific research has blossomed and its level of sophistication has increased dramatically. The deep-sea drilling vessel, the *Glomar Challenger*, and other advanced research vessels have contributed not only to greater knowledge of the nature of the oceans and their subsurface but also to an understanding of the basic processes which operate on and below the earth's crust. Evidence of sea-floor spreading and of plate tectonic movements have given us a greater understanding of earth processes, and of the modes of origin of many critically important mineral deposits.

During this century we have also experienced the gradual demise of several great surface fleets and the growing strategic importance of submarines. Great strides have been made in the development of means to detect submarines, which necessitated intensive research into ocean waves and currents in order to devise means of escaping detection.

The submarine fleets of the world have grown in number, sophistication and in their potential for destroying large parts of our planet. They are constantly involved in deadly games of tag and have assumed the world oceans as their playground. Harlow[1] and Hearn[2] have expressed the U.S. Navy's viewpoint that maximum freedom to use all dimensions of the sea must be maintained in order to exploit naval strength in the best national interest. Other major powers agree with this contention.

Several countries have stated publicly that scientific research of the oceans is of benefit to all mankind. They feel that there should be maximum freedom of such research which should be open to all. Some coastal States have denied the validity and equity of this reasoning on the basis of their inability to participate effectively in such research or to utilize the resultant data. These countries also feel that they are unable to protect their national interests regarding the resources in their areas of national jurisdiction, or to prevent environmental degradation of coastal waters by operations resulting from scientific research.[3]

Many coastal States favour the expansion of jurisdiction or control as a buffer against foreign intelligence. The principal issue is not the collection of scientific data by foreign nationals in the waters of a coastal State but the use to which the research data is put. What is beneficial scientifically to one country may represent a divulgence of vital economic or military intelligence to hostile or commercial adversaries.[3]

There has been little success in efforts to establish a sophisticated position regarding scientific research in coastal waters. Freedom of scientific research is easily compromised for more important economic and military interests.

The negotiations at the Third Law of the Sea Conference have centered around a coompromise between the commercial and security interests of coastal States, and the scientific and strategic interests of maritime States. These efforts have been complicated by a general realization of the fact that there is a thin dividing line between scientific research and espionage in the marine environment.

The Development of Marine Science

Modern marine science dates from the *Challenger* Expedition which sailed in 1872. This voyage was a huge undertaking for its time, and was made possible only by the prosperity of Victorian England. However, it also required skillful political negotiations by the scientists with the Admiralty and the Government. The Royal Society prepared the scientific plan for the expedition while the Hydrographer coped with the logistics and issued sailing orders[4]. The *Challenger* left Portsmouth on 21 December 1872.

This was a multi-disciplinary scientific expedition, and at each dredging and sounding station a number of observations were made.

The exact depth of water was determined, and a sample of the bottom material was recovered. The bottom water was examined physically and chemically, the bottom temperature was determined and at most stations a sample of the bottom fauna was procured by means of the dredge or trawl. In many instances the fauna of the surface and the intermediate depths was examined by the use of a tow net. Where possible, a series of temperature observations were made at different depths from the surface to the bottom, and at many stations samples of seawater were also obtained from various depths. The direction and rate of surface currents were determined and atmospheric and meteorological conditions were noted.

The *Challenger* returned to England on 24 May 1876 and an office was established in Edinburgh. Although the facilities were spartan, this virtually became the first college of marine science. Under the initial direction of John Murray the research was continued, and over the next 20 years 50 massive reports were published. These represented a quantum leap in man's knowledge of the biology, chemistry and geology of the oceans. The physics of the sea however had been relatively neglected.

Marine science in Britain became somewhat static after the *Challenger* Expedition, and the Scandinavians and Germans became more active. The mext important step in the development of marine science came about during World War II when the importance of military oceanography became apparent. After this war considerably more attention was devoted to international cooperation in oceanography under the auspices of organizations such as the Intergovernmental Oceanographic Commission.

The Deep Sea Drilling Project

The Deep Sea Drilling Project, lasting for several years, represents one of the outstanding projects in the history of science. It has been a unique effort to increase man's knowledge of the earth, the age and history of the oceans and the processes involved in the evolution of ocean basins. A great deal of information concerning the resource potential of vast areas of the ocean floor has also been collected.

The Deep Sea Drilling Project has been funded mainly by the U.S. National Science Foundation, although a number of countries have contributed in various ways to its success. The project has been managed by Scripps Institution of Oceanography and the drilling and coring operations were accomplished with the ship D/V *Glomar Challenger*. A number of foreign countries participated in various phases of the project.

The *Glomar Challenger* was constructed specifically for the Deep Sea Drilling Project and has many unique capabilities. Scientific planning for the Project has been provided by panels under the auspices of the Joint Oceanographic Institutions for Deep Earth Sampling (JOIDES). During the project several hundreds of holes were drilled in water depths of up to 2000 feet and to depths beneath the sea floor of up to 4265 feet. More than 165,000 feet of sediments were cored.

The project was responsible for a number of major scientific achievements.[5] Firstly, the recovery and radioactive dating of rocks in the Indian, Pacific and Antarctic oceans revealed a maximum age of about 160 million years. Compared to the ages of the oldest continental rock the ocean basins are therefore young features. This provides strong evidence in favour of the concept that the earth's crust is destroyed and renewed—the so-called theory of sea-floor spreading.

Drilling results have also confirmed a general increase in the age of the ocean floor at increasing distances from the area of crustal generation at the mid-ocean ridges towards the zones of destruction in the deep-sea trenches. This strongly supports other evidence of the movement of large earth plates. The drilling results also support earlier geophysical evidence of horizontal movements of these crustal plates at rates of 1-13 centimeters per year and provide evidence supporting the contention that substantial vertical movements have taken place in the oceans.

Drilling in the Mediterranean Sea revealed a mass of salt deposits and related sediments as well as plant and animal fossils, which indicate that it dried up about 12 million years ago.

Minerals such as zinc and copper were found in deep sea sediments in several areas. This has encouraged geologists to reexamine many ancient mineral deposits on land which may have originated in a similar manner.

The Attitudes of States towards Marine Research

Most countries now appreciate that scientific research in the marine environment is a prerequisite for resource exploitation and pollution control. In addition, marine scientific research is of great strategic importance to the super maritime powers whose nuclear submarines now constitute their most important line of defence. In view of these facts the control of marine scientific research has assumed a new importance. At the early sessions of the Third Law of the Sea Conference there were three main trends of thought in this regard.

In the first place, the majority of coastal States insisted on coastal State control over marine research in the territorial sea and in the proposed economic zone. In the view of these countries no marine scientific research could take place in these areas without the express consent of the coastal State, which should also have the right to participate in such research projects, to obtain samples of any material collected and to receive the results of such research. The insistence of the coastal States on such provisions is based on their desire to share in the benefits of research, to improve the competence of their own nationals and on their fears that marine scientific research may extend into exploration, which would give the larger States an advantage in the exploitation of marine resources within the economic zones of other States. Of course they also feared that scientific research could be used as a pretext for spying.

Some of these countries would have liked the proposed International Regime to control scientific research in the area beyond the limits of national jurisdiction, while others favoured freedom of scientific research in this area.

The U.S.S.R. and other socialist States favoured strong coastal State control over scientific research in the territorial sea and on the continental shelf (but not in its superjacent waters), and complete freedom of scientific research on the high seas. These countries strongly objected to any reference to the control of scientific research in the economic zone which they did not recognize. Their attitude is in line with present international law, including the 1958 Geneva Conventions. One suspects however that this was motivated largely by strategic considerations.

The United States favoured maximum freedom of scientific research in the marine environment. They were prepared to accept that the consent of the coastal State should be obtained for scientific research in the territorial sea but felt that they need only be notified of research in the economic zone. In the area beyond this limit of national jurisdiction they proposed that there should be complete freedom of scientific research. U. S. research organizations have been faced with endless bureaucracy when seeking permission to conduct marine

scientific research, particularly off the coast of Latin American countries. There is also a strong science lobby in the United States, which
insists on complete freedom of scientific research. However, there is
little doubt that strategic considerations also motivated this approach.

The definition of marine scientific research has given rise to
significant differences of opinion. The distinction between scientific
research on the one hand, and exploration or espionage on the other is
not always clear.

The dissatisfaction of developing countries with the traditional
law of the sea and particularly the freedom of the high seas was already
evident at the 1958 Geneva Conference on The Law of the Sea.[6] The
acceptance of the "common heritage" concept 12 years later provided a
basis for a legal system more compatible with their interests and has
led to attacks of increasing frequency on various aspects of the doctrine
of the freedom of the seas. Many of these countries perceive that at least
in the short term, they will profit more from the international management of deep sea-bed resources than from outright ownership of their
adjacent continental shelves or economic zones. Their bargaining
position is therefore one of claiming ownership of their shelves, and to
secure a share of whatever lies beyond through the mechanism of
common heritage. This means the creation of a strong International
Seabeds Authority which would control not only the resources of this
area but also restrict scientific research.

Preliminary Rules for Marine Scientific Research

After years of negotiation a series of draft articles has been prepared at
the various sessions of the Third Law of the Sea Conference.[7] Articles
40, 143, 202, 203, and 239 to 266 of this Informal Composite Negotiating
Text deal specifically with various aspects of marine scientific research.
Part XIII of the text deals exclusively with research in various areas of
the marine environment.

Section 1 of this part deals with general provisions for the conduct
of marine research. Article 239 claims that all States and competent
international organizations have the right to conduct marine scientific
research. In terms of article 240, States and competent international
organizations have an obligation to promote marine scientific research.
The general principles for the conduct of marine scientific research are
covered in article 241. According to this, marine scientific research
shall be conducted exclusively for peaceful purposes. Such a provision

appears to be naive and one finds it difficult to believe that the U.S. and Soviet navies would adhere to it. This article also specifies that such research shall be conducted with "appropriate" scientific methods and means but of course does not specify what these are. Scientific research is not to interfere with other legitimate uses of the sea, thereby relegating it to a lower priority. Marine research is to be conducted with due regard to the preservation of the marine environment.

According to article 242, marine scientific research shall not form the legal basis for any claim to any part of the marine environment or its resources. This clearly reflects the fears of developing countries which have been discussed above.[4]

Section 2 of part XIII deals with global and regional cooperation. Article 243 specifies that States and international organizations shall, on the basis of mutual benefit, promote international cooperation in marine scientific research for peaceful purpoes, through the conclusion of bilateral, regional and unilateral agreements (article 244).

States and international organizations are obligated to publish and disseminate information on major programmes and their objectives, as well as knowledge resulting from such research. They are also required to promote the flow of scientific data and the transfer of knowledge in particular to developing States, whose autonomous marine research capabilities they are to strengthen, for instance through programmes to provide education and training of their technical and scientific personnel (article 245).

Section 3 covers the conduct and promotion of scientific research in the various areas of the marine environment. According to article 246, coastal States have the exclusive right to authorize and conduct scientific research in their territorial sea. Research by other parties shall be conducted only with the express consent of and under conditions set forth by the coastal State.

In the exclusive economic zone and on the continental shelf coastal States shall have the right to regulate, authorize and conduct scientific research. Other States or organizations may undertake such research with the consent of the coastal State. However article 247 (3) does require coastal States to establish rules and procedures ensuring that such consent will not be delayed or denied unreasonably. Coastal States may withold their consent to another State if the proposed research project is of direct significance for the exploration and exploitation of natural resources, invloves drilling into the continental shelf, the use of explosives or the introduction of harmful substances, involves the construction or use of artificial islands, contains information which is inaccurate, or if the relevant State or organization has outstanding obligations to the coastal State from a prior research project. Scientific research in the exclusive economic zone or on the continental shelf should not interfere with other activities undertaken by the coastal State.

A coastal State which is a member of a regional or global organization, or which has a bilateral agreement with such an organization, shall be deemed to have authorized a research project by that organization if the State approved the project when the decision was made to proceed with it, or if the coastal State is willing to participate in the project (article 248).

Article 249 specifies the duty of researchers to provide information to the coastal State. It requires States or international organizations to provide that State, at least six months in advance of a research project, with a full description of the nature and objectives of the research project, the methods and means to be used (including a full description of the vessel and equipment), the precise geographical areas in which research is to be carried out, the date of first appearance and final departure of research vessels, the name of the sponsoring institution, its director and the person in charge of the particular project, and the extent to which it is considered that the coastal States in the exclusive economic zone and on the continental shelf are further protected by article 250, which specifies that States or international organizations conducting research in this area off a coastal State have to comply with the following conditions. They have to ensure the right of the coastal State to participate or be represented in the project, without obligation to contribute to any of the costs of the research project. They are also required to provide the coastal State with preliminary reports as soon as practicable, and with the final results and conclusions after the completion of the project. The coastal State also has the right of access to all data and samples, and to assistance in the assessment of such data. They have to be informed immediately of any major change in the research programme, and scientific equipment and installations are to be removed once the research is completed. According to article 251, communications concerning a research project should be made through appropriate official channels, and article 252 requires that States seek the promotion, through competent international organizations, of general criteria and guidelines to assist them in ascertaining the nature and implications of marine scientific research.

In order to avoid unnecessary delays, article 253 gives States and competent international organizations the right to proceed with a research project upon the six months expiry date after the coastal State was provided with the required information, unless the coastal State within four months of the receipt of this communication has informed them that it has withheld its consent in terms of some relevant article, or if the information given to the coastal State does not conform to the manifestly evident facts, or if it requires supplementary information relevant to the conditions and information provided for by the draft treaty, or if outstanding obligations exist with respect to previous research carried out by that State or organization.

The coastal State shall have the right to require the cessation of any research activities in progress within its exclusive economic zone or continental shelf if the project is not conducted in accordance with the information initially provided to the coastal State, or if the State or organization conducting the research fails to comply with the provisions regarding the rights of the coastal State (article 254).

The rights of neighbouring land-locked or other geographically disadvantaged States are protected by article 255, which requires that such States be notified of the proposed research project and provided with relevant information and assistance. Such disadvantaged States shall also be given the opportunity to participate in the proposed research project.

Most of the above articles appear very restrictive and would probably have an inhibiting effect on marine research in the economic zones and on the continental shelves. To a large extent, they reflect the interests and concerns of the developing countries. Article 256, which specifies that coastal States shall adopt reasonable and uniformly applied rules, regulations, and administrative procedures to States and organizations wishing to carry out research activities in these areas, and should adopt measures to facilitate access to their harbours, is an attempt on the part of the developed States to ameliorate the position.

The regulation of marine scientific research in the area beyond the limits of national jurisdiction was the subject of heated and even acrimonious debate for many years. The draft articles in the Informal Composite Negotiating Text reflect the extent to which the various interest groups had to compromise on this issue.

Article 257 specifies that all States, irrespective of their geographical location, as well as competent international organizations, shall have the right to conduct marine scientific research in this area.

Section 4 of the Negotiating Text deals with the legal status of scientific research installations and equipment in the marine environment. Articles 259 to 263 specify that such installations and equipment shall be subject to the same conditions as those for the conduct of scientific research in the area, that they shall not have the status of islands or possess their own territorial sea, that safety zones not exceeding 500 metres may be created around them, that they shall not constitute an obstacle or a hazard to international shipping routes and that they shall bear identification markings indicating the State of registry or the international organization to which they belong. They are required to have adequate internationally agreed warning signals to ensure safety at sea.

Section 5 deals with responsibility and liability, and article 264 requires States or competent international organizations to assure that marine scientific research is conducted in accordance with this convention. They are responsible and liable for contraventions, and shall provide compensation for damage resulting from such actions.

Section 6 determines the procedures for the settlement of disputes in accordance with the provisions of this convention, except that coastal States may exercise the right of discretion in accordance with article 247 which protects coastal State rights in the exclusive economic zone or on the continental shelf. The decision of a coastal State to terminate a research project in terms of article 254 is not subject to arbitration.

Discussion

Very few countries have the capability and financial resources to undertake sophisticated marine scientific research. They are all developed nations and have been outnumbered in the negotiations at the Third Law of the Sea Conference. Pure scientific research is not one of their vital or even primary interests and it appears that marine scientific research may be one of the victims of this conference if a comprehensive convention is agreed upon.

Although the Composite Negotiating Text is an informal document, it does reflect a fair indication of the extent to which a compromise has been reached with regard to marine scientific research. From this it would appear that political, strategic, and economic interests have been far more important to both developed and developing countries than scientific interests.

The lack of scientific understanding of most delegates at the Conference and the suspicion of the developing countries that scientific research is often an excuse for exploration or espionage, have further contributed to the apparent erosion of one of the traditional freedoms of the sea—the freedom to undertake scientific research.

References

1. Harlow, B. A. "Territorial Sea Concept." Mimeo., for Law of the Sea Institute, University of Rhode Island, 1966.

2. Hearn, W. A. "The Role of the United States Navy in the Formulation of a Federal Policy Regarding the Sea." *Natural Resources Lawyer*, 1, 1968. pp.23-31.

3. Ray, C. "Ecology, Law and the 'Marine Revolution.'" *Biological Conservation*, Vol. 3 (1), 1970. pp. 7-17.

4. Charnock, H. "H.M.S. *Challenger* and the Development of Marine Science." *Journal of Navigation*, Vol. 26 (1), 1973. pp. 1-12.

5. "The Deep Sea Drilling Project—A Hallmark in Ocean Research." *Sea Technology*, Vol. 15 (3), 1974. pp. 31-34.

6. Cadwalader, G. "Freedom for Science in the Oceans." *Science*, Vol. 182 (4107), 1973. pp. 15-20.

7. United Nations. Informal Composite Negotiating Text. United Nations Document A/CONF. 62/W.P. 10, 1977. 198 p.

Chapter Seventeen
The Oceans in Peace and War: Strategic Aspects

The strategic uses of the ocean may be regarded as the silent issue at the Third Law of the Sea Conference. However there is no doubt that this is a crucial issue, particularly to the superpowers. Although there has been a gentleman's agreement among the developing countries not to discuss this issue, they are very much aware of the fact that failure to comply with the vital strategic interests of the United States and the U.S.S.R. would inevitably lead to the failure of the Conference.

Strategic considerations impinge on many issues at the Law of the Sea Conference but nowhere more than on the issue of freedom of passage through international straits. Although countries bordering on such straits, led by Spain, have argued forcefully for a regime of innocent passage through such straits, they have conceded in private that this would never be acceptable to the superpowers who regard the right of overflight by military aircraft and of submerged passage by their submarines as being of vital importance to their defence interests. For this reason, countries like Australia tried to propose a compromise which they hoped would satisfy both sides.

With the increasing sophistication of nuclear weapons, anti-ballistic missiles and detection devices, both the United States and the U.S.S.R. have come to rely to an increasing extent on nuclear submarines as their most reliable and least vulnerable last line of defence. Defence-related oceanographic research in these countries receives far more financial support than pure oceanographic research as ever more advanced methods of detecting submarines and of escaping detection are pursued.

Strategic interests were largely responsible for the opposition of the superpowers to that new tide of history—the exclusive economic zone. Strategic interests also caused the United States to oppose the concept of a six-mile territorial sea and so to wreck the Second Law of the Sea Conference in 1960. Generally speaking, the strategic interests of the superpowers have been in conflict with the marine resource interests of the developing countries since the First Law of the Sea Conference of 1958.

These strategic interests are clearly also in conflict with the resource interests of the maritime powers, particularly insofar as the western European nations, Japan and the United States have become increasingly dependent on imported sources of energy and minerals and have neglected to maintain an adequate naval strength to protect the supply lines for these vital raw materials. Indeed it would appear that their vital interests would be better served by following an approach that would make it as difficult as possible for the Soviet navy to move freely through the oceans of the world.

One of the ironies at the Third Law of the Sea Conference is the cordial manner in which the Americans and Soviets have synchronized their efforts to secure the right for their naval forces to move freely through the oceans and thus secure the power of mutual destruction.

The Soviet Naval Build-up

During the past year there has been an intense debate among the strategists of NATO about the state of its defences. The already clear Soviet superiority in ground and air forces in Europe has been combined with a steady growth in Soviet naval capabilities.

Since World War II a once backward Soviet Union has emerged as a superpower.[1] The Soviet strategic nuclear capability now rivals and in some respects exceeds that of the United States. Perhaps even more importantly there has been an unprecedented expansion of the Soviet seapower. In the words of Admiral Gorshkov, "the Soviet navy has been transformed into an important strategic force, into a force capable of opposing agression for the sea and of accomplishing major operational and strategic missions on the world ocean . . ."[1]

The Soviet fleet now outnumbers the U.S. Navy by a considerable number of ships, particularly combat vessels. Soviet strategic submarines can fire intermediate-range ballistic missiles upon industrial centres in central and western Europe without leaving the protection of their home ports. The Soviet fleet of about 260 attack submarines could effectively seal off the northern and southern approaches to central Europe and their land-based aircraft could threaten the strategic sea lanes along the Europe's northern and southern flanks. Soviet naval strategy assumes as its primary military responsibility the isolation of the potential European battlefield from the resources of the United States.[1] In terms of major surface and sub-surface combatants, the Soviet navy now outnumbers the U.S. Navy by 497 to 246 vessels. The level of superiority is even more startling in the case of submarines.

With this formidable naval superiority the Soviets have gradually moved into parts of the world oceans which would allow them to disrupt the supply of oil and strategic metals to the West. One of their prime targets in this respect has been the vital Cape Sea Route along which more than 60 percent of the West's oil imports move. With a presence in the Horn of Africa, in Mozambique and in Angola, and in the absence of a significant Western naval presence in the South Atlantic and Indian oceans, they are already in a position to disrupt oil supplies to the West.

It has become increasingly clear that the Soviet Union's overall strategy includes resource diplomacy as an important element. Being almost self sufficient with regard to sources of energy and raw materials, they have come to appreciate that the increasing dependence of the West on imported sources of these materials is their Achilles heel and they have clearly adopted a policy based on the so-called weak-link principle, first proposed by Major General A. N. Lagovsky some 20 years ago. After pointing out that modern armaments are dependent on certain critical raw materials such as chrome, platinum, nickel, cobalt and titanium, he drew attention to the fact that the U.S. has virtually no chrome of its own. He expressed the view that the U.S.S.R. should exploit this and other weak links in the West.[2] Another Russian spokesman wrote in 1974 that "Africa holds a leading position in the world, both in reserves and output of many kinds of raw materials. The deposits of some of the minerals in Africa are unique . . . .most of them concentrated in Southern Africa."[3]

Behind the security of their naval forces in the region, and using Cuban troops as proxies, the Soviets have actively promoted the disruption of strategic minerals from this area by supporting terrorist movements in Rhodesia and Namibia, by assisting Marxist regimes in Angola and Mozambique, by cowing the President of Zambia and by supporting two invasions into the Shaba Province of Zaire—the world's most important source of cobalt.

In South America mineral supplies have been disrupted by Cuban supported "freedom fighters," while the Australian mineral industry has been rocked by communist infiltrated labour unions and by environmental groups of dubious affiliation.

What we are witnessing is clearly a policy of resource diplomacy on a global scale. In view of the West's vulnerability to such actions it is amazing that their response has been so muted. Kilmarx asserts that since the unfortunate experience of the U.S.A. in Vietman there has been a tendency to turn inward, to be preoccupied with domestic issues, to downgrade the importance of taking the lead in defending the interests of the free world and to revaluate the nature and magnitude of the Communist threat.[4] The era of detente emerged, nurtured by illusions from weak leadership that a generation of peace lay ahead and that the Cold War had been replaced by an era of arms limitation, growing cooperation with the U.S.S.R. and China and a diminution of the risks of war. However, Kilmarx believes that this period of "political malaise and foreign policy myopia" may gradually be ending.

At the Third Law of the Sea Conference the Russians have clearly attempted to pursue these interests, and have striven to obtain maximum freedom of movement for their naval forces. Many representatives from smaller nations privately expressed their fears about this but they are powerless to do much about it.

The Strategic Interests of the Smaller Nations

With the growing sophistication of the major fleets, the smaller nations are living in the shadow of naval intimidation. Clearly, there is not much that they can do effectively about this situation and many of their reactions signify frustration or politics for home consumption, rather than real defence interests.

One line of pursuit is the trend to ever increasing widths of the territorial sea by unilateral action. However if even the United States and the Soviet Union cannot effectively patrol a 200-mile territorial sea, it is ludicrous for a developing country to attempt to do so. Excessive claims in terms of the archipelago concept, and attempts to limit transit through international straits to a regime of innocent passage, also reflect measures aimed at securing a certain amount of control in their internal or coastal waters.

The only effective measure which the smaller coastal nations appear to have promoted in order to secure their countries from naval intimidation appears to be the concept of the exclusive economic zone. In an era where naval might has again assumed great importance in strategic planning, the smaller nations of the world have no option but to accomodate the vital interests of the superpowers in this regard. Whether the superpowers always correctly perceive their own best interests in this respect is an entirely different matter.

References

1.   Emery, D. F. "The Soviet Naval Threat to NATO Europe." *Strategic Review*, Vol. VI (4), 1978. pp. 62-70.

2.   Harrigan, A. "The Ultimate Target." *National Review*, May 14, 1976. pp. 496, 521.

3.   Vanneman, P. and James M. "The Soviet Intervention in Angola: Intentions and Implications." *Strategic Review*, Vol. IV (3), 1976. pp. 92-103.

4.   Kilmarx, R. A. "Minerals in the Assessment of World Powers." Conference on Strategic Raw Materials, Swaziland, June 1976 (unpublished report).

Chapter Eighteen
The Law of the Sea Makes Strange Bedfellows

During 1958 at the First Law of the Sea Conference held in Geneva, four conventions on the Law of the Sea were adopted. Apart from representing to a large extent a codification of existing law and customs, these conventions also established a number of new rules of law. Although the First Law of the Sea Conference was unable to solve all problems relating to the Law of the Sea, such as the breadth of the territorial sea, it is undoubtedly true that the four conventions which were born at this conference established a new legal code embodying the greatest measure of agreement which could be reached at that time.

The basic principles underlying the Law of the Sea as codified in 1958 are firstly, that the high seas were open to all nations for fishing, navigation, overflight and strategic purposes. Secondly, that the territorial sea over which international law permits the littoral State to exercise sovereign rights, subject only to the right of innocent passage, should be a narrow belt, and thirdly, that the continental shelf, being a natural prolongation of the land mass, forms part of the territory of the coastal State, and is therefore subject to its sovereignty.

This, briefly, was the situation when during 1967 Ambassador Pardo of Malta introduced to the General Assembly of the United Nations his draft resolution dealing with the legal status of the sea-bed and the ocean floor beyond the limits of national jurisdiction. Basically he proposed that this area of the sea-bed should be the common heritage of mankind, and that the resources of the area should be used for peaceful purposes and in the interests of all mankind.

Ambassador Pardo's resolution resulted in the establishment of an *ad hoc* Committee of 35 members which, during 1968, was changed into a standing committee named "The Committee on the Peaceful Uses of the Sea-Bed and the Ocean Floor Beyond the Limits of National Jurisdiction."

Initially this committee was assigned only four tasks, namely:

- to elaborate legal principles and norms which would promote international cooperation in the exploration and use of the sea-bed and the ocean floor;
- to study ways of promoting the exploration and use of the area's resources;
- to review studies concerned with exploration and research and;
- to examine proposed measures of cooperation aimed at preventing marine pollution which might result from the exploration of the resources of the sea.

It is clear that at that stage the mandate of the "Sea-Beds Committee" was restricted to reviewing one of the outstanding issues of the Law of the Sea, namely rules and practices for the exploration and exploitation of deep sea mineral resources. However, in 1970 the United Nations General Assembly passed Resolutions 2749 (XXV) and 2750 (XXV) which respectively proclaimed general principles on the Law of the Sea and conferred a new mandate on the "Sea-beds Committee" and increased its membership to 86 States. During 1971, in accordance with Resolution 2881 (XXVI), the membership of the Committee was further expanded to 91 States.

The new mandate conferred on the Sea-Beds Committee changed it in effect into a preparatory committee for a Third Law of the Sea Conference then envisaged to take place in 1973.

One may well ask why there was a necessity for a new conference on the Law of the Sea a mere 12 years after the successful conclusion of the 1958 Geneva Conventions. That the developed countries asked themselves exactly this question is clear from their initial reaction in this regard. They tried to restrict any future conference to a discussion of those subjects which remained unsolved at the Geneva Conference of 1958, including the problem of the legal status of the sea-bed and related matters, as envisaged by Ambassador Pardo. At that time, and this remains remains true to some extent today, the existing law as codified by the 1958 Geneva Conventions, generally suited the needs and interests of the developed nations.

The 1958 regime granted them freedom over the largest possible area of the seas for purposes of navigation, fishing and strategic uses. It also granted them freedom in principle to exploit the vast virgin area of the deep sea-bed with its mineral riches.

The developing countries on the other hand, grabbed the opportunity offered them by Ambassador Pardo with both hands and, for a variety of reasons, insisted successfully on a complete reexamination of the entire Law of The Sea. Their demands to rewrite the Law of the Sea should be viewed against the background of developments which took place after 1958. Most important probably was the rapid advance of sub-sea technology which rendered obsolete the 1958 Convention on the Continental Shelf, with its open-ended definition of the shelf. The exploitability of deep-sea minerals and hydrocarbons was no longer a mere possibility but within reach of the few technologically highly advanced nations. In addition, the depletion of fish stocks in many areas as a result of increased exploitation and improved fishing techniques by distant water fishing nations led to resentment amongst developing coastal States. They insisted that the old concept of freedom of fishing on the high seas should be discarded and replaced by coastal State jurisdiction extending over a large area of what previously was regarded as high seas. A third factor was the growing awareness of the dangers of pollution of the oceans which could ultimately lead to complete depletion of the living resources of the sea. Add furthermore the resentment of those States which were still dependent territories during the 1958 Conference on the Law of the Sea, against a regime which, according to them, was created by and for the developed States of the world, and the scene was set for an important clash between the maritime interests of developed countries, and the marine resource interests of developing countries.

If the initial developments indicated that the Third Law of the Sea conference was going to become a classical confrontation between the advanced and developing countries, sanity soon prevailed and States began to recognize that their real interests are dictated by physical, geographical, geological and biological facts of life. It soon became clear that many had conflicting interests (for instance, both coastal and distant water fishing fleets), that a community of interests often crossed political divisions and that few interests were universal or even commanded enough support to gain a two-thirds' majority. The non-interests of States, or the so-called floating vote, therefore assumed growing importance, and this vote was courted in informal negotiations.

For instance, Zambia, a land-locked State, has a vital interest in the right of access to the sea but no interest in navigation through international straits. The United States on the other hand, has no land-locked neighbours but a vital interest in freedom of navigation through international straits. An agreement in terms of which Zambia would support the U.S. on the straits issue in return for its support on the issue of access to the sea would therefore serve the interests of both nations.

As the individual States began to evaluate their own vital interests related to various issues on the Law of the Sea and as they progressed from there to an analysis of States with similar interests, and of those who represented floating votes on such issues, a number of strange courtships took place, in many instances between States with violent political differences. Evidence of such budding romances could be observed in the corridors of the Palais de Nation and in many secluded restaurants in and around Geneva.

The Law of the Sea was making some strange bedfellows.

Bloc-Forming and Common Interest Groups

The practice of bloc voting by the African, Latin American, and Eastern European groups has become an accepted phenomenon in the United Nations. Even members of the "Western European and Others Group" sometimes manage to bury their differences and to take a common stand. When it comes to representation of countries on U.N. committees, due regard is always paid to the principle of "equitable geographical representation" and the various groups nominate their own representatives in consultation with the chairman of the committee. This practice has also been followed by the Sea-Beds Committee and by the Third Law of the Sea Conference.

The normal schedule has often been interrupted by meetings of these regional groups, which take precedence over the meetings of the conference itself. Another common phenomenon is for the African, Latin American, and Asian regional groups to meet together in the so-called Group of 77, and to take a common stand among the developing countries in order to ensure lopsided majorities.

To what extent will the traditional regional concept influence the votes necessary to ensure the adoption of new concepts or the retention of established ones on the Law of the Sea? This is a difficult question and the answer will obviously vary from one issue to another. It should be stressed however, that the traditional United Nations regional groups represent a political division based on the polarization of developed versus developing, and "Free World" versus Communist countries on a geographical basis.

In March 1971 the representative of Singapore raised this issue when he stated emphatically that it would be unrealistic to apply the traditional regional concept to the negotiations for the Third Law of the Sea Conference, since the interests of countries with regard to the Law of the Sea were not governed by their politico-geographical groupings only, but rather by the realities of geology, geography, biology, ocean currents, climate, and other economic and strategic considerations. According to him there are nine major interest groups:

1. Land-locked States
2. Shelf-locked States
3. Coastal countries with extensive continental shelves.
4. Coastal States with little or no continental shelf but which front an open sea.
5. Coastal States whose economies are based on fishing in the waters adjacent to their coasts.
6. Countries with distant water fishing fleets.
7. Countries with economies based on minerals or hydrocarbons which are known to occur along their shores.
8. Maritime States.
9. States with an advanced underwater technology.

Many countries would fall into two or more of these groups. Subsequent events have amply revealed the realism of this classification as one country after another has promoted concepts in accordance with its own political, strategic and economic interests. But it should be emphasized that the groupings of the various interests has become much more complicated, while several countries have revaluated the priority of their interests and have changed sharply their positions on certain key issues.

The extent to which the traditional regional groups have failed to maintain a common front was first revealed by the reaction of States to a proposal by the Chairman of the Sea-beds Committee on 6 August 1973. The Chairman requested the various geographical groups to nominate between three and six members each to participate in a contact group which would attempt to reach political accommodations on issues which the sub-committees were not able to resolve.

There was strong opposition to this proposal and countries in the African, Asian, Latin American and Western European groups stated bluntly that there was no community of interests within their groups and that they were not prepared for other countries in their groups to negotiate on their behalf.

It would be unwise however to discount completely the traditional regional groups or their ability to secure a common position on at least some issues. One of the significant developments in this direction was the Addis Ababa Declaration of 1973 which represented a common stand on the major Law of the Sea issues signed by 41 African Heads of State.

This declaration indicated that the African States had secured the acceptance by their 13 land-locked members of the concept of a 200-mile economic zone in exchange for the right of participation in the exploitation of the living resources of this zone.

Members of the delegations of several Latin American States informed the authors as early as 1971 that they would buy the votes of their land-locked members by offering them similar benefits. This move appears to have been unsuccessful.

Faced with the realities of their own interests, members of the Sea-Beds Committee began to form new regional or common interest groups. During the early sessions the most significant of these was the land- and shelf-locked groups, which shared a common interest in their desire to secure access to the high seas, to limit the area of coastal State jurisdiction and to secure a share in the benefits of deep-sea mineral exploitation. This group had little to lose and did not have a strong bargaining position, apart from the fact that it could muster 50 votes or a blocking third. It could therefore prevent a successful Third Law of the Sea Conference. The attempts by the Organization of African Unity and the Latin Americans to buy the votes of their land-locked neighbours were aimed largely at breaking up this group.

As the concept of a 200-mile economic zone spread like wildfire through the conference the relevance of new regional groupings became apparent. A 200-mile zone has no significance for States bordering on enclosed seas like the Mediterranean or the Baltic, but is highly relevant and seductive to the countries of the Southern Hemisphere, and even to maritime nations facing an open sea. The concept of a 200-mile economic zone presented problems to certain States with acquired rights or potential resources beyond the 200-mile limit, so that a new group—the so-called plus 200-milers—came to the fore.

The problem of fisheries is another example. It is no longer realistic to consider this problem in terms of coastal and distant water fishing only. The sub-groups on this issue cover the whole spectrum of opinions from extreme distant water fishing claims, which would not recognize any coastal State rights beyond the 12-mile limit, through a group which recognizes preferential coastal State rights together with recognition of traditional distant water fishing rights, to strong coastal State rights but with distant water fishing nations being able to continue to some extent with their activities under licence to the coastal State and finally exclusive coastal State rights.

At the preparatory conferences, and during the various sessions of the Third Law of the Sea Conference, there has been a marked reluctance on the part of most countries to negotiate or to give in on any issues. Some, such as the Latin American countries, believed that time was on their side and that other nations would join them in supporting their stand on issues such as the 200-mile economic zone. They were at least partly correct in this attitude, as is evidenced by the remarkable swing in favour of this concept by the United States.

It should also be noted that concern with the ocean is for most countries only a small part of their total national interest. Problems such as internal cohesion, economic development or border disputes often weigh more heavily on the decision makers' minds than do those of national or international regimes of the sea.

There have been many shifts in position by various States on certain issues of the Law of the Sea. A certain amount of posturing has taken place, particularly among the developed States. The Composite Negotiating Text, while often containing vague or even ambiguous passages, does indicate a degree of compromise on many issues. While an attempt has been made to assess the attitudes of individual States on key issues, one should distinguish between their negotiating and fall-back positions and between vital interests and preferences. The early optimism about compromise, the hopes for a speedy resolution of complex issues and the dreams of a new Law of the Sea acceptable to all, have given way to pessimism, to an appreciation that the Third Law of the Sea Conference will take years to conclude and to the resignation to the fact that even if a new Law of the Sea Treaty finally emerges, it will not be entirely satisfactory to any nation.

The Interests of States According
to the Singapore Classification

The interests of States according to the nine groups proposed by the representative of Singapore, have been tentatively analysed and the results are presented in the tables at the end of this chapter. In addition to these nine categories, we have also considered a few other interest groups, such as those countries who may be expected to favour a 200-mile economic zone and those with interests beyond 200 miles, States in favour of free transit through international straits as opposed to those who favour only innocent passage, archipelagic States, and "zone-locked" States, that is States that would be enclosed by the proposed 200-mile economic zone.

This analysis was based wherever possible on an interpretation of statements made by the various countries. Where this was not possible the available geographical, geological, biological and physical evidence was used in making the assessments. It should be emphasized that such a classification does not in any way guarantee that States will vote according to it, nor that they perceive these as vital interests. Rather it attempts to show a community of interests which in many instances bears little resemblance to traditional political groupings.

Discussion

Probably no other international conference has ever had an agenda as broad in scope or as complex as the Third Law of the Sea Conference. It has become apparent that even highly sophisticated countries like the United States have great difficulty in determining what their best interests are relative to the various issues on the Law of the Sea, and what the priorities between these interests are. Even after more than a decade of debate it is apparent that many of the delegates from developing countries do not understand the implications of certain issues.

Clearly the interests of States are determined by a number of physical, economic and strategic factors—and not so much by their traditional geographical groupings. The interests of individual States within any of the traditional U.N. Caucus Groups may therefore differ considerably, while States with little political affinity may have vital common interests. Ambassador Koh of Singapore succinctly illustrated this by pointing out that:"The alliances at the conference are extremely complex and cut across economic and ideological groupings. You will find countries allied here that you will not find working together in any other international forum, such as Mongolia and Swaziland, or Jamaica and Iraq. Issues determine the alliances."[1]

Another problem which has slowed down the conference is that a decision was taken at a very early stage to adopt a draft treaty by consensus rather than by a simple or two-thirds majority. This has turned out to be an elusive goal.

There is a fear that failure to reach agreement on many issues will lead to the breakdown of the conference, which means that there may be chaos in the oceans, including a multiplicity of conflicting unilateral claims. However, the stakes are high and if progress has been slow, it has at least on some issues been evident.

Table 1

Countries in Favour of 200-Mile Economic Zone

Algeria	Ghana	Norway
Argentina	Guatemala	Pakistan
Australia	Guinea	Panama
Bangla Desh?	Guyana	Peru
Barbados	Haiti	Phillipines
Botswana?	Honduras	Portugal
Brazil	Iceland	Rwanda
Burundi?	Ireland	Senegal
Cameroon	India	Sierra Leone
Canada	Indonesia	Somalia
Central African Republic?	Ivory Coast	South Africa
Chad?	Jamaica	Spain
Chile	Kenya	Sri-Lanka
China	Lesotho?	Sudan
Columbia	Liberia	Surinam
Congo	Malagasy Republic	Swaziland?
Costa Rica	Malawi?	Tanzania
Dahomey	Malaysia	Togo
Denmark	Mali?	Trinidad and Tobago
Dominican Republic	Malta	Tunisia
Ecuador	Mauritania	Uganda?
Egypt	Mauritius	United Kingdom?
El Salvador	Mexico	Upper Volta?
Equatorial Guinea	Mongolia	Uruguay
Ethiopia	Morocco	Venezuela
Fiji	New Zealand	West Germany
France	Nicaragua	Yugoslavia
Gabon	Niger?	Zaire
Gambia	Nigeria	Zambia?

Newcomers

United States of America	U.S.S.R.?

Table 2

Plus 200-Milers (States with Continental Margin Extending beyond 200-Mile Limit)

Argentina	French Guyana	New Zealand,
Australia	Greenland (Denmark)	Norway
Brazil	Guinea	South Africa
Burma	Guyana	South-West Africa
Canada	Iceland	Spanish Sahara
China	India	Surinam
Equatorial Guinea	Ireland	U.K.
Faroes (Denmark)	Malagasy Republic	Uruguay
Fiji	Mauritius	U.S.A.
France—islands in Pacific	Mexico	U.S.S.R.
	Mozambique	

Table 3
Land-Locked Countries
U.N. Members

Afghanistan	Hungary	Paraguay
Austria	Laos	Rhodesia
Bhutan	Lesotho	Rwanda
Bolivia	Luxembourg	(Sikkim)
Botswana	Malawi	Swaziland
Central African Republic	Mongolian People's	Uganda
Chad	Republic	Upper Volta
Czechoslovakia	Nepal	Zambia
	Niger	

Non-U.N. Members

Andorra	Liechtenstein	San Marino
	Vatican City	

Source: Question of free access to the sea of land-locked countries. Annex II (1958) United Nations.

Table 4
Shelf-Locked Countries

Bahrain	Jordan	Singapore
Belgium	Khmer Republic (Cambodia)	Sweden
East Germany (F.D.R.)	Netherlands	United Arab Emirates
Finland	North Vietnam	West Germany (F.R.)
Iraq	Poland	Zaire
	Qatar	

Table 5
Developed Maritime Nations

France	Liberia (flag of convenience)	U.K.
Greece	Netherlands	U.S.A.
Italy	Norway	U.S.S.R.
Japan	Panama (flag of convenience)	West Germany (F.R.)
	Sweden	

Table 6
Developing Nations which Possess an Underwater Technology

France	Netherlands	U.S.S.R
Italy	U.K.	West Germany (F.R.)
Japan	U.S.A.	

Table 7
Pro-Free Transit Through Straits

Bulgaria	France	U.K.
Byelo-Russia	Norway	U.S.A.
Czechoslovakia	Poland	U.S.S.R.
East Germany	Romania	

Possibly

Albania	China	Mongolia

Other Maritime States e.g.

Greece	Liberia	Sweden
Italy	Netherlands	West Germany
Japan	Panama	

Table 8
Pro-Innocent Passage Through Straits

Latin American Countries	African Countries—O.A.U.	Spain

Possibly

Australia	Canada	Iceland
	New Zealand	

Table 9
Archipelagic States

States already committed unilaterally:
Phillipines   Indonesia

States claiming subject to LOS approval:
Bahamas   Fiji   Mauritius
New Zealand (claiming for the Cook Islands)
Tonga

States interested in the archipelago principle:
Denmark (for Faroes)   Ecuador (for Galapagos)   Iceland
Micronesia (Trust Territory in Pacific but unlikely to be independent)
Papua and New Guinea   Seychelles   Spain (claim for Canaries)

States which would qualify but have not committed themselves:
Maldives   Western Samoa

Table 10
Countries with Economies Dependent on Minerals or Liquids
which are Known to Occur in the Sea-Bed

Nickel (over 5,000 tons per annum)

Cuba   Rhodesia
(Also: Australia, Canada, Finland, Greece, New Caledonia (France), South Africa, U.S.A.,
U.S.S.R.)

Copper (over 300,000 tons per annum)

Chile   Zaire   Zambia
(Also: Canada, U.S.A., U.S.S.R.)

Cobalt (over 1,500 tons per annum)

Cuba   Zaire   Zambia
(Also: Canada)

Manganese (over 100,000 tons per annum)

Botswana   Gabon   Zaire
Brazil   India
(Also: Australia, China, South Africa, U.S.S.R.)

Phosphate (over 500,000 tons per annum)

Egypt   Morocco   Togo
Jordan   Nauru   Tunisia
(Also: China, Christmas Islands (U.S. and U.K.), Israel, Ocean Island (Gilbert and Ellice
Islands, U.K.), South Africa, U.S.A.

Crude Petroleum (10,000,000 tons per annum)

Algeria   Indonesia   Mexico
Argentina   Iran   Nigeria
Colombia   Iraq   Rumania
Egypt   Kuwait   Saudi Arabia
                              Libya
(Also: Canada, China, U.S.A., U.S.S.R.)

Natural Gas (10,000,000 cubic feet per annum)

Rumania   Tunisia
(Also: Algeria, Canada, France, Germany (F.R.), Iran, Italy, Netherlands, U.K., U.S.A.,
U.S.S.R.)

Mero considers it profitable to mine material such as PO_4, Ni, Cu, Co and Mn at today's
prices. Within the next generation the sea may also be the source of molybdenum,
vanadium, lead, zinc, titanium, aluminium, zirconium and several other metals.

Source: Mero, J. L. The Mineral Resources of the Sea. Elsevier Oceanography Series,
1965; U.N. Statistical Yearbook 1971. United Nations, 1972.; Statistical Summary of the
Mineral Industry World Production, Exports and Imports 1966-1970, Institute of Geological Sciences. H.M.S.O., 1972.

Table 11
Coastal States whose Economies are Dependent on Fishing in Waters
Adjacent to their Coasts (with a catch of 7,500,000 tons per annum)*

Chile   Indonesia   Philippines
Iceland   Korea (Republic of)   Thailand
India   Peru   Vietnam
*Many other countries have an interest in coastal fishing

Table 12
Countries With Distant Water Fishing Fleets

Major

France	Poland	U.S.A.
Japan	Portugal	U.S.S.R.
Korea (Republic of)	Spain	West Germany
Norway	U.K.	

Minor

East Germany	Italy	Taiwan
Ghana	Rumania	Thailand
	South Africa	

Table 13
Totally Zone-Locked Coastal States—By Region

The Americas

Cuba	Jamaica	Panama
Honduras	Nicaragua	Trinidad and Tobago

Europe

Albania	Greece	Poland
Belgium	Italy	Rumania
Bulgaria	Malta	Sweden
Denmark	Monaco	West Germany
East Germany	Netherlands	Yugoslavia
Finland	Norway	

The Near East and Africa

Algeria	Iran	Saudi Arabia
Bahrain	Iraq	Sudan
Cameroon	Israel	Syria
Congo	Jordan	Togo
Cyprus	Kuwait	Tunisia
Egypt	Lebanon	Turkey
Equatorial Guinea	Libya	United Arab Emirates
Ethiopia	Mauritania	Yemen
Gambia	Qatar	Zaire

Asia (except Near East) and Oceania

Cambodia	Malaysia	Vietnam (Dem. Republic)
Fiji	Nauru	Vietnam (Republic)
Korea (Dem. Republic)	Singapore	Western Samoa
Korea (Republic)	Thailand	

Table 14
Partially Zone-Locked Coastal States—i.e., Coastal States zone-locked on only one of two oceans on which they face.

Costa Rica (Atlantic only)
Colombia (Atlantic only—Pacific opening would be only a narrow corridor to south)
Guatemala (Atlantic only)   Mexico (Atlantic only)   U.S.S.R. (Atlantic only)

Table 15

**Land-Locked States Also Partially Zone-Locked—
i.e., dependent for their normal traffic routing on a
totally zone-locked State or States.**

Austria	Hungary	Luxembourg
Czechoslovakia	Laos	Switzerland

References

1. "Common Heritage of Mankind," *Newsweek*, 25 September 1978, Interview with Ambassador Tommy Koh of Singapore.

Chapter Nineteen
Wrapping Up The Package

Even as these words are written, the Eighth Session of UNCLOS III—the Third United Nations Conference on the Law of the Sea—will be in progress in Geneva.

It has been claimed that this will be a make or break session which will determine whether the whole effort will collapse or whether man will at last find the wit and wisdom to agree on an international code regulating his activities in the oceans of the world.

It is not the first time that such a claim has been made, and it is quite possible that it will not be the last. Admittedly, governments are showing signs of impatience at the fact that UNCLOS III is prolonging itself from year to year and from session to session without being able to come up with agreed solutions to the complex and interrelated problems before it. But so much has gone into the project over the last years, and so many States have set their hearts on a new dispensation, that it seems unlikely that the effort will be lightly abandoned.

The alternatives are stark enough. Either States must persevere even if it takes a few more years of debate to wear down the edges of disagreement and to reach the elusive consensus, or they must accept the law of the jungle under which the rich nations will take the lion's share, unilaterally and without benefit of a Convention.

There is nothing in the history of the United Nations over the last few years to suggest that this "winner-take-all" approach has a chance of succeeding. If anything, the pendulum has swung the other way. The countries of the Third World, together with the "land-locked and geographically disadvantaged" countries, command an overwhelming majority in the United Nations. They want to see a change since they stand to gain least under the "classical" Law of the Sea which, with only slow and evolutionary changes, will set the pace and determine the broad outlines if a new convention fails to be adopted. For them to allow the Conference to die would be tantamount to their standing aside and allowing the Great Powers to take over.

Some optimism about the outcome of the Eighth Session seems therefore to be in order. While it seems unlikely that all outstanding differences of substance will be resolved — leaving it to a future session or sessions to get down to perfecting the legal niceties of the code — one can at least hope that enough progress will be made to convince governments that it is worth their while to persist in their efforts. It is only to be expected that they should in the meantime take such legislative and other steps as would in their view be most likely to safeguard their position if the Conference were to fail.

This process indeed is already far advanced. The rush to proclaim 200-mile fishing zones at a time when the fate of the Convention itself is still in the balance, shows that States are not slow to stake their claims as soon as they perceive that the movement of international opinion is such as to lend respectability to their actions. In proclaiming exclusive control over the living resources within a 200-mile belt off their coasts, they are acting on the basis of a consensus which is emerging in regard to a single issue among all the issues before the Conference. Such claims however, are not without some legal basis. By the time that a majority of States, after long and thorough debate, have accepted the principle of 200-mile fishing zones, the principle has already moved a long way towards incorporation in the body of customary international law. In more practical terms, it would be difficult for other members of the international community to challenge the action of a State which was doing no more than what the others had advocated year after year, in successive sessions of the Conference.

Perhaps there is room for hope that the Conference will succeed in the long run: but this is not to imply that the difficulties which it faces at the current session are not daunting.

The confrontation which was shaping up at the resumed Seventh Session, held in New York in August/September 1978, will no doubt be toned down — or exacerbated — at the Eighth Session. It may be useful at this stage to highlight some of the main points of disagreement.[1]

The Group of 77 developing countries (a misnomer since the Group now numbers 119), has been taking an increasingly hard line against express or implied threats by the Great Powers that they might take matters into their own hands if the Conference failed to reach agreement on certain questions which they regard as crucial. Prominent among these are the roles to be played by the International Authority on the one hand, and national enterprises or consortia, on the other. The developing countries have a majority voice in the Authority: but only the Great Powers have the financial and technical resources to undertake to mine, with any hope of success, the resources of the deep sea-beds.

The former, understandably, are anxious that the wealth to be derived from the sea-beds—the "common heritage of mankind"— should be fairly apportioned "with due regard to the needs of the developing countries." The latter, equally understandably, are concerned that the mammoth investments (in terms both of money and of know-how), which the operation will involve, will not be dissipated. This could happen if the Authority were to impose conditions which they felt were unreasonable. Fair profits and sufficiently secure tenure of the areas to be allocated to them for mining, must be the starting point of any agreement. Without such incentives the massive investment will not be forthcoming—at least not in the countries having a free enterprise economy.

The differences of approach are highlighted by statements made at the resumed Seventh Session of the Conference by Ambassador Nandan of Fiji, representing the "Group of 77" developing countries, and by Ambassador Richardson, the United States delegate.

After the passage by the U.S. House of Representatives of H.R. 3350 in July 1978—amounting to unilateral legislation by the United States on deep-sea mining—Ambassador Nandan said:

> It is incomprehensible that at this time when the Conference is at an advanced stage in negotiating an internationally agreed regime for the exploration and exploitation of the resources of the deep sea-bed, States engaged in those negotiations should contemplate unilateral actions which would threaten to jeopardise the pursuit of the negotiations and indeed the successful conclusion of the Conference itself.[2]

To this, Ambassador Richardson opposed the standpoint of the United States that:

> States and their nationals have the legal right to use the mineral resources of the deep sea-bed beyond national jurisdiction . . . as . . . a freedom of the high seas.[3]

In a nutshell, the developing countries feel that unilateral action by the United States, which will probably be followed by similar action on the part of other developed countries, undermines their negotiating position, threatens the outcome of the Conference, and is in conflict with the understanding enshrined in the Moratorium Resolution[4] and the Declaration of Principles.[5] The United States position, as expressed by Ambassador Richardson, is that:

> Exploration and exploitation of the deep sea-bed beyond areas of national jurisdiction are freedoms of the high seas enjoyed by all nations. Legal restraints may be imposed on national action . . . only by their inclusion in rules of international law. With respect to deep-sea mining, we are unaware of any such restraints other than those that are generally applied to the high seas and the exercise of high seas freedoms . . . States will become subject to additional restraints when they adhere to a treaty that established an international authority to manage and oversee sea-bed mining. They will then have accepted voluntarily the alterations of those freedoms in the interest of creating a stable legal regime for the use and management of the world's oceans and their resources. But we cannot accept the suggestion that other States, without our consent, could deny or alter our rights under international law by resolutions, statements, and the like.[6]

The developing countries are full of forebodings that the unilateral action of the United States and such other developed countries as may be of the same opinion, will destroy the atmosphere of good faith and compromise which has been the hallmark of the Conference until now. The United States maintains that their legislation will act as a spur to the Conference to reach agreement: and Conference president Amerasinghe suggests, with his usual diplomacy, that the U.S. action should be regarded, not as an act of intimidation, but as an encouragement to the Conference.[7]

The polarisation of interests and attitudes between the advanced maritime nations on the one hand, and the Third World on the other—between the haves and the have-nots—is nowhere more clearly illustrated than with regard to this question of how, by whom and in what manner the wealth of the deep sea-beds should be exploited and how the proceeds of such exploitation should be divided. To change the metaphor, who is to bake the cake, using what ingedients, and how is the cake to be cut, if and when it turns out to be edible?

However interesting and complicated the other issues may be, this remains the nub of the question. When Ambassador Pardo proclaimed that the resources of the deep sea-beds should be exploited cooperatively, as the common heritage of mankind, there were those who doubted whether his ideal could be translated into reality and if it could, whether it would be such an unmixed blessing to humanity.

These questions have not yet been answered. Will the Conference succeed in setting up a Sea-Beds Authority which is capable of putting flesh on the bare bones of the "Common Heritage" concept? Will such an authority be able to hold the balance between diverse, powerful and often conflicting interests, to ensure than the advanced and wealthy nations will have the muscle and the elbow room which they need to prise open the treasure chest and that the poor nations or those whom Nature forgot to endow with a sea-coast should get their share of the bounty? Will there, in short, be a workable accommodation between the developed and the developing nations, for the benefit of all?

The wheel has come full circle, and the question facing the Eighth Session of the Conference in 1979 is no more and no less than the question which faced the Sea-Beds Conference from its inception.

It remains to be seen whether the Conference can solve this question. If it can, it is the authors' guess that all the other issues touched upon in this book can be solved eventually, however protracted the bargaining and that once agreement has been hammered out on the substantive issues, it will be a matter of legal drafting to embody such agreement in a comprehensive Code governing man's uses of the sea. Not that this task will be an easy one. There are issues of immense complexity from the legal, political, strategic and technical points of view but solution of the central issue should remove the log-jam which States have too often tried to ignore but which cannot, in the long run, be circumnavigated.

Should the Conference be unable to resolve the dichotomy of interests between the haves and the have-nots and to move on to the task of perfecting a comprehensive Code, it may well be that the whole effort will be written off by public opinion around the world as just another pipe-dream which came to nothing.

Such an extreme view would, in the authors' opinion, be wholly unjustified. Even without a Code, the international common law of the sea will have been enriched, informed and carried a long step forward by the years of debate in the Sea-Bed Committee and in UNCLOS III. There can be few angles of the complex of interrelated problems connected with man's use of the sea which have not been subjected to close scrutiny by some of the leading jurists, scientists and diplomats of the world in the course of the years of debate in this seemingly endless conference. Some common-law principles have already emerged through the interaction of State practices and the growing, if tentative consensus, with regard to issues like the delimitation of the territorial sea, the special status of archipelagic waters, the dangers of marine pollution, the need for conservation measures to protect the balance of life in the seas and numerous other matters: others will emerge as States feel their way through the maze, following leads which the debates at the Conference may have suggested.

There is a third possibility. What if the Conference manages to put together a paper tiger in the form of a treaty which proves unworkable either because States prove to be unequal to the challenge of working together within the framework provided; or because the cake on which so much energy has been expended and so many hopes have been based, turns out to be too small and too outrageously expensive to afford a worthwhile slice to anyone? The answer seems to be that even if the Convention should fail in its main objective of realizing and dividing up the common heritage of mankind, it would remain a source of conventional international law (and not only of customary law) on a wide range of other issues and as such, a massive contribution to the Law of Nations relating to the sea.

What may transpire during and after the Eighth Session of UNCLOS III is in the lap of the gods and it would be a bold man indeed who would venture to foretell it. But of one thing we can be reasonably sure—if a new regime of the sea is to emerge, based on compromise and the accommodation of States' interest, mankind will have to heed the biblical injunction of Ecclesiastes, the Preacher—"Cast thy bread upon the waters, for thou shalt find it after many days."

Notes

1.   An excellent summary of the "state of play" after the resumed session of UNCLOS III may be found in an article by Lee Kimball and Adolf R. H. Schneider entitled "UNCLOS III: The Resumed Seventh Session — A Shadow of Unilateral Actions?" published in *Environmental Policy and Law*, Volume 4, No. 4, December 1978. Elsevier Sequoia S.A., 1978.

2.   Press Release SEA/327, 28 August 1978: see Kimball and Schneider, op. cit.

3.   Press Release SEA/327.

4.   The Moratorium Resolution (General Assembly Resolution 2574D [XXIV]) was designed to discourage States from taking unilateral action which might anticipate decisions still to be reached by the Conference.

5.   The Declaration of Principles on the Sea-bed is embodied in General Assembly Resolution 2749 (XXV). It stresses, inter alia, the interdependence of the main issues before the Conference and the fact that they cannot be considered in isolation.

6.   Statement by Ambassador E. L. Richardson to the Plenary Meeting, 15 September 1978. Quoted in Kimball and Schneider, op. cit.

7.   Kimball and Schneider, op. cit.

General Reading List

In recent years – and especially during the last decade – a great deal has been written on the Law of the Sea, as well as on all those cognate disciplines which have a bearing on the present, ongoing task of codifying Sea Law in a new international Convention.

It would be invidious to try, within the confines of a book of this kind, to give anything like a comprehensive reading list. Such lists, which may run into volumes, are readily accessible to those who wish to delve deeper. Particular mention should perhaps be made of Professor Shigeru Oda's now famous compilation of basic documents under the title *The International Law of the Ocean Development*; of an excellent selection, in two volumes, of books and United Nations documents entitled *Bibliography of the New Law of the Sea* by Sybesma-Kol and Regout; and of the bibliographies issued from time to time by the United Nations Secretariat.

The list which follows refers to a few of the most useful of these bibliographies as well as to some of the books, articles and documents which are thought to be of topical interest or of more lasting value. The authors' involvement with the diverse issues covered, has meant that many more works than are listed here have helped them over the years and have influenced their thinking as one or other act in the long-drawn-out drama of the Conference unfolded. Any omissions – and they must be legion – should be seen in that context.

Amacher, Ryan C. and Sweeny, Richard James (Ed): *The Law of the Sea: U.S. Interests and Alternatives*: Washington, D.C., American Institute for Public Policy Research 1976.

Amerasinghe, Ambassador H. S.: The Third United Nations Conference on the Law of the Sea; Article in *UNITAR News*: Vol. 6 No. 1: 1974.

Amerasinghe, Ambassador H. S., Stavropoulos, C. A., Lee, Roy S. y el equipo de UNITAR: Las Naciones Unidas y el Mar; Secretaria de Relaciones Exteriores de *UNITAR*, Mexico-Nueva York 1974

Anand, R. P.: *The Legal Regime of the Sea-Bed and the Developing Countries*. A.W. Sijthoff, Leyden 1976.

Andrassy, Juraj: *International Law and the Resources of the Sea*. Columbia University Press, New York and London 1970.

Armstrong, P.: Mare Raptum: Government Proposals for Ocean Mismanagement: Caracas, 1974. In *Ocean Management*, March 1974: Elsevier Scientific Publishing Company, Amsterdam.

Barrie, G. B.: The Third law of the Sea Conference: A Preview of some of the Issues: Reprinted from *Tydskrif vir Hedendaagst Romeins–Hollandse Reg 1973*: Vol. 36 No. 1: Butterworths, Durban.

Barrie, G. N.: The Third Law of the Sea Conference: a Final Summation: Reprinted from *Tydskrif vir Hedendaagse Romeins-Hollandse Reg 1974*: Vol. 37 No. 3: Butterworths, Durban.

Beguery, Michel: *L'Exploitation des Oceans–L'economie de Demain*: Presses Universitaires de France, 1976.

Bourquin, Maurice: *L'Organisation Internationale des Voies de Communications*: Academie de Droit International: Recueil des Cours: No. 5: 1924 (IV) (Especially p. 168 ff.) Hachette, Paris, 1924.

Butler, William Elliott: *The Soviet Union and the Law of the Sea*; Johns Hopkins Press, 1971.

Cauchy, E.: Le Droit Maritime International Considere dans ses Origines et dans ses Rapports avec les Progrés de la Civilisation: Paris 1862 (2 vols) Cited by Ruth Lapidoth, *Freedom of Navigation*, *op. cit.*

Charney, Jonathan L. : *Law of the Sea: Breaking the Deadlock*: Foreign Affairs Quarterly: New York, 1977: Vol 55 No. 3.

Churchill, Robin, and Others: *New Directions in the Law of the Sea*: Collected Papers: Oceana Publications, Dobbs Ferry, New York 1973 onwards.

Colombos, C. John: *The International Law of the Sea*: Longmans, Green and Co., London (6th Edition 1967, reprinted 1968).

Committee On The Peaceful Uses Of The Sea—Bed and Ocean Floor Beyond The Limits of National Jurisdiction, Reports . . .: Official Records of the General Assembly.

Critchlow, Kenneth: *Into the Hidden Environment–Oceans Lifestream of our Planet*: George Philip and Son: London, 1972.

De Leener, Georges: *Règles Générales du Droit des Communications Internationals*: Recueil des Cours de L'Academie de Droit International: No. 55. 1936 Vol. 1: Librarie Hachette, Paris.

Dupuy, René Jean: *The Law of the Sea: Current Problems*: Dobbs Ferry, New York: Oceana Publications, 1974.

Fernandes, Javier Illanes: *El Derecho del Mar e sus Problemas Actuales*: Editorial Universitaria de Buenos Aires: 1974 (Cuestiones de Geopolitica).

Foigel, I.: The North Sea Continental Shelf Case: Article in *Of Law and Man — Essays in Honor of Haim H. Cohn*: Sabra Books, New York and Tel Aviv, 1971.

Friedmann, Wolfgang: *The Future of the Oceans*: George Braziller Inc, New York, 1971.

Gallardo, Victor A.: *Chile's National Interest in the Oceans 1976*: Chile, Universidad: Instituto de Estudos Internacionales. Ser. de Publicaciones especiales No. 10.

Garcia-Amador, F. V.: *The Exploitation and Conservation of the Resources of the Sea*: 2nd. Edition: A.W. Sijthoff, Leyden, 1963.

Gaskell, T. F.: Moving into Deeper Waters: Development and Promise of Off-shore Technology: Interregional Seminar on the Development of the Mineral Resources of the Continental Shelf: Port-of-Spain, Trinidad and Tobago: 5-16 April 1971: United Nations Technical papers Doc ST/TAO/SER.C/138: Sales No. E/F.72 II. A.6.

Gidel, G.-C.: Le Droit International Public de la Mer: Paris 1932-1934 (Vols I TO III).

Hambro, Edward: *The Case Law of the International Court*: A.W. Sijthoff, Leyden, 1966.

Hellman, Ronald G., and Rosenbaum, H. Jon (Ed.): *Latin America: The Search for a new International Role*: New York: Sage Publications, 1975.

International Court of Justice: *The North Sea Continental Shelf Cases*: ICJ Reports, The Hague 1969.

Interregional Seminar on the Development of the Mineral Resources of the Continental Shelf: Port-of-Spain, Trinidad and Tobago, 5-16 April 1971: U.N. Technical Papers, Doc. ST/TAO/SER. C/138.

Jessup, Philip C.: *L'Exploitation des Richesses de la Mer*: Recueil des Cours de l'Academie de Droit International: No. 29: 1929 Vol. IV Librairie Hachette, Paris.

Jones, Erin Bain: *Law of the Sea: Oceanic Resources*: Dallas, Southern Methodist University Press, 1972.

Johnston, Douglas M (Ed.): *Marine Policy and the Coastal Community: The Impact of the Law of the Sea*: St. Martins' Press New York 1976.

Joyner, Christopher C. (Ed.): *International Law Symposium on International Law of the Sea and the Future of Deep Sea Mining*: Charlottesville, Va., 1974: Accent Printing Co, 1975.

Labrousse, Henri: Le Droit de la Mer: Problèmes Economiques et Stratégiques: *Les Cahiers de la Fondation pour les Etudes de Défense Nationale*: 1977.

La Mer Et Le Milieu Marin: Numero hors Série No. 115 de *Science et Vie*: Excelsior Publications, S.A. Paris 1976.

Larson, David L. (Ed.) *Major Issues of the Law of the Sea*: University of New Hampshire 1976.

Law of the Sea Institute: 1st. to 10th Annual Conferences (1966-1976), Kingston, Rhode Island: Ohio State University Press (1967), University of Rhode Island (1968-73) and Ballinger Publishing Co. (1974-1977). (Especially the 8th Conference, devoted to "The Emerging Regime of the Oceans.")

Larson, David L. (Ed.), *Major Issues of the Law of the Sea*: University of New Hampshire 1976.

Law of the Sea Institute. Workshop, 4th: Hamilton, Bermuda Islands, 1974: Fisheries Conflicts in the North Atlantic: Problems of Management and Jurisdiction: Cambridge, Mass., Ballingen Publishing Co., 1974.

Llana, Christopher B. *et al* (Ed.): *Law of the Sea: a Bibliography of the Periodical Literature of the 1970s*: Kingston, University of Rhode Island, 1975.

Loftas, Tony: *The Last Resource: Man's Exploitation of the Oceans*: Revised edition, Pelican Books, Harmondsworth, England, 1972.

Martray, Joseph: *A qui appartient l'océan? Vers un nouveau régime des espaces et des fonds marins*: Paris, Editions maritimes et d'outre-mer, 1977.

McDougal and Burke: *The Public Order of the Oceans: a Contemporary International Law of the Sea*: New Haven and London, Yale University Press, 1965.

México Y El Regimen Del Mar: Compilation by the Secretaria de Relaciones Exteriores: Tlatelolco, Mexico, 1974.

Mostert, Noel: *Supership*: Warner Books, New York 1975.

O'Connell, D. P.: *International Law: Second Edition* (2 Vols): Steven and Son, London, 1970.

— — —. *The Influence of Law on Sea Power*: Manchester University Press, 1975.

Oda, Shigeru: *The International Law of the Ocean Development: Basic Documents*: A.W. Sijthoff, Leiden: Vol 1 1972, Vol 2 1975.

———. *The Law of the Sea in our Time/I: New Developments 1966-1975*: A.W. Sijthoff, Leiden, 1977.

Oppenheim's International Law: Ed. Lauterpacht, Hirsch: Eighth Edition: Longmans, Green and Co., Ltd., London 1955.

Pardo, Arvid: *The Common Heritage: Selected Papers on Oceans and World Order, 1967-1974*: Malta University Press, 1975.

Rao, P. Sreenivasa: *The Public Order of Ocean Resources: a Critique of the Contemporary Law of the Sea*: The M.I.T. Press, Cambridge, Massachusetts, and London, England, 1975.

Reuter, Paul: *Droit International Public*: Presses Univesitaires de France: 5th Edition, 1976.

Rosenne, Shabtai: *Documents on the International Court of Justice*: A.W. Sijthoff, Leiden and Oceana Publications Inc, New York, 1974.

Rüster, Berndt: *Die Rechtsordnung des Festlandsockels*: Duncker und Humblot, Berlin 1977.

Sanchez Rodriguez, Luis Ignacio: *La Zona Exclusiva de Pesca en el Nuevo Derecho del Mar*: Oviedo, 1977.

Schachter, Oscar, and Serwer, Daniel: Marine Pollution Problems and Remedies: United Nations Institute for Training and Research (UNITAR): New York, 1971.

Scorazzi, Tullio: *Gli accordi bilaterali sulla pesca*: A Giuffrè Milan, 1977.

Slouka, Zdenek J.: *International Custom and the Continental Shelf: A Study in the Dynamics of Customary Rules of International Law*: Martinus Nijhoff, The Hague 1968.

Sorensen, Max: *Les Sources du Droit International: Etude sur la Jurisprudence de la Cour Permanente de Justice Internationale*: Einar Munksgaard, Copenhagen, 1946.

Stavropolos, Constantin A.: Procedural Problems of the Third Conference on the Law of the Sea: *UNITAR News*: Vol 6 No. 1, 1974.

Swing, John Temple: Who will own the Oceans? *Foreign Affairs*, Vol. 54, No. 3: New York, April 1976.

Sybesma-Knol, Neri, and Regout, Alfreda: *Bibliografie van het nieuwe zeerecht: een Keuze uit boeken en UNO/dokumenten* (Bibliography of the New Law of the Sea: a Selective List of Books and U.N. Documents): Brussels, Vrije Universiteit, 1976.

— — —. *Bibliografie van het nieuwe zeerecht: een keuze uit de tijd-schriftenliteratuur sinds 1967* (Bibliography of the New Law of the Sea: a Selection from the Periodical Literature since 1967): Brussels, Vrije Universiteit, 1977.

Thomson, Jennifer: *The Law of the Sea, with Special Reference to Canada: a Select Bibliography*: Carleton University, Ottawa, 1976.

United Nations Legislative Series: National Legislation and Treaties Relating to The Law Of The Sea: United Nations Documents ST/LEG/SER.B/ 15-18

United Nations: Dag Hammarskjold Library: The Sea: a Select Bibliography on the Legal, Political, Economic and Technological Aspects, 1975-1976. U.N. Document ST/LIB/SER. B/16. Sales No. E/F. 75. 1.12 (An invaluable aid, prepared by the U.N. Secretariat for the Spring session of the Conference — New York March-May 1976).

United Nations: Dag Hammarskjold Library: The Sea: A Select Bibliography on the Legal, Political, Economic and Technical Aspects 1974-1975. U.N. Document ST/LIB/SER. B/16. U.N. Publication Sales No. E/F/. 75.1.7: New York, 1975.

United Nations (Second) Conference on the Law of the Sea: Official Records: Summary Records of Plenary Meetings and of Meetings of the Committee of the Whole: Annexes and Final Act: Geneva, 17 March-26 April 1960. U.N. Document A/CONF. 19/8.

United Nations Document ST/TAO/SER. C/138 (sales No. E/F. 72.II. A.6): Interregional Seminar on the Development of the Mineral Resources of the Continental Shelf: Port-of-Spain, Trinidad and Tobago, 5-16 April 1971.

United States Congress, House Committee on Foreign Affairs: Law of the Sea Resolution/Hearings before Subcommittee on international organisations and movements of the Committee: 93 Congress 1st. Session on H. Res. 216 and 296: Washington, D.C., 1973.

United States Congress. House Committee on Merchant Marine and Fisheries: National ocean policy — Hearings before the Sub-committee on Oceanography and the Committee: 94th Congress, 2nd. Session on oversight to examine general ocean policy: Washington D.C., 1976.

United States Congress. House Committee on Foreign Affairs: Status of the U.N. law of the sea conference — Hearing before the Committee — 93 Congress, 2nd. session — Washington, D.C., 1975.

Van Rensburg, W. C. J., and Granville, A.: National Institute for Metallurgy: Report No. 1644: Johannesburg, 1974.

Vargas, Jorge. (Ed.): *La Zona economica exclusiva de México: Nota explicativa y bibliografia selecta*: Mexico, 1976.

— — —. Repertorio bibliográfico: America Latina y el soberania sobre sus recursos oceánicos; contiene una selección de obras sobra: derecho del mar, documentos oficiales, organismos internacionales y trabajos cientifico-técnicos: Mexico, 1976.

Vicuna Francisco Orrega: *Los Fondos Marinos y Oceanicos*: Editorial Andres Bello 1976.

— — —. Tendencias del Derecho del mar contemporaneo: *UNITAR*: Buenos Aires, 1974.

Walker — Leigh Vanya: Law of the Sea: Time may be running out for World Maritime Committee: *Herald Tribune*, 30 January 1978.

Walsh, Don (Ed.): *The Law of the Sea: Issues in Ocean Resource Management*: Praeger, New York, 1977.

Zacklin, Ralph: *The Changing Law of the Sea: Western Hemisphere Perspectives*: Carnegie Endowment for International Peace: Inter-American Study Group of International Law: A.W. Sijthoff, Leiden, 1974.

Zacklin, Ralph (Ed.): *El Derecho del Mar en Evolución: La Contribución de los Países Americanos*: Fundo de Cultura Economica: México, 1975.

Index

Date Due

JAN 27 '93		